Lyotard and the Inhuman Condition

Technicities

Series Editors: John Armitage, Ryan Bishop and Joanne Roberts, Winchester School of Art, University of Southampton

The philosophy of technicities: exploring how technology mediates art, frames design and augments the mediated collective perception of everyday life.

Technicities will publish the latest philosophical thinking about our increasingly immaterial technocultural conditions, with a unique focus on the context of art, design and media.

Editorial Advisory Board
Benjamin Bratton, Cheryl Buckley, Sean Cubitt, Clive Dilnot, Jin Huimin, Arthur Kroker, Geert Lovink, Scott McQuire, Gunalan Nadarajan, Elin O'Hara Slavick, Li Shqiao, Geoffrey Winthrop-Young

Published
Lyotard and the Inhuman Condition: Reflections on Nihilism, Information and Art
By Ashley Woodward

Critical Luxury Studies: Art, Design, Media
Edited by John Armitage and Joanne Roberts

Forthcoming
Cold War Legacies: Systems, Theory, Aesthetics
Edited by John Beck and Ryan Bishop

Fashion and Materialism
By Ulrich Lehmann

The Afterlives of Georges Perec
Edited by Rowan Wilken and Justin Clemens

Lyotard and the Inhuman Condition

Reflections on Nihilism, Information, and Art

Ashley Woodward

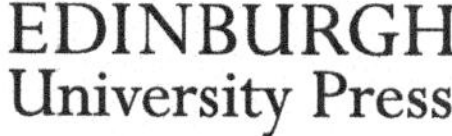
EDINBURGH
University Press

Edinburgh University Press is one of the leading university presses in the UK. We publish academic books and journals in our selected subject areas across the humanities and social sciences, combining cutting-edge scholarship with high editorial and production values to produce academic works of lasting importance. For more information visit our website: www.edinburghuniversitypress.com

Edinburgh University Press Ltd
The Tun – Holyrood Road,
12(2f) Jackson's Entry,
Edinburgh EH8 8PJ

First published in hardback by Edinburgh University Press 2016

Typeset in 11/13 Adobe Sabon by
IDSUK (DataConnection) Ltd, and
printed and bound in Great Britain by
CPI Group (UK) Ltd, Croydon CR0 4YY

A CIP record for this book is available from the British Library

ISBN 978 0 7486 9724 3 (hardback)
ISBN 978 1 4744 2580 3 (paperback)
ISBN 978 0 7486 9725 0 (webready PDF)
ISBN 978 1 4744 0491 4 (epub)

Contents

Series Editors' Preface   vi

Acknowledgements   vii

Abbreviations   viii

Introduction: Beyond the Postmodern? The *Inhuman* Condition   1

1   The End of Time: Evolution, Extinction, and the Fate of Meaning   11

2   Information and Event: Lyotard's Philosophy of Information   41

3   Economy, Ecology, Organology: On Technics and Desire   74

4   Nihilism and the Sublime: The Crisis of Perception   105

5   *Aesthēsis* and *Technē*: New Technologies and Lyotard's Aesthetics   134

6   Immaterial Matter: Yves Klein and the Aesthetics of the Sensible   151

7   Inhuman Arts: From Cubism to New Media   165

Conclusion: The Judgement of the Inhuman   189

Bibliography   196

Index   209

Series Editors' Preface

Technological transformation has profound and frequently unforeseen influences on art, design, and media. At times technology emancipates art and enriches the quality of design. Occasionally it causes acute individual and collective problems of mediated perception. Time after time technological change accomplishes both simultaneously. This new book series explores and reflects philosophically on what new and emerging *technicities* do to our everyday lives and increasingly immaterial technocultural conditions. Moving beyond traditional conceptions of the philosophy of technology and of techne, the series presents new philosophical thinking on how technology constantly alters the essential conditions of beauty, invention, and communication. From novel understandings of the world of technicity to new interpretations of aesthetic value, graphics, and information, *Technicities* focuses on the relationships between critical theory and representation, the arts, broadcasting, print, technological genealogies/histories, material culture, and digital technologies and our philosophical views of the world of art, design, and media.

The series foregrounds contemporary work in art, design, and media whilst remaining inclusive, in terms of both philosophical perspectives on technology and interdisciplinary contributions. For a philosophy of technicities is crucial to extant debates over the artistic, inventive, and informational aspects of technology. The books in the *Technicities* series concentrate on present-day and evolving technological advances but visual, design-led, and mass-mediated questions are emphasised to further our knowledge of their often-combined means of digital transformation.

The editors of *Technicities* welcome proposals for monographs and well-considered edited collections that establish new paths of investigation.

John Armitage, Ryan Bishop, and Joanne Roberts

Acknowledgements

First and foremost I want to acknowledge and thank James Williams, for the inspiration, support, mentorship, and collegiality he has generously provided me, in one form or another, for more than a decade. I also want to acknowledge Keith Ansell Pearson, whose work has been a significant inspiration. The occasional disagreements with each in these pages are the product of a much deeper debt, and formative influence, for what attempts to pass for scholarship and thought here. Finally I would like to thank Carol Macdonald at Edinburgh University Press for believing in this project.

Some of the chapters in this book, in slightly different form, have been previously published elsewhere, and I gratefully acknowledge permission to reprint material from the following sources. 'The End of Time' was originally published in *Parrhesia* 15 (2012): 87–105. 'Nihilism and the Sublime' was originally published as 'Nihilism and the Sublime in Lyotard' in *Angelaki* vol. 16, no. 2 (2011): 51–71. '*Aesthēsis* and *Technē*' was originally published as 'New Technologies and Lyotard's Aesthetics' in *Litteraria Pragensia* vol. 16, no. 32 (2006): 14–35. 'Immaterial Matter' was originally published in *Sensorium: Aesthetics, Art, Life*, ed. Barbara Bolt, Felicity Colman, Graham Jones, and Ashley Woodward (Newcastle upon Tyne: Cambridge Scholars Press, 2007).

Abbreviations

Below are abbreviations of Lyotard's main books, and frequently referenced other texts, which will be used throughout. Lyotard's essays and other minor works, along with other texts referenced, appear in the Bibliography.

Works by Lyotard

A   *The Assassination of Experience by Painting – Monory*, trans. Rachel Bowlby. Jean-François Lyotard. Writings on Contemporary Art and Artists, ed. Herman Parret. Vol. 6. Leuven: Leuven University Press, 2013.

D   *The Differend: Phrases in Dispute*, trans. Georges Van Den Abbeele. Manchester: Manchester University Press, 1988.

DF   *Discourse, Figure*, trans. Antony Hudek and Mary Lyton. Minneapolis: University of Minnesota Press, 2011.

DP   *Des Dispositifs pulsionnels*. Paris: Galilée, 1994.

DT   *Duchamp's TRANS/formers*, trans. Ian McLeod. Jean-François Lyotard. Writings on Contemporary Art and Artists, ed. Herman Parret. Vol. 3. Leuven: Leuven University Press, 2010.

DW   *Driftworks*, ed. Roger McKeon. New York: Semiotext(e), 1984.

E   *Enthusiasm: The Kantian Critique of History*, trans. Georges Van Den Abbeele. Stanford: Stanford University Press, 2009.

HJ   *Heidegger and 'the jews'*, trans. Andreas Michel and Mark S. Roberts. Minneapolis: University of Minnesota Press, 1990.

I1   (ed.) *Les Immatériaux*. Vol. 1: *Epreuves d'écriture*. Paris: Centre Georges Pompidou, 1985.

I2   (ed.) *Les Immatériaux*. Vol. 2: *Album. Inventaire*. Paris: Centre Georges Pompidou, 1985.

IN   *The Inhuman: Reflections on Time*, trans. Geoffrey Bennington and Rachel Bowlby. Cambridge: Polity Press, 1991.

JG   (with Jean-Loup Thébaud) *Just Gaming*, trans. Wlad Godzich. Manchester: Manchester University Press, 1985.

KA   *Karel Appel: A Gesture of Colour*, trans. Vlad Ionescu and Peter W. Milne. Jean-François Lyotard. Writings on Contemporary Art and Artists, ed. Herman Parret. Vol. 1. Leuven: Leuven University Press, 2009.

LAS   *Lessons on the Analytic of the Sublime*, trans. Elizabeth Rottenberg. Stanford: Stanford University Press, 1994.

LE   *Libidinal Economy*, trans. Iain Hamilton Grant. London: Athlone, 1993.

LR   *The Lyotard Reader*, ed. Andrew Benjamin. Oxford and Cambridge: Basil Blackwell, 1989.

LRG   *The Lyotard Reader and Guide*, ed. Keith Crome and James Williams. Edinburgh: Edinburgh University Press, 2006.

MP   *Misère de la philosophie*. Paris: Galilée, 2000.

MTI   *Miscellaneous Texts I: Aesthetics and Theory of Art*. Jean-François Lyotard. Writings on Contemporary Art and Artists, ed. Herman Parret. Vol. 4.I. Leuven: Leuven University Press, 2012.

MTII *Miscellaneous Texts II: Contemporary Artists*. Jean-François Lyotard. Writings on Contemporary Art and Artists, ed. Herman Parret. Vol. 4.II. Leuven: Leuven University Press, 2012.

P   *Peregrinations: Law, Form, Event*. New York: Columbia University Press, 1988.

PC   *The Postmodern Condition: A Report on Knowledge*, trans. Geoff Bennington and Brian Massumi. Manchester: Manchester University Press, 1984.

PE   *The Postmodern Explained to Children: Correspondence 1982–1985*, trans. Julian Pefanis and Morgan Thomas. Sydney: Power Publications, 1992.

PF   *Postmodern Fables*, trans. Georges Van Den Abbeele. Minneapolis: University of Minnesota Press, 1997.

PW   *Jean-François Lyotard: Political Writings*, trans. Bill Readings and Kevin Paul. Minneapolis: University of Minnesota Press, 1993.

SM   *Signed, Malraux*, trans. Robert Harvey. Minneapolis: University of Minnesota Press, 1999.

SR   *Soundproof Room: Malraux's Anti-Aesthetics*, trans. Robert Harvey. Stanford: Stanford University Press, 2001.

TP   *Toward the Postmodern*, ed. Robert Harvey and Mark S. Roberts. Atlantic Highlands, NJ: Humanities Press, 1993.

WP   *What to Paint?*, ed. Herman Parret. Jean-François Lyotard. Writings on Contemporary Art and Artists, ed. Herman Parret. Vol. 5. Leuven: Leuven University Press, 2013.

Other Works

CJ   Immanuel Kant, *The Critique of Judgement*, trans. James Creed Meredith. Oxford: Clarendon Press, 1961.

SE   *The Standard Edition of the Complete Psychological Works of Sigmund Freud*, 24 vols, ed. James Strachey. London: Hogarth, 1953–75.

Beyond the Postmodern?
The *Inhuman* Condition

Man's anxiety is that he is losing his (so-called) identity as a 'human being'.

Lyotard 1985a: 49

Man is perhaps only a very sophisticated node in the general interaction of emanations constituting the universe.

Lyotard PE: 32

In that very complex regulation which is due for us, man is no longer the measure. He needs to consider himself as one of the elements of this extraordinarily complex structure in which he finds himself, and at every level: biological, familial, physical, etc. He doesn't need to fear this situation, this condition.

Lyotard, in Lyotard and Théofilakis 1985: 13

Jean-François Lyotard was one of the leading French philosophers of his generation, whose wide-ranging and highly original contributions to thought were overshadowed by his brief, unfortunate association with 'postmodernism'. He is still most widely known as the prophet of the 'end of metanarratives'. In today's climate of the new pantheon of Olympian continental philosophers (Badiou, Žižek, Agamben, Rancière, Stiegler, and so on), the backlash against postmodernism appears to have triumphed: truth, metaphysics, realism, the subject; Marxism, Plato, Descartes, Hegel, and other figures and notions unpopular in the heyday of postmodernism are once again on the agenda. Whither, then, Lyotard? If there is any philosopher with whom we can no longer afford to *waste our time*, and can confidently remove from our reading lists, surely it is he?

Against such an assumption, my hope is that this book demonstrates what a new generation of scholars are now discovering: that

Lyotard's extensive work moves in a vast scope beyond the postmodern. As Douglas Kellner rightly asserts:

> Lyotard's significance as a philosopher is certainly not limited to his popularization of the problematic of the postmodern. He has many provocative positions in theory, aesthetics, and politics and his philosophical itinerary is a complex one that has not been properly explored – a task for the new generation! (Kellner 1999)

Moreover, the first English-language presentations of Lyotard, excellent as they were, inevitably reflected the trends of the time, tending to emphasise his similarities and differences in relation to Derrida, deconstruction, and the 'theory' then popular in literature departments (Bennington 1988; Readings 1991). My hope is that the essays collected here will contribute in their own small way to the newly developing image of a hitherto *unknown Lyotard*, an image that has been appearing over the last few years, as more of his diverse work comes to light, and new studies are updating the way we see this important thinker.[1] Like other diverse and complex writers, it is possible (and probably necessary) in any study to extract and focus on some elements of Lyotard's work, while marginalising or ignoring others. Thus, it is not uncommon to feel that we do not even recognise the portraits others paint of thinkers whose corpus we think we know well. While staking no high claim to radical originality, I nevertheless hope that the studies collected here will bring out aspects of Lyotard that can transmit something of the freshness I never fail to find in returning to his works. The Lyotard I present here is a contemporary thinker of nihilism in the Nietzschean tradition who updates this problematic for the new century, a critical interrogator of information theory whose ideas have the potential to incisively intervene in the so-called 'informational turn' in philosophy, theory, and culture, and an art writer and theorist of contemporary – and in particular, new media – art.

Before moving into this terrain, it is perhaps worthwhile to address, briefly and directly, what someone at a recent Lyotard conference noted is for all those working on him today the 'elephant in the room': the postmodern. The term 'postmodern' and its variations remain vexed, and a large part of the problem of clarifying it is that it emerged in different fields (literature, sociology, architecture, the arts, philosophy) with widely varying meanings, yet many then attempted to unify these meanings in the name of a general cultural trend, a *Zeitgeist* felt to be emerging in the last decades of the twentieth century, under the name of postmodern*ism*. In philosophy, postmodernism has come to be understood primarily as a combination of epistemic and ontological relativism: there is no truth or reality, but only perspectives on these. This position was popularly associated with figures such as Foucault, Derrida, Baudrillard, and the whole poststructuralist generation of French intellectuals, but was explicitly embraced by only a very few significant philosophers (such as Rorty and Vattimo).

I would argue that Lyotard's thought can only be properly situated with this type of postmodern philosophy in a specific period of its development, roughly the latter half of the 1970s. It was then that Lyotard was enthusiastic about Nietzsche and the sophists, and developed a pagan, pragmatic philosophy which rejects any grounding in truth or reality, promotes the multiplication of perspectives, and asserts that argumentative philosophical discourse is one literary genre among others, in which the feeling of conviction which follows from a convincing argument is just another rhetorical effect.[2] However, although Lyotard would never lose his critical attitude towards the categories of 'truth' and 'reality', understanding them as complexes which need to be analysed rather than as basic givens, already by 1979's *Just Gaming* he was expressing serious doubts about the adequacy of sophistical relativism in the face of the problem of justice. This motivated his well-known move to Kant and Levinas, and the adoption in *The Differend* of a much more complex and nuanced philosophy, which retains aspects of perspectivism whilst foregrounding the necessity of judgement.

Moreover, Lyotard's deployment of the term 'postmodern' (he almost never used the term postmodern*ism*) was arguably never well understood by the majority of those who took it up.[3] This misunderstanding is well presented around the issue of metanarratives. While the term itself is rather plastic, it does maintain a certain specificity often overlooked by many, who understand a metanarrative as simply a 'big story'; as any claim to truth, or principle of explanation, or justification, or appeal to reason. Certainly, Lyotard meant something much more specific than this (see Chapter 1 for a detailed discussion). Famously, Lyotard defines the postmodern as 'incredulity toward metanarratives' (PC: xxiv). This claim that such an incredulity should be embraced is justified in several ways, but cannot be understood as a simple rejection of truth, reasons, and principles (see Williams 2000a). For Lyotard, 'the postmodern' signals a complex of problems which call for specific and careful philosophical thought, and it cannot be reduced to any simple position or body of doctrines signifiable with an 'ism'. Regarding the postmodern, then, when approaching Lyotard we need to keep two things in mind: first, his work traverses a vast field beyond the orbit of this term; and second, for him it has a specific meaning (or number of meanings) irreducible to wider discussions of postmodernism.

I have chosen the phrase 'Inhuman Condition' as part of the title of this book strategically. In part, it suggests that Lyotard's work examined here is work which moves beyond the postmodern condition, at least as it is presented in the influential book of that title. Moreover, it is adapted to the thought that our own condition has perhaps changed (a notion widely believed), and seeks to avoid the easy dismissal which Lyotard's continued association with the postmodern continues to invite. There is a significant sense, I would argue, in which the first point is true. Lyotard quickly realised that his suggestion that we have 'completed our process of mourning' for narrative meaning, made in *The Postmodern Condition* (41), was premature, and he engaged with the persistence of this narrative by other means. I explore this theme in Chapter 1, arguing that what Lyotard called the 'postmodern fable' operates as something like a 'post-metanarrative', continuing to offer a narrative form of legitimation in a posthuman, or inhuman, mode. Thus, after *The Postmodern Condition*, in the years when he was writing the essays collected in *The Inhuman*, Lyotard does enact a shift in his thinking about the contemporary condition. Thus we might perhaps be justified in making a strategic distinction between the *postmodern* condition for which he is best known – characterised by the demise of metanarratives – and the *inhuman* condition, characterised by the persistence of the post-metanarrative of 'development', and all its consequences. However, strictly speaking he makes no such clear distinction, and continues to characterise the contemporary condition as postmodern. In following his thought, I will sometimes use the expression 'postmodern condition', and the question mark in my title above – *Beyond the postmodern?* – signals that the 'inhuman condition', as I am calling it, is better thought as a further complication or inflection within the postmodern, than as anything like a decisive break or definitive overcoming.[4]

A significant number of authors have connected Lyotard's work with the 'posthuman',[5] and the '*Posthuman* Condition' would have been another legitimate title I might have chosen under which to refocus Lyotard's work.[6] The posthuman is a term quickly developing a widespread popularity, and like any such term, it is used in a number of varying ways. Yet I suggest that most of its significant uses may be broadly glossed by the suggestion that it is a meeting point for developments in science, theory, and culture which register a radical displacement of the human, and thus of humanism. The latter (also of course a diverse and contested idea) may itself be glossed in this context as an understanding of the human as determinable according to an essence which makes us distinct from the natural and from the artifactual, and which typically also centralises and privileges the human. Most frequently in the history of Western thought, this human essence has been identified with reason. Moreover, it has often been thought to possess the key features of autonomy and individuality.[7]

Posthumanism registers the breakdown in coherence of this idea of the human. This breakdown has resulted from technological advances and scientific paradigm changes which have increasingly erased the lines which have been thought to distinguish the human from both the natural world and the artificial (technological) world. Sciences and technologies such as cybernetics, ecology, artificial intelligence (AI), and artificial life (AL) have overturned the sovereign uniqueness of the human by emphasising the similarities, continuities, and complex interactions between differentiated systems. Humans are animals, and machines can think. Yet humans, animals, and machines can all be seen as varieties of living systems inhabiting relational networks. Throughout the twentieth century and into the twenty-first, at the same time that these scientific and technological developments have been taking place, philosophical developments in Germany, France, and elsewhere have been deconstructing the essential components of humanism on the theoretical level. As we shall see, Lyotard's work intersects with posthumanism on both these levels, and his reflections on these issues in the 1980s were prescient of the debates gaining increased urgency and attention today.

While in the following chapters I sometimes engage with discourses of the posthuman – and also of the transhuman, that particular posthumanist movement which prescribes the progressive evolutionary development of humanity through technological enhancement – I have chosen to retain Lyotard's term 'the inhuman' in order better to keep to the specificity and rigour of his own thought. As Lyotard explains in his introduction to *The Inhuman*, the titular term has a double meaning for him. On the one hand, it designates something inhumane: the contemporary global system which no longer functions even in the pretence of bettering humanity, but according to the criterion of performativity or efficiency which is the result of the combined logic of capital and technoscience. This inhuman is the nihilism of the contemporary situation as Lyotard analyses it, in which thought, art, and life are threatened. On the other hand, the inhuman also designates that which resists this first inhuman, the condition for thought, art, and life, which he sees as 'preceding' the human, and necessary for constituting it (IN: 2).

The way in which other scholars have linked Lyotard's thought to the posthuman has sometimes been problematic. In an otherwise insightful essay, Paul Harris writes:

> It is tempting to read the essays in *The Inhuman* as Lyotard's contribution to the mounting discourse on the 'post-human.' And in thinking through some of the consequences of 'complexification' on a transhuman level, Lyotard's speculations seem ripe for such use. But I would rather think that Lyotard is pleading for a reassertion of the human mind in its contingency and finitude. [...] we see Lyotard's 'inhuman' contributing to a cartography not of the post-human, but the *ana-human*—the work of reworking the body and soul, of recuperating 'humanity' in the midst of its initial, supposed erasure or absence. (Harris 2001: 147–8)

The problem with Harris's sentiment here is that with his insistence on seeing Lyotard's work as either a contribution to the posthuman or a defence of the human, he misses the unique character of Lyotard's positive conception of the inhuman, which – unlike 'the human' – allows it to be connected with, and located as a site of resistance within, the negative inhuman.[8] Importantly, what Lyotard defends and celebrates is not what humanism understood as essential to the human (rationality, autonomy, and so on), but rather what it repressed and sought to eliminate in constructing this supposed essence (which Lyotard names in a number of ways: the unconscious, affect, *infantia*, and so on).

Most of the chapters of this book were originally written as standalone essays. In collecting them here, I have made some alterations to those previously published. I have attempted to remove repetitions and to make links between the chapters so that they may be coherently read in sequence. Yet I have also sought to preserve something of the singular style and tone of each, such that each might be read independently, and, I hope, stand up on its own. The unity of the chapters is given by their common themes, as indicated by the title and the subtitle of this book: they explore Lyotard and the inhuman condition through the themes of nihilism, information, and art. These themes are closely connected in Lyotard's thought, and accordingly, many chapters deal with more than one of these themes. Yet, roughly speaking, the chapters are ordered according to their focus, and may be read accordingly. In particular, I would suggest that a reader only interested in Lyotard's philosophy of art might begin with Chapter 4 ('Nihilism and the Sublime') and focus on the later essays. The earlier essays, more focused on Lyotard's analysis of nihilism in the contemporary situation and on philosophy of technology and information, tend to be longer and more technical.

The last several centuries are replete with influential diagnoses of, and attempts to respond to, the dark side of modernisation – Nietzsche's nihilism, Spengler's *Decline of the West*, Heidegger's retreat of Being, Husserl's *Crisis*, Adorno and Horkheimer's *Dialectic of Enlightenment*, Henry's *Barbarism*, and so on. In agreement with Williams (2000a) and Crome (2013), I see *nihilism* as a central theme in Lyotard's work, and it is my contention that in this respect he is one of the most important figures to have worked and thought in Nietzsche's wake. Lyotard offers us a series of powerful and unique insights into the nature of nihilism, and his work in this area still leaves much to be explored, assessed, and extended.

In my earlier study *Nihilism in Postmodernity* (2009), I largely followed Williams (2000a) in locating Lyotard's most significant and effective response to nihilism in his libidinal philosophy of the early 1970s. The essays collected here, most of which have been written since that earlier work, effect a shift to an attempt to think more deeply about how nihilism is presented and challenged in Lyotard's later thinking (see in particular Chapter 4). In my view this move does not invalidate the libidinal philosophy so much as indicate a deepening (and darkening) reflection on the state of the contemporary condition on Lyotard's part, and although the resistance to nihilism becomes more minimal, it arguably also calibrates itself more effectively to the current situation. As I argued in my previous work, I don't think one need side with the earlier or later Lyotard and reject the other, but can take the entire field of his thought and forge our own connections in light of our own researches.

Information is a key theme I have chosen through which to characterise Lyotard's later reflections on nihilism and the current situation, and which most strongly galvanises a dimension of his thought I believe to have been significantly under-appreciated. While some commentators have highlighted Lyotard's contribution to new media theory and posthuman thought, it has so far not been given the close and systematic analysis it deserves, particularly with regard to information theory. I attempt to situate Lyotard here as an important thinker of the 'philosophy of information', and to place this contested concept at the heart of the inhuman condition. Many of the chapters focus attention to those frequent, if generally schematic, discussions in many of his essays of information theory, cybernetics, artificial intelligence, telematics, computing, and so on, which remain in many respects prophetic and insightful with respect to one of the most dominant forces of rapid transformation in the world today, information technologies. In this regard, Lyotard's fascinating provocation with respect to contemporary nihilism is that, given the displacement of

the human by contemporary technosciences, our resistance should
not take the form of resuscitating any humanism, but of attempting to
think what is meaningful and valuable in and through the categories
of information theory itself (see especially Chapter 2).

Yet most centrally for Lyotard, *art* is what plays the role of resisting nihilism. This is no surprise: it has been a familiar theme in continental philosophy at least since Nietzsche, canonically expressed
in Heidegger's contention that for the latter, '[a]rt is the distinctive
countermovement to nihilism' (Heidegger 1981: 73). As is well
known, art is a central concern for Lyotard. But his extensive work
on the arts has also suffered the ambiguous fate of being associated
with *The Postmodern Condition*, and specifically with the essay
'Answering the Question, What Is Postmodernism?' appended to its
English translation. Lyotard's aesthetics is perhaps still best known
for the distinction he makes here between modern and postmodern
art, and for a few essays on the sublime aesthetic published in art
journals and then collected in *The Inhuman*. What is not very widely
known or well understood is Lyotard's recognition of a *crisis* in the
arts brought about, in part, by the application of new technologies
– what we today tend to call 'new media art' (which is known by
many alternative names and contains multiple sub-genres: computer
art, digital art, video art, electronic art, glitch art, bio art, information art, robotic art, virtual art, telematic art, systems art, and so on).

According to Lyotard, the degree of conceptual mediation introduced by such new technologies (which for him are technologies
which precisely have the quality of cognitive processes – they are
mechanical means of 'thinking') means that the old, Kantian conception of the aesthetic experience relying on a free, precognitive
synthesis of sensations is now called into question. Lyotard's work
around this area remains characteristically ambivalent, but at times
he underlines the great positive experimental value of these works,
and he points towards the aesthetic of the sublime as a way of understanding new media art from a philosophical perspective (see in particular Chapter 5). Moreover, Lyotard curated what has increasingly
become recognised as one of the first, and one of the most ambitious,
exhibitions of new media art, *Les Immatériaux*, held at the Pompidou Centre in 1985 (see Chapter 7). Recalling and drawing attention
to these facets of Lyotard's aesthetics, this book seeks to place him as
an early theorist of the new media arts, whose importance continues
to persist as these arts evolve.

Lyotard mobilises these engagements with the arts in such a way
that their countermovement to nihilism becomes evident, often in
ways which are highly original and distinctive – in particular, through

investigations of the aesthetic of the sublime (see Chapters 4, 5, and 6), the question of art and technology (Chapters 2, 5, and 7), the idea of immateriality (Chapters 6 and 7), and the inhuman itself (Chapter 7). For Lyotard, art acts as a countermovement to nihilism not only in the most general sense established by Nietzsche – by reasserting of the value of the sensible against its negation by the intelligible – but also because he sees the experiments of the avant-gardes as paralleling and prefiguring the changes wrought by technoscience. For him, the anxiety we feel today as the human appears to be revealed by technoscience as 'only a very sophisticated node in the general interaction of emanations constituting the universe' (PE: 32) can be confronted with the more positive promise their experiments reveal. As Lyotard underscores, in exploring the limits of meaning and sensation, art explores the inhuman in a manner which preserves and extends what the nihilism of the inhuman condition threatens: an openness to 'the event', that which is uncalculated, unexpected, and unthought.[9]

In sum, Lyotard presents a unique and acutely insightful position on nihilism in contemporary thought and culture. While Nietzsche, Heidegger, and many others have contributed much to such reflection, they often remain in important respects nostalgic for the meanings and values we have lost. While not necessarily proposing any final or adequate solutions, Lyotard frames these questions in a more progressive manner by remaining open to the positive potentialities of the new conditions of existence, while at the same time remaining sensitive to the urgent need to critically challenge destructive tendencies. By thinking through meaning and value at the horizon of cultural change, under the rubric of 'the inhuman', Lyotard's work helps probe the limits of how it is that life may be meaningful, and provides intellectual resources which help us to negotiate the continuously changing world. The reflections developed in this book explore our inhuman condition, through, with, and at times against, Lyotard.

Notes

1. Of particularly notable importance are the bilingual collected volumes of Lyotard's art writings edited by Herman Parrett and published by Leuven University Press (2009–13), the long-awaited English translation of *Discourse, Figure* (D), and the renewed attention given to the exhibition Lyotard directed, *Les Immatériaux*, signalled by a number of retrospective events around its thirtieth anniversary in 2015. Recent significant scholarly works in English include Bamford 2012, Jones 2013, Bickis and Shields 2013, Milne et al. 2013, Sawyer 2014, Boeve 2015, and Hui and Broeckmann 2015.

2. See the two volumes of Lyotard's 'paganism', *Instructions païennes* and *Rudiments païens*. The first is translated as 'Lessons in Paganism' in LR. A selection of essays from the second is translated in TP. But see especially 'Theory as Art: A Pragmatic Point of View' (Lyotard 1981b).
3. In an interview, Lyotard explains: 'I never used the term *postmodernism*, only "the postmodern" or "postmodernity" – it's not an *ism*. The major misunderstanding is to transform into an *ism* what wasn't at all an *ism*. I hate *isms* because I'm not a theorist' (Lyotard 2006).
4. This strategic decision to displace the postmodern with a focus on the inhuman does not mean that I believe Lyotard's concept of the 'postmodern' is now without value. For a recent interpretation and defence of this concept, see Jones 2013.
5. See Sim 1997; Badmington 2000; Harris 2001; White 2006; Martin 2009; Miccoli 2010; Herbrechter 2013.
6. In fact, both the terms 'postmodern' and 'posthuman' find an important common source in the work of Ihab Hassan, and it is interesting to note that Lyotard's first essay to discuss the postmodern (Lyotard 1977) was published alongside one by Hassan (1977) on the posthuman, in the proceedings of a conference at which they both presented.
7. These are the main features of the 'liberal humanist subject', which N. Katherine Hayles, in her deservedly influential study *How We Became Posthuman*, identifies as the relevant sense of the 'human' which has been deconstructed by scientific and cultural developments, giving meaning to the term 'posthuman'. Following C. B. Macpherson, she conceives of the liberal humanist subject as owning itself, and owing nothing to society. See Hayles 1999: 3.
8. This is also what Stuart Sim misses by reading Lyotard as being in fact a defender of humanism. See Sim 1997 and various of his entries in Sim 2011.
9. On the event in Lyotard's thought, see Chapter 2, and for a more detailed discussion, Woodward 2006.

Chapter 1

The End of Time: Evolution, Extinction, and the Fate of Meaning

When a philosopher announces a discourse on time, one can expect the worst.

Lyotard 2002: 30

0. According to some recent and contemporary philosophers, we are no longer having the time of our lives.[1] What this means is that a certain way of understanding time – time on the scale of human life – has been displaced by recent developments. Most significantly, in the last several decades science has opened up vast vistas of previously unimagined time, the 'deep' or 'cosmic' time of the earth's archaic past and of the universe's future, with the suggestion that, in any meaningful sense, time will end in a trillion, trillion, trillion years from now, with the heat death of the universe. 'The end of time' of this chapter's title envelops these two senses: the end of cosmic time, and the end of human time brought about by the revelation of the former. But my question here turns this movement back around to the question of human beings and their lives, and asks about the import of cosmic time for the meaningfulness of human lives: how does the revelation of cosmic time, and its inevitable end, impact on existential meaning?

For some prominent twentieth-century philosophers, notably those working in the phenomenological tradition, no such problem arises: existential significance may be restricted to the world of everyday perception, and thus the 'time of our lives' isolated from scientific developments. Referencing Husserl and Merleau-Ponty, historian of philosophy Pierre Hadot argues this point succinctly:

[I]t is essential to realize that our way of perceiving the world in everyday life is not radically affected by scientific conceptions. For all of us – even for the astronomer, when he goes home at night – the sun

11

> rises and sets, and the earth is immobile. [...] The analyses of Husserl
> and Merleau-Ponty thus let us see that the Copernican revolution,
> of which so much is made in philosophy handbooks, upset only the
> theoretical discourse of the learned *about* the world, but did not at
> all change the habitual, day-to-day perception we have *of* the world.
> (Hadot 1995: 253)[2]

One philosopher who has resisted this phenomenological line of
defence is Jean-François Lyotard.[3] Lyotard fruitfully explores the
problem of the meaning of cosmic time for human life in a number of
essays in the 1980s and 1990s through the fable of the 'solar catastrophe' – the death of our sun several billion years from now. I want
here to engage this fable, and also the works of several commentators who have previously engaged it – notably Keith Ansell Pearson
and Ray Brassier – in order to shed light on the general problem
itself. Ansell Pearson brings these issues in contact with transhumanism, and critiques the postmodern fable told by the transhumanists
from the perspectives of Nietzsche and of modern science, as still too
anthropomorphic (negentropy and complexity are still expressions
of human, all too human values). Brassier wants to accede entirely
to science and to nihilism, seeing it as a vector of creativity and intelligibility rather than as a threat to values which need preserving.

1. This is the fable Lyotard narrates:
Our sun will expend its fuel in roughly 5 billion years, and the resulting nuclear reactions of its death throes will incinerate the earth.[4]
By then, it will be all over for human beings, unless we find a way
to exodus from the earth and to survive in the conditions prevalent
in other parts of the cosmos. Lyotard suggests that this problem is
the most important and pressing one facing us today, and it is what
drives the process we call 'development'. Everything happening in
the sciences and in cutting-edge technologies is aimed towards preparing us for extraterrestrial survival:

> logic, econometrics and monetary theory, information theory, the
> physics of conductors, astrophysics and astronautics, genetic and
> dietetic biology and medicine, catastrophe theory, chaos theory, mili-
> tary strategy and ballistics, sports technology, systems theory, linguis-
> tics and potential literature. (PF: 91)

A couple of decades later, we can update Lyotard a little in terms
of what are widely regarded as the most cutting-edge sciences and
technologies today: genetic engineering, nanotechnologies, quantum

computing, robotics, prosthetics, cognitive enhancement, artificial life, and so on – and who knows what currently unimagined technics might be invented in the next 5 billion years?

All these technologies are aimed, Lyotard suggests, towards remodelling the human body so that it may survive in the conditions of the cosmos. And what will the result be? What will 'the human' have become, such that it will be capable of an extraterrestrial existence? This is something that the fable does not tell us. But taking into account the likelihood of a radical transformation, Lyotard prefers to pose the problem of survival not for the human as such, but for 'the Brain and its Human'. And this, more broadly, because the brain is the most complex matter we know of in the cosmos, and the hero of the story is not the human as such – which in fact is threatened with disappearance through such a radical transformation – but complex processes. The fable of solar catastrophe Lyotard tells presents the crisis not as one of the survival of the human, but rather at the deeper level of the energy in the universe and its organisation.

Energy is distributed in the cosmos such that disorganisation is more probable than organisation. But it happens, against the odds, that some energy forms into organised systems. Closed systems will quickly dissipate their energy and collapse, reverting to the more probable state of disorganisation: this is described by the second law of thermodynamics, and called *entropy*. But open systems – systems capable of exploiting energy from outside their organised structure – are much more stable and can preserve themselves for much longer. Increasing complexity of the organised system allows for greater capacity for the exploitation of external energy, and prolonged preservation of the organisation itself. The tendency towards organisation in energy is termed *negentropy* (or 'negative entropy'). Norbert Wiener, the founding father of cybernetics, describes the drama of energy in the universe as follows:

> We are swimming upstream against a great torrent of disorganisation, which tends to reduce everything to the heat death of equilibrium and sameness [...] This heat death in physics has a counterpart in the ethics of Kierkegaard, who pointed out that we live in a chaotic moral universe. In this, our main obligation is to establish arbitrary enclaves of order and system [...] Like the Red Queen, we cannot stay where we are without running as fast as we can. (Wiener 1964: 324)

Wiener's image of us 'running as fast as we can' captures well the accelerating pace of development, and places it on the level where Lyotard presents it: the drama of the organisation and disorganisation of energy in the cosmos. Ultimately, the hero of the fable is the negentropic system. Contingently, this is the human brain, since it is the most complex system in the known universe. Lyotard presents some of the main stages of increasing complexity in the historical adventure of negentropic forces in the cosmos:

Life: on our planet, approximately 4 billion years ago, the complex and improbable systems called living cells synthesised themselves out of molecular systems.

Scissiparity: the reproduction of single-celled organisms through division into two parts almost identical to the original.

Sexual reproduction: the ontogenesis of living organisms proceeding from the aleatory combination of two separate genetic codes, allowing for greater differentiation of organisms and greater probability of survival of the species (more efficient processing of energy).

Humankind: selected through evolutionary processes which favour the survival of the best-adapted (most complex, negentropic) systems. Lyotard writes that '[t]his was an extremely unlikely system – [...] as unlikely as it is for a four-legged creature to stand up on the soles of its rear paws' (PF: 87–8).

Symbolic language: dramatically increases complexity through being *recursive* (it has the ability to recombine its elements infinitely while still making sense) and *self-referential* (being able to take itself as its object; symbolic language thus bestowed its user, the human system, with memory and critique, allowing it to deliberately modify itself and improve its performance).

The Neolithic and Industrial Revolutions: these two revolutions marked increases in efficiency in the way humans lived together in communities, allowing the exploitation of new energy sources, and the greater preservation of the negentropic human system.

Liberal democracies: the emergence, by the same processes of natural selection which govern the natural world, of the most efficient form of social organisation. Liberal democracies, in allowing a great deal of openness and flexibility in the social organisation itself, allow the most efficient way of exploiting energies and ensuring the preservation and increasing complexity of the collective human system. This system proved to be much more efficient at exploiting energy than closed systems with fixed social hierarchies. (See PF: 85–90)

The process of which these have been some of the most remarkable stages is called 'progress'. The only thing which looks like it might now be a threat to this progress is the death of the sun in 5 billion years. Against this inevitable eventuality (the sun is a closed system, and its lifespan a law of physics), the human system engages in 'development', preparing itself – or whatever it will be by the time it is ready to leave the earth – for existence in the cosmos. According to Lyotard, we have no right to assume that what will have survived will be human, or will even be 'alive' in any sense in which we currently understand these terms. We can therefore only properly call it 'the negentropic system'.

2. What is Lyotard doing in recounting this strange narrative of solar catastrophe? His fable regarding the death of the sun has frequently enough been commented on, but has rarely been well understood.[5] Most commentators discuss only the brilliant and ambiguous essay 'Can Thought Go On Without a Body?' (in IN), but Lyotard in fact discusses this fable in numerous essays written in the late 1980s and early 1990s.[6] Lyotard remains most well known for his claim regarding the end of metanarratives, and a common enough response to his solar fable has been the confused suspicion that he is unwittingly presenting us with another metanarrative, so soon after proclaiming their obsolescence. But in fact wit (and perhaps too much, which explains his readers' confusion) is on Lyotard's side here. He addresses this issue directly (in an essay that many seem not to have read), and gives a number of reasons why the fable is *not* a metanarrative.

What is a metanarrative? It is a 'grand story' told to justify research and development, and to give meaning to human life and all of its projects and activities. For Lyotard, metanarratives are characterised by a certain understanding of time, which he calls 'historicity' (according to him, a modern invention, of which the ancients were ignorant). Grand narratives are built around a metaphysics of the subject: they tell of a subject alienated from an originary, utopian wholeness, afflicted with a lack, and they present a *telos*, a denouement of the narrative in which the subject's lack is overcome and the originary wholeness restored. Modern historicity is thus an eschatology: it construes the end of time as a *redemption*. According to Lyotard, modern historicity has its origins in the Christianity of Paul and Augustine, but also manifests itself through the grand narratives of the Enlightenment (such as Marxism and Hegelianism), which construe the essential project of Humanity as one of progress and emancipation. Though often secularised, the Enlightenment metanarratives maintain an eschatological structure and a modern historicity: the individual subject of the soul affected by sin is transformed into the collective subject of Humanity, affected by ignorance, and the *telos* of redemption is no longer salvation through Christ but the emancipation of the human race through the full development of reason.[7]

According to Lyotard, the fable of solar catastrophe is of course a narrative, but it is not a *meta*narrative in the same sense as those to which he claims we have become incredulous, because it presents none of the traits of modern historicity (PF: 98). And this for the following reasons:

1. It is thoroughly *materialist*. It is a physical history about energy, and matter as states of energy. Humanity is presented as a complex material system; consciousness as an effect of language; and language itself as a highly complex material system (PF: 98).
2. The time of this narrative is *diachrony* (not historicity). Temporal succession is based on the partitioning of regular physical movements, and not on the time of consciousness, in which past and future are synchronous with a 'present' (such a time, according to the fable, is possible only for systems capable of symbolic language usage).
3. The fable does not have a *telos* of emancipation.[8] It *does* project an end, which is the survival (the salvation) of a highly complex negentropic system, 'a kind of super-brain' (PF: 98) from the fiery hells of solar incineration. But this end is not inscribed in the 'hermeneutic circle' through which it would mirror an origin, the reclaiming of a lost state of grace. Instead, Lyotard presents this end as simply a development from insensible matter, 'the effect of a "cybernetic loop" regulated toward growth' (PF: 99).
4. The future presented is not an object of *hope*. We cannot hope for the perfection of Humanity as the subject of history. The Human will be sacrificed for complexity. What it is that will be saved from solar catastrophe (if anything is), we can only dimly imagine.

Finally, Lyotard makes perhaps the most important point, implied by some of the above:

5. The hero of the story is not a *subject*. Rather, it is simply *energy*, and specifically, that tendency towards organisation in transformations of energy known as negentropy. As such, the fable has nothing to do with the emancipation of Humanity as the subject of history, and even underlies the current bankruptcy of such a project (since current 'development' is already oriented towards the inhuman horizon of extraterrestrial survival).[9]

Moreover, contrary to some confused commentators, Lyotard certainly does not endorse the story of solar death he tells, nor does he present it as a 'fact'. It is, precisely, a 'fable', and it is what the section title of the book *Postmodern Fables* in which its most extended presentation appears designates it: a 'system fantasy'. That is, it is a fable, or fantasy, told by what Lyotard often simply calls 'the system', by which he means the contemporary technoscientific and capitalist system of 'development'. In the essay 'The Wall, The Gulf, and the Sun', which contains an earlier version of 'A Postmodern Fable', the fable itself is put in the mouth of the system: it begins, 'The system said: .' It is not presented as factual, and Lyotard says that it does not require belief, nor is even expected to be believed (PW: 152; Lyotard 1994b: 192). Although it draws on science and the stories sometimes accredited by scientists, Lyotard notes that if they are asked, the scientists are clear that it is no more than a hypothesis (PW: 101). Lyotard suggests that it is a fable which circulates as a rumour (Lyotard 1994b: 192). He also insists that it is a *metaphysical* story, by which he means (in a broadly empiricist sense) that there is no evidence to verify it, and that it fails to criticise the presuppositions implied by the terms of its own argument (1994b: 194). It is not a metaphysics of the subject, but a metaphysics of energy. And he asserts that there is no more evidence for the existence of 'energy' than there is for the existence of a subject (1994b: 194).

3. Given all these ironic, sceptical, and critical caveats, then, why does Lyotard have recourse to the fable in so many places; what philosophical *work* does he want it to do? I want to suggest that the story of solar death is, according to Lyotard, the form that the metanarrative – the dream of emancipation – takes on in the postmodern era, that is, the era defined by the end of metanarratives.

It has frequently been commented with respect to Lyotard's well-known thesis on the end of metanarratives that he spoke too soon.[10] However, it is plausible to suggest that we may understand Lyotard's claim in a similar fashion to Nietzsche's proclamation of the death of God (with which it has important similarities): Nietzsche noted that the dead God's shadow would continue to haunt us a long while yet before it can be fully vanquished (Nietzsche 2001: §108), and the same might be said of metanarratives. Lyotard's postmodern fable of solar death is presented as the 'shadow' of a metanarrative: it is 'the great narrative that the world persists in telling itself after the great narratives have obviously failed' (PF: 81–2); 'the unavowed dream that the postmodern world dreams about itself' (PF: 81). It bears both important similarities and important differences in relation to a metanarrative, and for this reason we might be justified in using the ungainly term of 'post-metanarrative' in order to describe it.

In several places at least, Lyotard's opposition to the values expressed in the fable – its limitations and undesirability as a narrative of legitimation – is clear. He suggests that 'in his darker moments' he imagines the human project of emancipation as merely the effect of the inhuman drama of negentropy struggling against entropy (PW: 151). What's wrong with the fable, then? Ethically and politically: the drive towards development is governed by the principle of efficiency (or performativity, as Lyotard calls it), and what matters is only the optimum way of transforming energy such that organisation is preserved and entropy kept at bay. In terms of the overall performance of the human negentropic system, it would seem to be maximised if inefficient systems are eliminated. The fable thus suggests that according to some natural right liberal democracies have achieved their own legitimacy, while – Lyotard suggests – the entire Third World, as a poorly performing system, might be eliminated (PW: 99; IN: 76–7). As Stephen J. Gould notes, natural selection is actually a kind of natural 'decimation' – 'killing off nine so that the best tenth might survive' (Gould 1990, as cited and explained by Jencks 1996: 71). If we accede to a legitimation discourse based on natural selection, then we accede to the decimation of the human population.

Moreover, Lyotard suggests some 'existential' reasons for a critical reaction to the fable: the understanding of human life as simply a part of the drama of complexity risks eliminating those things which currently make human life valuable and worthwhile. As Lyotard says, we do not know if what leaves the earth in the great exodus before the sun's final death throes will be capable of truly thinking, of feeling, or will even be 'alive' in any recognisable sense. Yet Lyotard does not oppose the inhuman threat of development with the humanism of phenomenology, hermeneutics, or existentialism; of the subject, consciousness, the lifeworld, and so on. Instead, he opposes it with an alternative conception of the inhuman, which draws on Freudian psychoanalysis and on movements in the arts such as cubism (on the latter, see Chapter 7). What he values, and fears will be eliminated by development, are what he sees as the conditions of thought and art: sexual difference, suffering, and childhood (IN: 16–23; PW: 106–7). Lyotard insists that we should not decide in advance what artificial bodies might be capable of, but rather simply insist on what they *must* be capable of if what is valuable in the current version of the Brain and Its Human is not to be fully betrayed. Lyotard speaks of thought and art as another kind of complexity, and defends it in the name of another kind of 'inhuman'. In short, he seeks *resistance* to the fable, understood as an explanation for our contemporary nihilism, that is, what's wrong with the current socio-political-existential condition. He explains his use of the fable as a *strategy*, and one which deliberately presents the enemy as strongly as possible in order to present the strongest possible resistance (Lyotard 1994b: 195). It has the form: Even if things are really as dire as this, we might still resist.

Crucially for our interests here, Lyotard argues that the 'time implied in the story no longer has a human shape' (Lyotard 1994b: 194). In recounting this fable as an 'explanation' for the contemporary condition, Lyotard is giving us at least one reason for the end of 'human' time: *the end of metanarratives means the end of historicity as the modern imaginary of time, and the opening of our understanding of time onto a horizon (the death of the sun) which seems to destroy humanism (the image of man as the source and limit of meaning and value)*. The fable of the solar catastrophe rips our existential reflections from a rootedness in the earth (*à la* Husserl, Heidegger) and submits them to an alien takeover by inhuman forces. Yet Lyotard, despite his ironic and subtle critiques of this fable, and his gestures towards inhuman resistance, leaves the question of *how* we ought to respond to it largely in question. He presents it as something which asks to be reflected on.

4. If Lyotard is trying to present the (post-)metanarrative which governs contemporary life, why does he choose what might appear to many to be such a strange story, perhaps little more than a bizarre science fiction? In fact, such a story is presented by others, who (unlike Lyotard) ask us to take it seriously. First, Charles Jencks, the preeminent theorist of architectural postmodernism, presents such a story precisely *as* a persistent metanarrative (and quite explicitly against Lyotard and others who proclaimed their bankruptcy) in the final chapter of his book *What Is Post-Modernism?*.[11] Jencks agrees with Lyotard and others that both religious and Enlightenment metanarratives have lost much of their currency (their power to be believed), but suggests that the cosmological story of the universe might be a credible metanarrative for contemporary times. He writes that:

> It certainly would replace humanism – man the measure of all things – with the larger picture in which the cosmos is the measure of all things. It could possibly give direction, orientation and meaning to human activity, but not result in a reductive anthropocentrism. (Jencks 1996: 71)

Drawing on Brian Swimme and Thomas Berry's *The Universe Story, From the Primordial Flaring Forth to the Ecozoic Era* (1992), Jencks states that there is a kind of teleological or purposeful growth in the tendency of matter to self-organise, and the story of the universe recounts 'the tendency of all material systems to develop towards greater complexity' (Jencks 1996: 71). This tendency is expressed first through 'crystallised evolution' – the formation of stars and planets as a result of the interactions of the four fundamental forces of the universe (gravity, electromagnetic force, the strong and weak nuclear forces) – and then also through the 'natural evolution' of organic life.

For Jencks, despite the catastrophic decimations Gould notes (see above), the universe story is an optimistic one, in which the universe progresses insofar as it creates ever-greater complexity, feeling, sensitivity, mental power, and organisation (Jencks 1996: 71). Moreover, Jencks asserts that while scientists themselves might not see it, the universe story is 'spiritual',

> [b]ecause the universe is a single, unbroken, creative event which is still unfolding with human beings as essential parts of its story; because it inevitably produces surprising, humorous creations of beauty; because its laws are mysteriously complex and finely tuned; because it is so enjoyable and because there is strong evidence that, given enough time, it must produce culture. (Jencks 1996: 72)

In support of his vision, Jencks cites Ilya Prigogine and Isabelle Stengers, the complexity scientists at the Santa Fe Institute, supporters of the cosmological anthropic principle, scientists such as Freeman Dyson, Paul Davies, and Fred Hoyle, and evolutionists such as Allan Wilson (Jencks 1996: 72–3). Jencks draws on this last to emphasise the important role the brain plays in evolution (as does Lyotard's fable). He asserts that the tendency of complex adaptive systems (CAS) to learn and create is a 'spiritual quest' (73). Moreover, Jencks criticises philosophers such as Heidegger, Wittgenstein, Sartre, and Derrida for over-emphasising contingency and our alienation from the universe, and for refusing to acknowledge the beautiful emergent cosmic order (73).

In sum, what Jencks recounts is the story of cosmogenesis: the generative nature of nature (Jencks 1996: 77). For him it is a teleological or purposive narrative, where the purpose is the production of complexity, understood not only in inhuman terms as systems ordered for the efficient transformation of energy, but as necessarily and inevitably producing human beings, consciousness, culture, creativity, and beauty. While it displaces humanism by asserting that the human being is no longer the measure of all things, it does give human beings, and the things we have traditionally valued, a home in nature. Because of this, and because of the supposedly superior plausibility of this narrative over the religious and modernist ones (to paraphrase Lyotard, Jencks is suggesting that the universe story is a metanarrative towards which we may still be credulous), for Jencks, this metanarrative is a story 'that can orient a global civilization' (77).

From a Lyotardian perspective, Jencks's 'new metanarrative' begs for critique. First, it is simply not presented with compelling intellectual rigour. It is as though Jencks has applied his principle of double coding, a kind of pastiche, to concepts – anything can be mixed with anything else, regardless of apparent lack of fit.[12] For example, he asserts that the initial conditions of the universe – from which what is commonly called the 'Big Bang' emerged – might be called 'the Mind of God' or 'the Platonic World of the Forms', and that it contained 'the laws of justice, harmony, balance, aesthetics' (Jencks 1996: 75). From a philosophical perspective, such unlikely claims need a great deal more argumentative support than Jencks gives them. Perhaps most significantly, however, Jencks's 'universe story' seems to contain a version of the Hegelian apologetics to which Lyotard refuses to accede: for Jencks, the universe is justified by its production of complexity, despite the decimation of life required for such a production (just as for Hegel all the evil in the world is justified by the dialectical motor of history[13]). For Lyotard, an ethical sensitivity demands that we not accept such an apologetics; to do so is to justify the existence of evil, and to risk perpetuating it. (Jencks in fact presents this apologetics in banal bad taste, appealing to his readers not to let nature's 'undeniable nasty part' distract us from the beauty to be heard in the sounds of birds and dolphins (1996: 76).) Ironically, perhaps, Jencks's dangerously blithe presentation of a new metanarrative helps us to understand the significance and force of Lyotard's critical engagement with the post-metanarrative of the fable of solar catastrophe.

5. Second, a story similar to Lyotard's fable is evident in some forms of transhumanism. Although Lyotard never indicates precisely where he derived the ideas presented in the fable, one possibility is that he picked them up while working in California in the 1980s (he held posts at the University of California, Irvine and San Diego), a time and place during which the loose collection of ideas known as transhumanism began to coalesce. A landmark in this coalescence was the publication, in 1990, of Ed Regis's satirical volume recounting the way-out ideas of various fringe scientists in the California area, *Great Mambo Chicken and the Transhuman Condition*. Ansell Pearson's

discussion of Lyotard in *Viroid Life: Perspectives on Nietzsche and the Transhuman Condition* (1997) calls attention to the similarities between Lyotard's fable and transhumanism. These similarities are readily apparent from the first two articles of the *Transhumanist Declaration*:

> 1. Humanity stands to be profoundly affected by science and technology in the future. We envision the possibility of broadening human potential by overcoming aging, cognitive shortcomings, involuntary suffering, and our confinement to planet Earth.

> 2. We believe that humanity's potential is still mostly unrealised. There are possible scenarios that lead to wonderful and exceedingly worthwhile enhanced human conditions. (In More and Vita-More 2013: 54)

Broadly speaking, as these lines indicate, the key idea of transhumanism is the desirability of transcending the human condition through the development and application of new technologies. This includes, but is not limited to, the artificial enhancements and transformations of the human body by technological means which Lyotard discusses in his fable. One significant branch of transhumanism, known as 'extropianism', presents an evaluative structure based on energetic concepts, similar to the one Lyotard recounts: 'extropy' designates the opposite of entropy (it is thus an alternative term for negentropy), and extropian transhumanism seeks to use technology to promote 'extropian principles'.[14] Transhumanists are overtly concerned with life extension and survival, the most extreme expression of which is the 'Omega Point' cosmology proposed by Frank J. Tipler. Tipler (1994) argues that intelligent life will eventually colonise the cosmos, use elementary particles as information processors, and run a simulation which will effectively resurrect the dead by emulating all the possible alternate universes since the Big Bang. Tipler identifies this 'Omega Point' with God and the Christian conception of Heaven, since he sees most of the traditional criteria for such as being fulfilled in this way.

Like so many others, Ansell Pearson unfortunately misreads Lyotard by taking him too literally (a misreading for which Lyotard's texts, with their subtle irony, must take at least a little responsibility), and misses the critical dimension. Let us get the details of this misreading out of the way first, in order better to concentrate on the positive contributions Ansell Pearson offers to the problems we are considering here. After briefly recounting Lyotard's fable of the escape of the negentropic system from the solar catastrophe as presented in the essay 'Time Today', Ansell Pearson complains that

> [i]n the case of Lyotard's thinking on time today, the monstrous logic of capitalism is granted a logic of autonomy which in reality it does not enjoy. His presentation of the inhuman time of our neg-entropic destiny results in an abstract and ahistorical opposition between a pure ethicism on the one hand and the unstoppable – because cosmic – accumulation process on the other. Is this not to be seduced by capital's own desire to construct itself as the transcendental ground of all change and innovation? (Ansell Pearson 1997: 171)

And further:

> The real problem with Lyotard's fantastical account is that it ascribes to capital a vitalism and a teleology. He thus ends up, ironically, offering us the kind of meta-narrative which he had sought to show in the earlier essay on the postmodern condition was now discredited. Grand narratives concerning a neg-entropic future end up being complicit with the image that the system of control likes to project of itself, that is, portraying advanced technological life as if it were simply a mere continuation of natural history. (Ansell Pearson 1997: 172)

We need only recall Lyotard's description of the fable as precisely that, and as motivated by a strategy for making the enemy appear as strong as possible in order to critique it as strongly as possible, in order to see where Ansell Pearson goes wrong here. The far greater interest of Ansell Pearson's otherwise brilliant book, however, concerns his critiques of the discourse of transhumanism, which we can read as usefully applicable to Lyotard's fable (despite his misinterpretations). As such, Ansell Pearson provides a way of interpreting the fable according to the value structure that it embodies, and also a certain way of resisting this value structure (a way which is far more literally and factually oriented than Lyotard's ironic and suggestive strategies).

Throughout the chapters of *Viroid Life*, Ansell Pearson delivers a scathing critique of transhumanism, conducted on two primary fronts: on one, he deploys Nietzsche's critique of anthropomorphic thinking to find deep-seated anthropocentrisms in the discourses which proclaim the transcendence of the human; on the other, he effectively attacks the supposedly scientific basis of transhumanist discourse by exposing many of its main contentions as factually outdated or simply false on the basis of contemporary science. Both of these lines of argument might be applied to Lyotard's fable.

6. In contrast to Lyotard, Ansell Pearson asserts that the transhumanist discourses of evolution as increasing negentropy and complexity *are* a new form of metanarrative, and this because they project anthropocentric biases onto supposedly natural processes, giving human life meaning in the context of the natural universe. Where Lyotard sees the erasure of the figure of the human in the valorisation of negentropy, Ansell Pearson sees a deeper and more hidden inscription of the human in the supposedly inhuman. Transhumanist discourse is a metanarrative because it remains teleological, citing complex organisation as the purposiveness of the universe itself, and giving meaning to human life as an essential part of the development of this goal (even if 'the human' as such is destined to transcend itself). According to Ansell Pearson, '[t]he new grand narratives are as anthropomorphic as hell' (1997: 170). What is most anthropomorphic in this metanarrative is the very ascription of *purpose* to the universe, which is – from a Nietzschean perspective – an anthropocentric conceit, finding no basis in fact, but rather existing because of the deep-seated human *desire* for purpose and tendency to interpret the world in purposive terms.

Ansell Pearson further argues that transhumanism is an expression of the ascetic ideal (that is, it preserves the religious values Nietzsche criticised and sought to overcome) (1997: 25). The ascetic ideal cannot affirm suffering in life, and hence devalues life in its wholeness, projecting a better world elsewhere. Transhumanism preserves and reflects the ascetic ideal insofar as it seeks to leave the corporeal and earthly conditions of human existence and become 'pure mind' in the form of informational abstraction. Moreover, we may understand transhumanism as a manifestation of the ascetic ideal insofar as it denies the value and legitimacy of entropic processes, of degeneration, deregulation, disorder, and death, seeing value only in order, preservation, and growth. For Nietzsche, this structure of values can be effective in preserving life, but it maintains the will to power at a low level, hampering its creativity and flourishing. Transhumanism reflects and perpetuates those Christian and Platonic values which, according to Nietzsche, preserve life at the cost of mutilating and destroying what is most valuable *in* life, its capacity for creative transformation.

The narrative of the adventure of negentropy is pernicious because it provides a supposedly naturalist ground for what are really just human, all-too-human values, insulating them from much-needed critique and interrogation. As Ansell Pearson characterises it, transhumanism in its most popular form is the new 'Platonism for the people' (a characterisation Nietzsche once famously applied to Christianity) (Ansell Pearson 1997: 172). Ansell Pearson also notes, here following Lyotard, that this discourse also functions as an apologetics for capitalism and imperialism, by claiming that the liberal democracies to which they have become wedded are the 'chosen' (and hence, solely legitimate) forms of social and political organisation of the natural forces of the universe (170–4).

7. Further, Ansell Pearson calls into question the factual legitimacy of the supposedly scientific claims on which transhumanism founds itself. First, he questions the claim that the story of the development of life in the universe can plausibly be read as a kind of necessary, progressive development. Transhumanists tend to assert that the production of complex systems such as human beings was somehow inevitable: while only a stage within the cosmic drama, we appear as a *necessary* stage, within an arc of gradually increasing complex systems. Ansell Pearson calls this gradualist, progressivist interpretation of the history of the universe into question by citing scientific works which suggest, to the contrary, that cosmic history is in fact a highly contingent series of events, displaying nothing of gradualness, progress, or inevitability. For example, the geophysicist Stuart Ross Taylor suggests that if the asteroid thought to be responsible for the extinction of the dinosaurs had missed colliding with the earth in its path through space, human life would likely never have evolved in its current form (Taylor 1992: 294, cited in Ansell Pearson 1997: 185).

Moreover, and perhaps *most* tellingly, Ansell Pearson points out that the idea that nature 'selects' in such a way that it progressively develops complexity is not upheld by current science (1997: 171). The idea that the 'arrow of complexity' drives evolution is a Lamarckian (hence, pre-Darwinian) idea, which is not supported by Darwin or by more recent biology. Significantly, as anyone who has anything more than a popular, superficial grasp of Darwinian evolutionary theory ought to know, Darwin effectively eliminated teleology from natural processes by demonstrating how complex systems *could* arise through blind and arbitrary processes of natural selection operating over vast expanses of time. However, evolution does not *select* complexity; some simple organisms survive much better than complex ones in certain environments, and in fact evolution can have a difficult time explaining complexity when simple systems often seem better adapted for survival (171). Moreover, evolution does not consist in a progressive adaptation of an organism to its environment, since environmental factors are also constantly in flux.

Finally, Ansell Pearson indicates that the work of Ilya Prigogine – popularised in his book with Isabelle Stengers, *Order Out of Chaos* (1985) – enables us to question the supposed antagonism of entropy and negentropy that forms the matrix of the transhumanist fable. The work on dissipative structures by Prigogine and Stengers shows that entropy and negentropy are not antagonists, but 'partners in crime': in dissipative systems, entropic processes can contribute to the formation of complex adaptive systems. According to Prigogine's research, then, entropy is not simply the enemy of organisation; the two processes admit of a complex interweaving (Ansell Pearson 1997: 185).

8. What Ansell Pearson's discussion of transhumanism interrogates is the attempt to recuperate traditional structures of meaning – religious and modern – within the context of new scientific developments. In terms of time, what this effectively means is that *transhumanism tries to make cosmic time conform to the basic structural model of modern, eschatological temporality*. It does so by ascribing purposiveness to natural processes, identifying the subject of history with negentropic complexity, and projecting the redemption of this complexity through its eventual salvation from the entropic forces of the universe. Entropy is easily and loosely identified with original sin, originary lack, or the basic *problem* of existence from which existence needs to be redeemed, and this redemption is understood as the development of negentropy to the point at which it is able to save and preserve itself from the menace of entropy. Just as much as any religious narrative, the fable can be understood as promising salvation from death. In this way, transhumanism can be seen as a discourse which tries to show how our present sense of what gives meaning and value to human life can survive the death of our bodies and the evolutionary take-over of the flesh by metal and silicon.

In short, what Ansell Pearson effectively demonstrates is that, despite Lyotard's insistence that the fable itself is not a metanarrative, and that it calls into question the human, *it can be and is* understood by many as a metanarrative, suffused with anthropocentric bias. Thus, a humanism, based in human, all-too-human values, stubbornly persists in the face of the thought of the end of time. The problem with trying to save meaning by anthropomorphising cosmic time into eschatological historicity is twofold: first, it preserves values which we might be better off without, and second, it is already implausible and will forever be fighting a rear-guard action, since it depends upon (and is all too ready to indulge in) an illegitimate 'fudging' of scientific facts. However, Ansell Pearson also shows a way of resisting this dangerous persistence of humanism through both Nietzschean value-critique and appeals to science itself in order to demystify the pseudo-scientific post-metanarrative, restoring to us our *properly* inhuman, or posthuman, future(s).

9. Ray Brassier takes up Lyotard's fable in the essay 'Solar Catastrophe: Lyotard, Freud, and the Death Drive' (2003) and in the final chapter

of his book *Nihil Unbound* (2007) (which is a reworked version of the essay, contextualised within the overall argument of the book). Brassier in a sense takes up Lyotard's fable in the opposite direction to Ansell Pearson, radicalising its inhuman potential and mobilising it in service to the destruction of the 'manifest image' of the human. This manifest image – as contrasted with the scientific image, a distinction introduced by Wilfrid Sellars – is the image of human beings as they have typically perceived themselves up to now, possessing psychological attributes such as 'beliefs', 'desires', and 'intentions'. This image views human beings as *persons*, as loci of rational agency, and fulfils a normative role insofar as it grounds our view of human activities as purposive and meaningful. In other words, the manifest image is the 'humanist' image of the human. The scientific image, by contrast, views human beings simply as complex physical systems. While Sellars wants to recognise both images as essential, Brassier wants to destroy the former in light of the latter (see Sellars 1963; Brassier 2007: 3–6).

Through Brassier (and significantly, via Meillassoux), we see that the displacement effectuated by the discovery of cosmic time has the potential to destroy both the manifest image of the human, and the very metatheory of meaning which has supported discourses on human meaning and value since Kant ('correlationism', and phenomenology in particular). Rather than decry such an eventuality under the name of nihilism, as so many have done, Brassier asserts the legitimacy of nihilism and pushes it to the limit. For Brassier, 'the disenchantment of the world deserves to be celebrated as an achievement of intellectual maturity, not bewailed as an intellectual impoverishment' (2007: xi). Brassier understands nihilism primarily as

> the unavoidable corollary of the realist conviction that there is a mind-independent reality, which, despite the presumptions of human narcissism, is indifferent to our existence and oblivious to the 'values' and 'meanings' which we would drape over it in order to make it more hospitable. (Brassier 2007: xi)

Brassier asserts (following Nietzsche) that the interests of thought and of life are not necessarily in concert, but, in contrast to Nietzsche, unambiguously takes the side of thought, and expresses contempt for attempts to take the side of life:

> Philosophy would do well to desist from issuing any further injunctions about the need to re-establish the meaningfulness of existence, the purposefulness of life, or mend the shattered concord between man and nature. It should strive to be more than a sop to the pathetic twinge of human self-esteem. Nihilism is not an existential quandary but a speculative opportunity. (Brassier 2007: xi)

10. Brassier attacks the humanist attempt to defend the lifeworld against the encroachments of positivism and naturalism in twentieth-century philosophy by way of Quentin Meillassoux's attack on correlationism in *After Finitude* (2009). Meillassoux explains correlationism as follows:

> By 'correlation' we mean the idea according to which we only ever have access to the correlation between thinking and being, and never to either term considered apart from the other. We will henceforth call *correlationism* any current of thought which maintains the unsurpassable character of the correlation so defined. (Meillassoux 2008: 5)

Meillassoux identifies the origins of correlationism primarily in the Kantian attempt to disqualify dogmatic metaphysics. Kant introduced a new sense of objectivity, whereby it no longer indexed extra-subjectivity, but rather intersubjective agreement (that is, agreement of subjects within the correlation, rather than reference to what lies outside it) (Meillassoux 2008: 4). Correlationism, he asserts, is the dominant characteristic of all post-critical philosophy (which according to him is most contemporary philosophy, the most significant currents of which have been phenomenology – which identifies consciousness as the medium of correlation – and various currents of analytic philosophy – which identify language as the medium) (6). By mounting an argument against correlation, Meillassoux seeks to restore the privileges of speculative metaphysics, which claims to think things in themselves, outside the correlation. Meillassoux is thus an appropriate resource for Brassier's valorisation of nihilism as 'speculative realism', the assertion that we can think mind-independent reality. Furthermore, however, he shows how an extension of Meillassoux's work on the significance of 'deep time' effectively destroys the correlationist theory of meaning which has upheld the manifest image of man, with its humanist meanings and values, in nineteenth- and twentieth-century philosophy, the most prominent representative of which is phenomenology. But let us begin with Meillassoux's argument against correlationism.

This proceeds by way of the 'deep time' of the age of the earth confirmed in the 1930s.[15] He defines the key terms of his argument here as follows:

- I will call 'ancestral' any reality anterior to the emergence of the human species – or even anterior to every organized form of life on earth.

- I will call 'arche-fossil' or 'fossil-matter' not just materials indicating the traces of past life, according to the familiar sense of the term 'fossil,' but materials indicating the existence of an ancestral reality or event; one that is anterior to terrestrial life. An *arche*-fossil thus designates the material support on the basis of which the experiments that yield estimates of ancestral phenomena proceed – for example, an isotope whose rate of radioactive decay we know, or the luminous emission of a star that informs us as to the date of its formation. (Meillassoux 2008: 10)

According to Meillassoux, the revelation of ancestrality (the 'deep time' of the past) by the arche-fossil presents a problem for the correlationist because what it tells of is a time before the emergence of the correlation (that is, before the emergence of human thought), and is thus something which cannot be contained *within* the correlation as such. For the correlationist, the correlation itself is the condition of the intelligibility of any knowledge claim; claims which fall outside the correlation are to be dismissed as dogmatic metaphysics. The correlationist must therefore modify the (naïve realist) claims of the scientist by adding to any claims about ancestrality the epistemic caveat *'for us'* (that is, any claims supposedly about a time before the correlation emerged must be reformulated *within* the correlation, and retrojected onto the past). Yet for Meillassoux, this will not do. To see what is wrong with this correlationist move, all we need to do is to ask (phrasing the general question by way of a specific example): *'what is it that happened 4.56 billion years ago?* Did the accretion of the earth happen, *yes or no?'* (Meillassoux 2008: 16)

Meillassoux suggests that the correlationist is likely to say both yes *and* no; yes in the sense that science gives us objective facts (objective understood as intersubjectively verifiable), and no in the sense that ancestral events could not possibly have actually taken place in the way science describes (because, the correlationist must insist, they are described from within, and thus conditioned by, the correlation, but what they describe was prior to the correlation and thus not itself conditioned by it). For the correlationist, what science describes as ancestral has no possible object and is a *non-sense* (since objectivity and sense are themselves held to only make sense from within the correlation). Meillassoux suggests that the correlationist will split the scientific claim into two senses: a superficial, naïve realist sense which the scientist him- or herself might believe, and the more profound philosophical, correlationist sense. Yet Meillassoux insists that this precarious partitioning is unacceptable. He explains: 'if ancestral statements derived their value solely from the current universality of their verification they would be completely devoid of interest for the scientists who take the trouble to validate them' (2008: 17). Thus, the correlationist attempt to compromise with the scientist's ancestral claim evacuates any relevance and meaning from the claim, which (according to Meillassoux) needs to be literal and realist if it is to have any scientific value. Therefore, Meillassoux insists, '[t]here is no possible compromise between the correlation and the arche-fossil: once one has acknowledged one, one has thereby disqualified the other' (17). Thus if Meillassoux is correct, the scientific revelation of the deep time of the earth invalidates correlationism, including the existential-phenomenological framework of human meaning.

11. Yet Brassier thinks that Meillassoux's argument from the arche-fossil is not on its own strong enough to refute correlationism. In short, he contends that the argument from anteriority can too easily be appropriated by the correlationist, since – however unhappy scientists may be with this, and despite Meillassoux's inadequate rejoinders – the correlationist can always say that it is possible to *think* being before the correlation existed, so that anterior being is postulated as being *for us*.[16] In order to expand the argument against correlationism so that it has a properly devastating force, Brassier points to a time we *cannot think*: this, he believes, is the future extinction of the human race. It is here that he has recourse to Lyotard's fable of 'solar catastrophe'. He writes that '[w]hat defies correlation is the thought that [and here he quotes Lyotard:] "after the sun's death, there will be no thought left to know its death took place"' (Brassier 2007: 229; IN: 9). While Lyotard contemplates the possibility that thought might survive solar death, Brassier asserts that this is irrelevant, since in any case it will not survive the heat death of the universe in one trillion, trillion, trillion (10^{1728}) years from now, when entropic forces in the universe will have made the formation of matter impossible, and we will have reached the end of space–time as we know it.[17] At the end of time, Brassier proposes, there will be an insurmountable external limit to thought. He calls this limit *extinction* (2007: 228–9).

Extinction, for Brassier, is not the death of a biological species, but something which *levels* the supposed transcendence of human beings (consciousness or *Dasein*) as the locus of correlation, by reducing it to the level of natural phenomena. The key point for Brassier here is that – unlike ancestrality – the thought of extinction, taken as an object, transforms *thought itself* into an object. He writes:

> Extinction turns thinking inside out, objectifying it as a perishable thing in the world like any other (and no longer the imperishable condition of perishing). This is an externalization that cannot be

appropriated by thought [...] because it indexes the autonomy of the object in its capacity to transform thought itself into a thing. (Brassier 2007: 229)

Whenever in time the extinction of thought will occur, Brassier contends, it has a transcendental status, in the sense that it is *as if it has already happened*. And this is precisely because of the levelling effect he points to: the very fact that we know thought will suffer the catastrophe of extinction, whenever it will occur, shows that thought itself *never is* anything more than another perishable object. As Brassier phrases it, the inevitable fact of extinction means that *everything is already dead*. Again he quotes Lyotard: 'Everything's dead already if this infinite reserve from which you now draw energy to defer answers, if in short thought as quest, dies out with the sun' (IN: 9, quoted in Brassier 2007: 223).

This, then, is why Lyotard's solar death gives a stronger argument against correlationism than Meillassoux's arche-fossil: ancestrality says there is a time before thought, but leaves the correlation more or less intact, just limited in its scope. But according to Brassier, the inevitability of future extinction is more than an empirical fact, it has transcendental scope; it ruins the privilege of thought and cedes it to the object. In short, Brassier argues that there is a much more radical disjunction between the time of *extinction* and the space–time of correlation than between *ancestrality* and the space–time of correlation. While the latter can be reduced to and incorporated within chronology, and can become a relatively unproblematic thought *for us*, the former cannot be reduced to chronology or to a thought that can be grasped *for us*. This argument hinges on time, because transcendence is bounded by human time, and levelled by cosmic time.

12. In order to construe thought as something which can go beyond correlationism (and thus be capable of realist speculation), and to give an account of what motivates such thought, Brassier has recourse to a reading of Freud's death drive, and an interpretation of Lyotard's solar catastrophe in terms of this. He explains the points that interest him in Freud's explanation of the death drive in *Beyond the Pleasure Principle* (SE XVIII) as follows. Freud arrives at the hypothesis of the death drive by posing the question of traumatic repetition: why are people driven to a psychic repetition (for example, in dreams) of traumatic experiences? His answer is that such repetitions are an attempt to retroactively protect the organism from the trauma itself, by generating the degree of anxiety required to bind the excess energy released by the traumatic event. A traumatic event is one for which the organism is not prepared; it introduces into the psychic

apparatus an excess of energy which it does not have the resources to bind, to incorporate into its psychic economy. Traumatic repetition is thus an attempt to bind this excess energy so that it ceases to trouble and destabilise the psychic apparatus.

Second, Brassier highlights and develops Freud's speculative suggestions regarding the origins of organic life in the same essay. According to Freud, the birth of organic life is dependent on, and coincides with, the death of outer layers of the organism which are thereby able to act as filters, protecting the organism from excess bombardment by exogenous stimuli. Organic individuation is thus dependent on, and generated by, a kind of death. Brassier argues that it is the originary split between the organic and inorganic, indexed on the death of the external part of the organism, which makes this possible, and which constitutes a kind of 'aboriginal trauma' on which any other traumatic repetition is based. What thought does, essentially, is attempt to bind death, to come to terms with death itself, understood as the inorganic origin of the organic. This, then, is the death drive: the process by which thought attempts to bind, invest, come to terms with, death itself. On this reading, thought is the product of the traumatic trace of the inorganic in the organic; it is motivated by the attempt to bind the aboriginal death synchronous with the birth of the organism (Brassier 2007: 234–8).

Next, Brassier transposes Freud's death drive to the solar/cosmic register. According to him, Lyotard's solar catastrophe is an analogue to the aboriginal trauma of death as the death of part of the organism in organic individuation. Brassier, through his reading of Freud, suggests that philosophy's task is to 'bind' (invest, cathect) extinction, understood as aboriginal trauma. He argues that thought can successfully bind the trauma of extinction by *becoming* death; that is, by effectuating an 'identity-without-synthesis' with the object. The possibility of this is explained with recourse to François Laruelle's 'non-philosophy', a new form of transcendental reasoning which in effect solves the 'problem of access' to the real for Brassier's speculative realism.

13. The Laruellean component of Brassier's argument regarding extinction is outlined extremely briefly in the closing paragraph of the 'Solar Catastrophe' essay, with no attempt to explain the many technical terms introduced, and likely leaving the reader unfamiliar with Laruelle (which would have been most, at the time of publication) baffled. The explanation of this argument is more forthcoming in *Nihil Unbound*, and we are today in a somewhat better position to appreciate it, as Laurelle's work (in its basics, if not its

details) is becoming more widely known.[18] Its main pertinent points are these. According to Laruelle, all philosophy is determined by a structural invariant he calls the philosophical 'decision', which consists in positing a basic division between the real and philosophical thought (the 'dyad'), then positing that philosophical thought can mix or synthesise these two in order to ground its own purchase on the real and establish its authoritative claim to think the real. Philosophy thus, according to Laruelle, involves an imposture insofar as it grounds itself through a viciously circular reasoning. By contrast, Laruelle's 'non-philosophy' begins with an axiomatic decision to consider the real as the One, an indivisible pure immanence. Thought is then understood as part of the real, as unilaterally determined by it ('in the last instance'), but as having no grasp on it. As Brassier expresses it, Laruelle's thinking of the real conceives of the real as grasping thought and forcing thought to think it – such that thought is 'of' the real, without being able to represent it.

Non-philosophy and its various stages of development (called 'Philosophy II', 'Philosophy III', etc.) are the result of Laruelle's attempt to find a methodological solution to the difficult problem of how to think the real *from* the real. In general, his solution is to maintain a strict *dualism* between thought and the real, which insists on the unilateral relation explained above. Since it makes no claim to a new theory which would better represent the real, non-philosophy continues to use philosophical concepts as its material, but divested of their transcendental assumption to represent the real. Instead (in the language of Philosophy III), thought is considered as a 'transcendental clone' of the real.

Brassier applies these non-philosophical concepts to a thinking of extinction by suggesting how, with Freud, we can understand thought itself as radically immanent to the real. In suggesting that the death drive is 'consummated' with this thought, Brassier suggests that thought divests itself of all transcendence when it thinks itself as part of the 'inorganic' materiality of the universe. In *Nihil Unbound* he argues that all forms of philosophical vitalism retain a trace of transcendence, a distinction between the transcendent animation of life, associated with thought, and the bare immanence of death. In proposing an 'identity-without-synthesis' between extinction and the thought that thinks it, he is drawing on Laruelle to reject the transcendence associated with the synthesis of the philosophical decision (that is, philosophy's synthesis of the dyad, of concepts and the real), in order to assert that thought itself is nothing but a material process, part of an immanent material unity. For all the persistent strangeness of the non-philosophical terms he uses, Brassier's invocation of a 'subject-(of)-death' as a 'transcendental clone' is nothing other than an attempt to think, in a transcendental register, the materialist monism he believes must be the ontology of hard science. The death drive, understood in the above sense, is what gives Brassier's nihilist project its motive force. Following but displacing Nietzsche, he revalues the will to know *as* the will to nothingness, asserting its primacy over the will to life-affirmation. In effect, Brassier aligns thought with death and nothingness, and champions it over life, value, and meaning.

14. Brassier argues that the attack on correlationism destroys the position from which many of the most influential twentieth-century responses to nihilism have proceeded: in particular phenomenology and existentialism, but arguably also the philosophies of the linguistic turn, including at least some forms of poststructuralism. And more generally, a quite broad form of humanism, in which human thought and language in general (and not just the consciousness of the individual) receive a privileged place. This is so because correlationism gives a special status to the human as the locus in which *all* meaning becomes operative: it responds to the nihilistic encroachment of the sciences by arguing that even scientific knowledge is a secondary derivative of the primary givenness of the correlation as such. Briefly put, correlationism provides an argumentative framework in which it can seemingly be shown that human meaning trumps scientific discourse.[19] Brassier wants to show that this argumentative framework collapses, and the order of trumping is reversed. For Nietzsche, the nihilism of contemporary natural science is expressed in the fact that '[s]ince Copernicus man has been rolling form the centre toward X' (1968: §1.5). For Brassier, this X might be understood as the in-itself which Kant also designated as an X, because, he believed, we could not know it.[20] Brassier's nihilism means that the destruction of the manifest image of man ('we' roll further from 'Man' *as* centre) gets us closer to an adequate thinking of the X. At the same time, the more adequately we think the X, the further we roll into our nihilism, away from our familiar horizon of meanings and values. For Brassier, this price is worth paying for the gain thought makes in rational intelligibility (Brassier 2007: 238).

15. To return, in conclusion, to Lyotard. First, Lyotard's ironic, fabling, writerly response to the 'post-metanarratives' of development as physical eschatology might appear to be a much less effective rejoinder than Ansell Pearson's direct debunking on the basis of hard science. Yet, there is a very deliberate strategy at work here, one which we may see as analogous to Lyotard's treatment of Holocaust deniers

(in particular, Robert Faurisson). In the latter case, Lyotard resists the usual move of most historians simply to stake the claims of historical evidence for the reality of the Holocaust against the deniers, since he does not believe that any appeal to historical evidence captures what it is about the Holocaust which needs to be acknowledged and remembered: not its reality as a historical event, but the unthinkable magnitude of its very *wrongness* (see D; HJ). Similarly, in critiquing the post-metanarrative, it is not the scientific veracity or otherwise which Lyotard sees as being at stake. Rather, the stake concerns the values it embodies, and their political and existential implications. Lyotard's strategy is thus in line with his general agreement with the critique of metaphysics (following Kant, Heidegger, and Adorno, among others), and with the fact/value distinction (most famously proposed by Hume). Lyotard seeks to engage critically with a metaphysical story which claims to ground values (as we have seen, this claim is explicitly made by Jencks) from a perspective which rejects the possibility of any such grounding. Thus, he does not seek to simply challenge the factual bases of the (meta)physical story, but rather to draw out the value-implications of such a story and try to show that they lead to undesirable consequences, ones which would likely not be endorsed by most promulgators of the post-metanarrative themselves.

Ansell Pearson's admirable method of scientific refutation certainly has its power and its uses, but it maintains the problematic in its present position. In order to respond, the transhumanists (and others) need simply update their science. Whether or not the latest scientific developments can be reconciled with 'historicity' is largely a matter of interpretation. As the example of Jencks shows, there is a great deal of flexibility possible here, and there is every reason to believe that, with enough interpretive ingenuity, almost any new scientific development could be incorporated within such a framework. Lyotard's strategy, while more subtle and elusive, has the advantage of shifting the ground of the debate. If successful, such a shift should make us realise the necessity of thinking values on their own terms, independent of physical and metaphysical discourses, while increasing our critical awareness of any and all attempts to ground values in such a way.

We may summarise the various other perspectives we have reviewed here in the following way: Jencks and the transhumanists try to resolve the crisis for the meaning of human existence announced by the end of time by trying to collapse the new image of existence into the old structures of meaning, while Brassier wants to eradicate the old structures of meaning entirely for the sake of the new image of existence. Lyotard, however, offers a third way: he insists on the intractability and incommensurability of both categories, of meaning and existence.[21] On the side of existence, Lyotard departs from Jencks, the transhumanists, and those who think cosmic time can be reconciled with human historicity, as well as those such as Husserl, Merleau-Ponty, and Hadot who believe that it can be bracketed as irrelevant to the human construction of meaning. For Lyotard, contemporary science needs to be taken seriously, and has a real gravitational force which pulls contemporary thought from its orbit around the manifest image of the human. However, on the side of meaning, Lyotard would likely have objected to Brassier's nihilism (as he did against positivist reductions of meaning to science) that it illegitimately levels all forms of reason to a single conception (the will to *knowledge*, or as Lyotard would put it, the cognitive genre). One of the key elements of Lyotard's thought is the defence of a kind of rational pluralism, in which modes of thought such as the ethical and the aesthetic are defended in their own specificity, as heterogenous to, and incommensurable with, the cognitive.[22]

A Lyotardian strategy, then, would be *to insist on the abyss between meaning and existence*,[23] to hold them as incommensurable, to allow thought a space where it has responsibility only to itself and not to life (a *speculative* space), as well as a space where life has responsibility to itself and not to thought: yet not to strictly police their boundaries, keeping them hermetically isolated, but to attempt to think 'passages' between them: this is what Lyotard calls *judgement*. As is well known, Lyotard's understanding of judgement is derived from readings of Aristotle and (especially) Kant. For him it refers to thinking which of necessity has to judge without recourse to any pre-existing rule or set of criteria which would determine in advance what is to be judged, and which must proceed on a case-by-case basis (JG: 14). Suggesting the symbol of an archipelago for the entire realm of thought, in which the islands are Kantian faculties or Wittgensteinian language games (or 'phrase families', as Lyotard calls them) with their own proper objects and rules for validating claims regarding those objects, judgement is like an admiral who launches expeditions over the seas between the islands, presenting what is discovered on one island to another island (E: 12). Judgement proceeds guided by *feeling*, not by concepts (JG: 15). It is prior to the rules and criteria established by the islands of the archipelago; it establishes those islands, and creates 'passages' between them. The significance of the image of the archipelago is that it asserts the heterogeneity of thought, and the incommensurability – lack of a common measure, which would be like an established bridge or trade agreement between the islands – between its different forms of operation. Judgement signals that thinking, of a certain kind (called 'philosophical'), requires that the seas be perilously crossed each and every time.

Despite its largely Kantian origin, judgement need not be understood as a model of thought which necessarily reduces everything to correlation, but rather one which seeks to think the implications of the inside and the outside of the correlation for each other, refusing any common measure which would *reduce* the one side to the other. Judgement might be adopted as a model with which to think both the manifest and the scientific images of man, to allow them to oscillate, without the teleology of either modernist historicity or the eliminativist programme, but rather with an (at least) equal concern to develop what the revelation of the scientific image of man, and of cosmic time, means *for us*, such that although radically displaced, the time of our lives is not, for all that, quite over yet.

Notes

1. This chapter, in an earlier version, was first presented at the 2011 conference of the Australasian Society for Continental Philosophy, held at LaTrobe University, on the theme 'The Time of Our Lives'.
2. Hadot references Husserl 1981 and Merleau-Ponty 2012.
3. Whether or not science does in fact leave everyday *perception* intact is an issue I will leave to one side here in order to focus on some different issues concerning time and meaning that Lyotard develops. However, we may note in passing that Lyotard does not agree with Hadot's assessment. For further discussion of this issue, see Chapter 4.
4. Lyotard always gives the figure as 4.5 billion years, but current science puts it closer to 5 billion. Lyotard also suggests that the sun will explode and the earth will be engulfed in a nova (PF: 83). In fact, the sun does not have enough mass to go nova, and when, in 5 billion years, it no longer has enough fuel to continue the fusion reaction which converts hydrogen into helium, it will expand and become a red giant, before contracting into a white dwarf. However, the fate of the earth remains the same: it will be incinerated as it is engulfed by the expanding photosphere. While there has been some speculation that the earth might survive because the reduction of the sun's mass will allow it to enter a wider orbit, recent research has shown that this will still not prevent the earth from being engulfed. See Shröder and Smith 2008, in particular section 4.3, 'Doomsday confirmed', pp. 160–1. However, Shröder and Smith do note the possibility (suggested by Korycansky et al. 2001) of a potential method of saving the earth or at least extending its lifespan by increasing its orbit with the aid of the gravitational effects of arranged encounters with an appropriate asteroidal body. Interestingly, echoing Lyotard's concerns that his fable is meant in part to dramatise, Shröder and Smith note that such a scheme 'would have the advantage of improving conditions for the whole biosphere, whereas any scheme for interplanetary "life rafts" that could move slowly outwards to maintain habitable conditions would, on

cost and energy grounds, necessarily be confined to a small fraction of the human population – with all the political problems that would produce – plus perhaps a tiny proportion of other species' (2008: 161).

5. See for example Sim 1997; Ansell Pearson 1997; Badmington 2000; Germain 2009.

6. Lyotard's most extensive discussion of the fable is the essay 'A Postmodern Fable' in PF, but see also 'Time Today' in IN; 'The Wall, the Gulf, and the Sun: A Fable', 'The Grip (*Mainmise*)', and '*Oikos*' in PW; 'The Survivor' in TP; and 'A Postmodern Fable on Postmodernity, or: In the Megalopolis' (Lyotard 1994b).

7. In one essay Lyotard gives the following list of modern metanarratives: 'the progressive emancipation of reason and freedom, the progressive or catastrophic emancipation of labour (source of alienated value in capitalism), the enrichment of all humanity through the progress of capitalist technoscience, and even – if we include Christianity itself in modernity (in opposition to the classicism of antiquity) – the salvation of creatures through the conversion of souls to the Christian narrative of martyred love' (PE: 29).

8. This is Lyotard's claim in the essay 'A Postmodern Fable'. Elsewhere, in the essay 'The Grip', he presents this point in a far more nuanced way, suggesting that the fable proceeds from and is an extension of the desire for emancipation, but crosses a threshold beyond which emancipation no longer makes sense, precisely because the value of development (the means) takes precedence over, and ends up destroying, the end (the meaning of the 'human' which was to be emancipated).

9. 'The hero is not a subject. The word energy says nothing, except that there is some force. [...] it knows nothing and does not *want* any of it. It obeys blind, local laws and chance' (PF: 93).

10. See for example Ansell Pearson 1994: 3–4.

11. Lyotard and Jencks, as two of the most prominent theorists of the postmodern, commented occasionally on each other's works, primarily in order to distinguish their positions. Jencks's 'new metanarrative' discussed here explicitly distinguishes his position from Lyotard's. Lyotard, for his part, in one place notes 'Jencks's "postmodernism" in architecture, which the reader will do me the favour of not confusing with what I have called "the postmodern condition"' (IN: 127). As far as I am able to determine, Lyotard discusses the 'post-metanarrative' before Jencks does, his first presentations appearing in 1987 with the essays 'Can Thought Go On Without a Body?' and 'Time Today'. While Jencks's book *What Is Post-Modernism?* is based on lectures first delivered in 1985, its four editions undergo significant revision (so much so that Jencks says he is tempted to coin a new term for what seems to him to be a new genre, and suggests 'transitext', 'metamorphibook', 'rescription', or 'evolvotome' (Jencks 1996: 8), and the chapter on the 'new metanarrative' appears only with the fourth edition (1996). There is no evidence in Jencks's discussion that he was aware that Lyotard had already critiqued just such a 'new metanarrative' based on cosmology.

12. Jencks's 'double coding', a key idea of his theory of Post-Modern architecture, combines two heterogenous approaches – typically modern techniques and traditional or local building – in a single construction, irrespective of their lack of stylistic fit. Among other things, the approach is aimed at addressing the divide, which so beset modernist architecture, between the visions of professional architects and the needs and tastes of the public who use their buildings. See Jencks 1996: 29–30.

13. See for example Richard J. Bernstein's discussion of Hegel in chapter 2 of his book *Radical Evil* (2002).

14. See Max More's 'Principles of Extropy' (2003). One of the many meanings given to extropy in this manifesto is this: 'Extropy means seeking more intelligence, wisdom, and effectiveness, an open-ended lifespan, and the removal of political, cultural, biological, and psychological limits to continuing development.'

15. The earth is roughly 4.5 billion years old, as established largely through work in the radiometric dating of rock by Arthur Holmes. A report published by the National Research Council of the US National Academy of sciences and co-authored by Holmes, published in 1931, provided detailed and convincing data and saw the general acceptance of this geo-chronological dating by the scientific community. See Knopf et al. 1931.

16. Brassier's argument against Meillassoux here is in fact a complex one, drawing on several arguments suggested by others. One key strand of this argument, in a little more detail, is as follows. Brassier notes that Meillassoux's appeal to anteriority hangs on the scientific (Einstein–Minkowski), empirical conception of space–time, and the way this space–time coordinates the past, present, and future in what Brassier calls 'chronology'. However, Brassier notes, 'a simple change in the framework which determines chronology would suffice to dissolve the alleged incommensurability between ancestral and anthropomorphic time, thereby bridging the conceptual abyss which is supposed to separate anteriority from spatiotemporal distance' (2007: 59). Meillassoux admits that it is simply an empirical, contingent fact that ancestral time preceded manifestation (the world as it appears within the correlation), and he is also committed to the idea that the coordination of space–time which establishes such a chronology *might* change, since this is a corollary of his 'principle of factiality', or the assertion of absolute contingency, which is a further key argument of *After Finitude* (see chapter 3 of that book). In short, Brassier argues that while Meillassoux's argument takes place in a *logical* register, it necessarily hinges on an *empirical* contingency (58). Brassier wants something more: an argument with a robustly transcendental scope.

17. Brassier properly notes that this 'end' of time will be asymptotic (2003: 428): the breakdown of all matter, leaving only photons dancing in a cold, chaotic void, will end space–time as we know it (with any capacity to support life), but the universe in this minimal state will continue to expand indefinitely. Brassier references Odenwald 2002: 163 and Krauss and Starkman 2000. In 2011, the Nobel Prize in Physics was awarded to Saul Perlmutter, Brian P. Schmidt, and Adam G. Riess for

the discovery of the accelerating expansion of the universe through the observation of supernovae, a discovery which supports the hypothesis of 'heat death'. However, this thesis on the end of time is not uncontested. A recent scientific paper suggests that time will end in 5 billion years, roughly synchronous with the death of our sun. This hypothesis draws on the calculation of probabilities associated with the theory of a 'multiverse' cosmology. See Bousso et al. 2011. (The authors clearly state that '[w]e do not know whether our conclusion is empirically correct. What we have shown is that it follows logically from a certain set of assumptions' (14).)

18. The most important of Laruelle's works on which Brassier draws have now appeared in English translation. See Laruelle 2013a, 2013b. For a remarkably perspicuous introduction to Laruelle's notoriously difficult work, see James 2012: ch. 7, and for a useful collection of secondary texts, see Mullarkey and Smith 2012.

19. This characterisation requires the caveat that 'human meaning' is being used in such a broad sense here (simply as contrasted with scientific discourse) that it encompasses many perspectives – such as those of Heidegger and of structuralism – which portray themselves as challenging humanism. For example, for all Heidegger's decentring of *Dasein* and stressing of Being in his later works, *Dasein* remains that *to which* Being discloses itself and the world. (For an argument that Heidegger remains a humanist, see Welsch 2007.) It is this very broad sense that Brassier is concerned with.

20. More precisely, it is the transcendental object (the thing 'behind' appearances which appears) which Kant designates with an X, but he sometimes uses this term synonymously with the thing-in-itself, precisely because they are both unknowable as such (since they can be thought, but cannot be an object of experience). See 'Transcendental object' in Caygill 1995: 401.

21. This theme is developed in more detail in Chapter 4.

22. This argument is developed at length in *The Differend*, but for a brief summary of Lyotard's views, see 'Dispatch Concerning the Confusion of Reasons' in PE. In this essay he summarises a number of the key points in his position which I have mentioned here, by indicating what he sees as 'the stake confronting philosophical thought today. We must follow metaphysics in its fall, as Adorno said, but without lapsing into the current mood of positivist pragmatism which, beneath its liberal exterior, is no less hegemonic than dogmatism. We must trace a line of resistance to both of them. We must counter-attack the confusions without forming a new "front." For the time being, the defence of reasons is conducted by "micrologies"' (77).

23. On this theme, see Chapter 4.

Chapter 2

Information and Event: Lyotard's Philosophy of Information

Contemporary man is unable to hope for the unexpected, for anomalous events that don't correspond with 'normal' logic: still less is he prepared to allow even the thought of unprogrammed phenomena [...] the spiritual emptiness that results should be enough to give him pause for thought.

Andrei Tarkovsky 1989: 228

The Informational Turn

The contemporary theoretical context witnesses many claims to some kind of significant 'turn'[1] – ethical, theological, speculative, neuroscientific, nonhuman, and so on[2] – which would perhaps be comparable to the 'linguistic turn' in philosophy which dominated much of the twentieth century. Each declaration of a 'turn' stakes a claim as to what is at issue in thought today. One of the most plausible claims is to that of an *informational* turn, plausible both because of the way it traces its development to the linguistic turn itself, and because it undeniably has a much broader cultural resonance: we are living today in an 'information age', as few would dispute, resulting from what some term the 'fourth revolution', that of computation (Floridi 2014). The historical emergence of the informational turn is described by Luciano Floridi, one of the most prominent proponents of the 'philosophy of information' (PI), as follows:

The scientific revolution made seventeenth-century philosophers redirect their attention from the nature of the knowledge object to the epistemic relation between it and the knowing subject, and hence from metaphysics to epistemology. The subsequent growth of the information society and the appearance of the infosphere, the

> semantic environment in which millions of people spend their time nowadays, have led contemporary philosophy to privilege critical reflection first on the domain represented by the memory and languages of organised knowledge, the instruments whereby the infosphere is managed – thus moving from epistemology to philosophy of language and logic [...] – and then on the nature of its very fabric and essence, information itself. (Floridi 2011: 25)

During the 1980s, Floridi explains, various areas of activity and research became more accepted, and they converged in the historical emergence of the 'philosophy of information' late in the decade. These areas included disciplines such as AI and information theory, concepts such as complexity, computation, and dynamic systems, phenomena such as electronic communities and digital arts, and issues like the nature of artificial agents and virtual reality (Floridi 2011: 6).

Floridi defines the philosophy of information characteristic of the informational turn as follows:

> PI The philosophy of information (PI) is the philosophical field concerned with (a) the critical investigation of the conceptual nature and basic principles of information, including its dynamics, utilisation, and sciences; and (b) the elaboration and application of information-theoretic and computational methodologies to philosophical problems. (Floridi 2011: 14)

He contends that PI can lay claim to being a new *philosophia prima*, in both the Aristotelean sense of the primacy of its object (information) and the Cartesian–Kantian sense of the primacy of its methodology and problems (those which derive from and relate to information technologies) (Floridi 2011: 25).

Lyotard as Philosopher of Information

Lyotard made frequent remarks about information, primarily in his writings in the 1980s. The remarks are primarily (though not exclusively) critical, and I wish to argue here that we may reconstruct a kind of philosophy of information from these remarks. However, it is worth noting at the outset that Lyotard was not an expert on information theory. (In fact, he tends to confuse his references when he invokes the subject.[3]) He seemed to know relatively little of the technical specificities of information theory, and I will argue in one section of this chapter that this deficiency gives us need to critically revise his work on information if we are to make the most effective use of it. In particular, we shall see that he fails to appreciate the distinction – crucial to information theory – between *semantic information* and *data*.

Why then, it may well be asked, should we give any attention to Lyotard's thoughts in this area? What can he bring to the field of the philosophy of information as such?

First, Floridi notes that we can talk of PI in philosophers who lived before the information revolution (Floridi 2011: 15), and this diachronic consideration might also be synchronically extended to contemporary philosophers – such as Lyotard – who do not fully embrace PI in an explicit and technically rigorous way, but whose reflections have implications for it. Second, Lyotard was fully aware of his limited expertise on many of the issues with which he engaged, and incorporates a legitimation of this relative ignorance within his critical perspective. Following Lyotard, one way of drawing a distinction between an expert and a philosopher would be to suggest that experts deal with *technical* questions, while philosophers deal with *reflective* questions (Lyotard and Théofilakis 1985: 4–5). It is precisely a philosophical reflection on information which Lyotard contributes; a reflection on information which brings it into contact with a whole range of issues outside the scope of information theory and its *technical* questions and solutions. Lyotard explores aspects of PI acknowledged by Floridi and others as important, but which are often given little attention by those who style themselves as philosophers of information: the socio-political, existential, and artistic implications of information (see Floridi 2011: ch. 2).

In Floridi's taxonomy of the various branches of PI, Lyotard deals with 'cyberphilosophy': reflection on the 'psychological, anthropological, and social phenomena characterising the information society and human behaviour in digital environments' (Floridi 2002: 139). Here we are on the 'macro' level of the socio-political. Moreover, Lyotard explores information from the perspective of the tradition of continental critiques of language, and of the 'ontological' (as opposed to the so-called 'informational') perspective on language. Here, Lyotard examines the 'micro' level, the ontology of information and how it relates to the semantic and existential constitution of meaning as such.

It is in both these senses, I wish to argue, that Lyotard may be positioned as a philosopher of information. The value of his reflections are not to be found in his (rather meagre) understanding of information theory as such, but in his wider philosophical reflections within which the problematic of information is then inserted, often in strikingly original and insightful ways. This is his uniqueness, and relevance, in this field. More specifically, Lyotard critically examines the dangers and potentials of information in relation to 'the event'. This term has been established as central in Lyotard's work since Geoffrey Bennington's seminal study (Bennington 1988). As in the works of other prominent French philosophers (such as Derrida, Deleuze, and Badiou), for Lyotard the event designates a happening or occurrence, the eruption of something new from within an established structure. For him an event is unpredictable; it arises in an unexpected way, and cannot be fully captured in any retrospective system of representation. Events are what generate and give content to structures, theories, and representations, but something of them will always resist incorporation, remaining elusive and inexplicable. Crucially, for Lyotard events are what inspire philosophical thought and artistic work, key things he maintains give existence value, and which find themselves threatened by the 'ideology' of information. As we shall see, what is at stake in Lyotard's philosophy of information is the question of whether it is possible to think the event in an information-theoretic context.

In what follows I will outline the two main dimensions – the macro and the micro – of Lyotard's critical philosophy of information. Following this, I will indicate some necessary corrections to Lyotard's critique of information in relation to information theory, and then finish with a programmatic outline of how the critical philosophy of information Lyotard sketches in silhouette might be developed and extended.

Lyotard's Critique of Information

> I say that our role as thinkers is to deepen our understanding of what goes on in language, *to critique the vapid idea of information*, to reveal an irremediable opacity at the very core of language.
>
> Lyotard 1986–7: 218; italics mine

I. Cyberphilosophy

In a number of places – the essays 'Matter and Time' and 'Time Today' collected in *The Inhuman* in particular – Lyotard presents a kind of metaphysical hypothesis which is intended to illustrate how we can understand information technologies, and to throw into relief the social, political, and existential implications of such technologies. As elsewhere in Lyotard's writings, however, we must be careful in not attributing to Lyotard a belief in this metaphysical thesis; he presents it as a hypothesis which allows a critical perspective, a perspective which ends up undermining the hypothesis itself (as discussed in Chapter 1). In short, Lyotard uses a metaphysical 'fiction' in order to facilitate a critique of the socio-political implications of information technology. This metaphysical fiction is drawn in part from Bergson, Stiegler, and a critique of time in capitalism, but principally from Leibniz, and Lyotard tends to refer to it under the moniker of 'the Leibnizian hypothesis' (IN: 65). Let us outline this hypothesis in its various modalities, and then examine the critical perspective on information Lyotard draws from it.

The Leibnizian Hypothesis

Lyotard's concern with the social impact of information takes place at the level of 'legitimation', the subject of his best-known work *The Postmodern Condition*.[4] As Aristotle suggests, we may seek the justification for any action by following an ever-regressing chain of reasons. What Lyotard means by 'legitimation' may perhaps be thought of as the end-point of such a chain of reasoning about social and political activities: why do we do what we do, as a people? How do we justify it to ourselves, and to others? How do we understand, at the highest level, the purpose of human life, insofar as this is given expression in the reasons we give to justify social undertakings? Lyotard sees in the development and use of information technologies an implied answer to this question; a transformation in the nature of legitimation which is an extension of his thesis in *The Postmodern Condition* that the Enlightenment tradition of legitimation by metanarratives (principally, expressing an ideal end in emancipation) has given way to legitimation by 'performativity' (exclusive focus on technical means to the neglect of reflective ends). According to Lyotard, in Leibnizian terms it is as if contemporary humanity sees itself as part of a 'monad in expansion' (IN: 67).

Lyotard explains that the major intuition which guides Leibniz's work, and in particular the *Monadology* (in Leibniz 1956), is the assumption of two extreme limits to the capacity to synthesise a multiplicity of information, one minimal, the other maximal (IN: 60). These limits are two possible states of a monad. Leibniz's ontology posits that everything consists at bottom of monads, which are simple substances. Monads are non-divisible and non-extended, formal, unified, and ideal, or 'mind-like'. Monads are all endowed with perception (*Monadology* §14) and with what Leibniz calls appetition (or appetite), the action internal to the monad which brings about changes in perception (§15). Every monad contains within itself a reflection of the entire universe. However, not everything is reflected clearly: monads contain clear reflections over only a limited range of things, those close to them, while containing confused reflections (or 'representations') of things further away. Each monad gives a differ-ent perspective on the universe, according to which some things are represented clearly while others are not, and it is these differences in perspective which distinguish the monads from each other (§60). As Anthony F. Beavers notes, 'since monads are individuated on the basis of differences in what they perceive, they can be conceived of as information-based agents' (Beavers 2012: 6).

The two limit states of the monad are given by the degree to which it represents the rest of the universe clearly. At the minimal limit is what Leibniz variously calls the 'bare monad', 'entelechy', or 'material point', endowed with only very simple perceptions and little or no memory (*Monadology* §19). At the maximal limit point is God: only God is the most perfect monad, which contains a per-fect reflection of everything in the universe. Between these two limit points are varying degrees of the capacity to clearly represent or contain knowledge of the universe, indexed to an extent (and this is important to Lyotard's interpretation) on the capacity for memori-sation (§26). Memory allows previous perceptions to be compared with current perceptions, in order to build a clearer representation. Such representations, by allowing a knowledge of the regularities in the behaviours of objects, also allow an anticipation of future perceptions. To put all this in information-theoretic terms, monads are arranged in a hierarchy according to their capacity to synthe-sise and store information (where we are understanding information as what Leibniz called clear representations or simply knowledge). All monads have incomplete information except God, who can be imagined as a supreme archivist or databank which contains all the information in the universe.

Importantly for Lyotard's analysis, this Leibnizian hypothesis bears directly on *time*: the synthesis of information is a synthesis of time. In Leibniz, the fact that every monad contains a reflection of the entire universe, however indistinct, means that it bears marks and traces of everything that happens in the universe throughout time – in the past, present, and future. God exists 'outside' time, insofar as He has per-fect knowledge of all events at all times: the all-encompassing point of view of Eternity. As we have seen above, the capacity to synthesise information also bears on time, through *memory*. Bare monads have little capacity to synthesise and store events which take place at dif-ferent times, since they have no, or only a very minimal, memory. Memory allows the synthesis of a multiplicity of times in a single time (the present moment in which one remembers). Moreover, this allows an understanding of the world to develop which recognises regularities and in turn allows prediction and anticipation of future events. Commenting on Leibniz, Daniel Garber suggests that each monad is created by God 'with a kind of internal programme, as it were, which determines all the states that it will take, and the order in which it will take them' (Garber 1998: 547). The 'ideal programme' would be the one which contains not simply a succession of perceptual states, but the perception of all states – all times – in a single totalising perspective, and 'God alone has or is the memory of the whole, and of its programme' (IN: 39).[5]

Lyotard develops this Leibnizian hypothesis by supplementing it with several other perspectives which draw out its implications for a social critique of information.

Bergson: Matter and Mind

First, in the essay 'Matter and Time', Lyotard notes the similarities between Leibniz's perspective and the views Bergson develops in *Matter and Memory* (1911). Here, Bergson develops a metaphysics of 'images',[6] designed to respond to the problems of (Cartesian) realism and (Berkeleyan) idealism, to break down the distinction between the ways of construing matter and mind in the philosophical tradition. While Bergson presents his own conclusions as defending a form of dualism – insofar as they uphold the reality of both matter and spirit or mind (in contrast to realism and idealism, which seek to reduce one to the other) – he believes it is a dualism which overcomes much of the problematic nature of previous dualisms (Bergson 1911: vii). In fact, some commentators have thought Bergson's position to be better understood as a kind of monism. In any case, what interests Lyotard is the way that Bergson's work on mind and matter breaks with the Cartesian understanding of matter, and makes matter – at least to a far greater extent than does Descartes – *continuous* with mind. Bergson's philosophy of mind displaces the traditional distinction between matter and mind through the categories of *time* and *memory*. He writes: '*Questions relating to subject and object, to their distinction and their union, should be put in terms of time rather than of space*' (77). It is this focus on time which allows a move away from the problem of interaction which has proved so intractable for Cartesian dualism. Descartes' understanding of matter and mind as separate substances with differing properties of a spatial type (matter is located in space and is infinitely divisible; mind is not located in space and is not divisible) institutes a divide between them which makes it difficult to see how they might interact. In contrast, Bergson's *temporalisation* of these categories allows a displacement of the problem.

Bergson occasionally references Leibniz in support of his argument, and in his essay 'Matter and Time' Lyotard seeks to show that Bergson's position is profoundly Leibnizian. Like Leibniz, Bergson proposes a hierarchy of beings more or less endowed with mind, ranging between minimal and maximal points, and indexed on memory. Bergson's minimal point, roughly equivalent to Leibniz's bare monad, is the 'material point', endowed with what he calls 'pure perception'. Bergson explains:

> I mean a perception which exists in theory rather than in fact and would be possessed by a being placed where I am, living as I live, but absorbed in the present and capable, by giving up every form of memory, of obtaining a vision of matter both immediate and instantaneous. (Bergson 1911: 26)

This minimal point, perception without memory, is matter. At the other end of the spectrum is the most developed mind, which – like Leibniz's God – we can imagine as a being endowed with absolute memory. (Bergson presents this limit as eternity – see Bergson 1946: 221; Lacey 1989: 129.)

Bergson understands perception pragmatically as aimed primarily towards the *action* of the perceiver in relation to the world (rather than, as is often thought, aimed towards the gathering of disinterested knowledge). At the minimal point of pure perception, what perceives reacts immediately to any stimulus, like a mechanical impulse (Bergson 1911: 21). At this point reactions are a matter of necessary cause and effect. Bergson then understands the increasing complexity of a material organism in terms of the endowment of a greater memory.

This memory is interposed between the initial contact of a perception, and the motor reaction of the organism in response to the perception. The more memory interposed, the greater the possibilities of different reactions, the more a particular action is *delayed*, and the less necessary any particular reaction to perceptual stimuli is over another reaction. Bergson explains this complexity in animal organisms in terms of the increasing complexity of nervous relays between the afferent (sensitive) and efferent (motive) fibres (Bergson 1911: 3). Every reaction to a given stimulus chooses one course along these nervous relays, while all other possible courses and the actions to which they would give rise remain *virtual*. Memory stores all of these virtual ways of reacting as well as the actual reactions, creating a greater range of possible reactions. This virtual store of non-actualised reactions are registered as mental *representations*, which thus differ in degree, but not in kind, from perceptions themselves. The immediate 'shocks' of pure perception are 'condensed' by perception, which is no longer pure, insofar as it now has a memory. The more complex the virtual store of memory, the greater the range of options for reaction, and the longer immediate reaction is delayed as these various possibilities for reaction are processed. In the case of a very complex organism such as a human being, a sophisticated memory enables such a degree of uncertainty between perception and reaction that according to Bergson we are justified in understanding ourselves to have free will.

Bergson presents the difference between matter and mind as one of *rhythm*. Mind contracts or condenses material vibrations so that we are able to experience in a shorter duration what actually takes place in the material world in a comparatively longer duration. This contraction is enabled by memory, which according to Bergson mixes with perception in conscious experience. In explaining this point, Lyotard references Bergson's own example of seeing the colour red (IN: 42; Bergson 1911: 272–3). Red light has the longest wavelength of the visible spectrum, and hence the least frequent vibration – 400 billion vibrations in a second. Bergson reasons – drawing on a claim by Sigmund Exner that the smallest instant we can consciously distinguish is one five-hundredth of a second – that if consciousness had to count each of these vibrations, it would take more than 25,000 years to register a one-second burst of red light (Bergson 1911: 272–3). Bergson concludes then that we must distinguish between time in general and our own duration, and that in our duration we contract the extremely multiple vibrations which take place in the material world so that we may perceive them instantaneously. Bergson summarises:

> In short, then, to perceive consists in condensing enormous periods of an infinitely diluted existence into a few more differentiated moments of an intenser life, and in thus summing up a very long history. To perceive means to immobilise. (Bergson 1911: 275)

Bergson presents these different rhythms as different degrees of tension or relaxation. Matter may thus be considered as a relatively relaxed rhythm, while mind is a more tense rhythm, which contracts the vibrations of matter into a shorter time. The difference between matter and mind is thus indexed on time rather than space. Memory plays a crucial role here, because it is what allows the contraction to take place: memory supplements perception so that often what we experience is to a large extent what we remember from the past, and memory also plays a role in selecting from immediate perceptions according to our pragmatic needs (perception for Bergson, as noted above, is always directed towards practical action). The greater the memory, the greater the capacity for contraction, and the greater tension and higher mental life we have.

Lyotard summarises what he takes from Bergson as follows:

> So we must imagine that from matter to mind there is but a difference of degree, which depends on the capacity to gather and conserve. Mind is matter which remembers its interactions, its immanence. But there is a continuum from the instantaneous mind of matter to the very gathered matter of minds. (IN: 40)

Lyotard insists that 'whatever Bergson may have thought about it', the transformations he effects on the concept of matter 'can easily be linked with the ambient technologism or techno-scientism' (IN: 44).[7] This link has at least two important senses. First, computer science has allowed the creation of material devices able to take over a process previously thought to have been the exclusive purview of mind (a process André Leroi-Gourhan ([1964–5] 1993) calls 'exteriorisation'). Information technologies therefore seem to perform the same kind of displacement of the matter/mind distinction as Bergson's philosophy. Second, one of these important processes is memory – the storage of information. For Lyotard, the information technologies extend the capacities that Bergson identifies in more complex organisms for synthesising a multiplicity of times into a single time, by storing these times as data in a memory bank. He writes:

> If we have at our disposal interfaces capable of memorizing, in a fashion accessible to us, vibrations naturally beyond our ken, i.e. that determine us as no more than 'material points' (as is the case with many forms of radiation), then we are extending our power of differentiation and our memories, we are delaying reactions which are as yet not under control, we are increasing our material liberty. (IN: 43)

With this focus on memory and control of the future, Lyotard thus sees information technologies as essentially technologies of *time*. This view is given more detail through two further perspectives which Lyotard also integrates into the 'Leibnizian hypothesis'.

Stiegler: From Ethnoculture to Technoscience

Drawing on the early work of Bernard Stiegler, Lyotard suggests that all technologies have been technologies of time, that is, means of stocking information with the aim of gaining greater control over the future.[8] In trying to determine what all 'new technologies of communication' have in common, and their philosophical stakes, Stiegler argues that they are essentially means for the artificial preservation of memory. Stiegler's more original thesis, now well known, is that they produce time and memory themselves. Extending the Derridean logic of seeing phenomena that are typically characterised as secondary and derivative as in fact primary and conditioning, Stiegler argues that memory is profoundly *objective* and *technological*, well before being psychological (Stiegler 1986: 63). Retrospectively, such technologies may be seen to include writing (a 'proto-neo-technology'), and even earlier, the oral narratives of ethnocultures.[9] Taking up this analysis, Lyotard explains that these ethnocultural narratives were for much of human history the most efficient apparatuses available for memorising and transmitting information and organising space and time (IN: 62). Such narratives store and transmit a stock of memory across generations, and enable a degree of control over the future through the idea of destiny. Destiny assumes that all events are already determined, and unfold according to a pre-established sequence. This idea reduces our sense of contingency about the future, and introduces the possibility that we might be able to gain knowledge, in the present, of events due to unfold in the future. Moreover, the narratives of ethnocultures organise all events into a single story, thereby giving them meaning. This meaning allows us a sense of purchase, of control, and removes the sense of contingency regarding what happens. Lyotard explains: '[N]arratives are like temporal filters whose function is to transform the emotive charge linked to the event into sequences of units of information capable of giving rise to something like meaning' (IN: 63).

However, ethnocultures have the relative disadvantage of tying a people to a given time and place, to a historical and geographical context, and in that sense are relatively inflexible. Lyotard argues that what he calls the metanarratives of modernity follow the same basic structure and function as ethnocultural narratives, though they ground their legitimacy in the future (as the projected ideal of an emancipated humanity) rather than in the past (with myths of origin, venerated ancestors, and so on). These narratives may be more robust than ethnocultures because they allow for greater geographical and historical displacements, but they remain fragile because they are predicated on the possibility of giving meaning to all events in relation to a projected ideal, one for which we can have no evidence with which to ground our belief (and which some events – such as the Holocaust – seem to give us reason *not* to believe).

Yet for Lyotard a major displacement arises in accord with the 'incredulity toward metanarratives' he famously analyses in *The Postmodern Condition*. One major reason for this incredulity is simply that we have found more efficient technologies of time than the narrative. These more efficient technologies are the new information technologies and capitalist economy (discussed below). As Lyotard explains, information technologies provide a much more efficient means of controlling time than ethnocultural myths and modern metanarratives because they are far more flexible and resilient; they are tied neither to a particular time and space, nor to any particular teleology. The information technologies, as Lyotard sees them, are simply aimed at creating an ever-increasing store of information, which will allow us to have greater control over the future, but without specifying any particular goals for that future. The store of information which the new technologies enable allows for the development of a far more open future, and even the possibility of life in other parts of the cosmos:

> The importance of the technologies constructed around electronics and data processing resides in the fact that they make the programming and control of memorizing, i.e. the synthesis of different times in one time, less dependent on the conditions of life on earth. (IN: 62)

Capital: Money Is Time

Lyotard adds an important politico-economic dimension to his analysis by arguing that the Leibnizian hypothesis also admits of a 'tight and relevant correlation' with capitalism (IN: 67). He also views capitalism through the lens of time, seeing it as an attempt to stock times in order to control the future. Time, he suggests, is central to exchange, which he analyses as follows: 'Someone (X) gives someone (Y) an object a at time t. This giving has as its condition that Y will give X an object b at time t'' (65–6). Now, exchange assumes that at time t it is as if time t' had already happened, though in practice, the further apart these times, the more contingency is introduced, and the greater the risk that Y will not in fact give X object b. So capital, Lyotard argues, is geared towards assuring that future events are programmed to occur with as great a certainty as possible (in order to ensure growth and avoid loss). Capital thus appears as a technology of time aimed at controlling probabilities. Money can be understood from this perspective as stockpiled time, since the more one has available, the greater the neutralisation of the significance in the event that Y fails to give X object b at time t', and the greater the overall possibilities for investments which reduce any such risk of loss. Capital invested in research and development is aimed at anticipating the future, and thereby reducing the possibility of any unforeseen occurrences. Another way this can be expressed is to say that capitalism consists in *gaining time*.

Both the Leibnizian hypothesis and capital, Lyotard argues, are aimed at predicting and controlling the future to the greatest possible extent, and thus in effect they are aimed at neutralising events (unpredictable and unforeseen occurrences). The synergistic stockpiling of information and money is aimed at incorporating all times and events into a programmed synthesis in which nothing escapes mastery and control: in an ideal situation, all future 'events' will be already bought and paid for, insured against loss, programmed, foreseen, and effectively neutralised (insofar as they are no longer 'unforeseen occurrences'). Both information technology and capitalism, Lyotard suggests, develop autonomously in relation to human beings and their interests, and may be understood as the effect of *a cosmic process of complexification*.

We are now in a position to summarise Lyotard's 'Leibnizian hypothesis', which synthesises these ideas drawn from Leibniz, Bergson, Stiegler, and the critique of capitalism. In fact, Lyotard suggests that such views are compatible with developments in contemporary physics, and that the Leibnizian hypothesis presents a kind of 'general physics' (which, Lyotard tells us, is equivalent to a metaphysics, presumably because physics is extended beyond the empirical to realms traditionally treated of by metaphysics, such as mind or soul), which would give us a metaphysical picture of reality, along with an integrated understanding of the nature of human beings, information technologies, and capitalism. In this generalised physics, the distinctions between time and space, matter and mind, are broken down.[10] In contemporary physics, Lyotard suggests, elementary particles are about as 'naked' as Leibniz's 'material point'. A particle (material point) may be understood to have an elementary memory and temporal filter in the form of properties allowing it to enter into relations with others according to specific regularities (IN: 61). The cosmos may then be understood in Leibnizian/Bergsonian terms as consisting of beings of varying degrees of complexity with respect to their organisation, with matter at one end of the spectrum (low complexity) and mind at the other end (high complexity). Thus complexity is enabled by memory, and understood in terms of time: matter is instantaneous time, while mind is a synthesis of many times into a single time. In the region of the cosmos inhabited by human beings, the human brain and language are the most complex systems which have so far developed. Yet the new information technologies are beginning to supplement, extend, and in some ways exceed, these complex systems:

> The new technologies, built on electronics and data processing, must be considered [...] as material extensions of our capacity to memorize, more in Leibniz's sense than Bergson's, given the role played in them by symbolic language as supreme 'condenser' of all information. (IN: 43)

Lyotard suggests that the process of development in which humanity is currently caught up can be understood on the model of the Leibnizian hypothesis as the production of an ever-increasingly complex monad, or as he calls it, a 'monad in expansion' (IN: 67). With God, or perfect information, as the ideal limit, what we are seeing is the development of complexity towards this limit, through both technoscience and capitalism. With regard to capitalism, Lyotard suggests that

> [o]ne could go so far as to say that the desire for profit and wealth is no doubt no other than this process itself, working upon the nervous centres of the human brain and experienced directly by the human body. (IN: 71)

And with regard to the role of information technology in this process:

> [c]omputers never stop being able to synthesize more and more 'times', so that Leibniz could have said of this process that it is on the way to producing a monad much more 'complete' than humanity itself has ever [been] able to be. (IN: 64)

Technologies of time synthesise a multiplicity of times into a single time insofar as they gather the past and the future into the present; the past is gathered in order to make the future predictable and controllable; the future is gathered insofar as it is programmed as predictable and controllable; and the present is the 'point of access' to the multiplicity of times. With their aid, humanity is taking part in a generalised process of the production of a 'monad in expansion'. As discussed in the previous chapter, one of the ideas Lyotard frequently uses in his writings in the 1980s to dramatise the question of what development aims at is the question of what might be able to survive the death of the sun. His suggestion is that this will not likely be anything we would be able to recognise as humanity, but rather the 'most complete monad' with which it was pregnant (IN: 65), thus linking his 'Leibnizian hypothesis' with his 'postmodern fable'.

With the metaphysical fiction of the Leibnizian hypothesis, Lyotard gives expression to the common view that information technology is *dematerialising* the world.[11] It is a kind of *informational metaphysics*, which considers every being as an information processor, from the bare monad or material point understood as a being 'which could only convey or transmit the "bits" of information as they are received' (IN: 60), to God as the ideal of perfectly complete information. Such an informational metaphysics is also not unique; it resonates broadly with John Archibald Wheeler's 'It from Bit' ontology (Wheeler 1990), Luciano Floridi's informational realism (Floridi 2011: ch. 15), pancomputationalism (Zuse [1970] 2012; Schmidhuber 1997), and various other information-based metaphysics. However, the distinctiveness of Lyotard's analysis lies in its emphasis on the role of *time*. This emphasis allows him to link the critique of information with the critique of capitalism (considered as saving time), and, as we shall see, a resistance to development through the category of 'the event'.

2. Postinformation

In proclaiming what he sees as the great power of information in a philosophical context, Floridi also indicates what Lyotard sees as its danger. Floridi writes:

> PI possesses one of the most powerful conceptual vocabularies ever devised in philosophy. This is because we can still rely on informational concepts whenever a complete understanding of some series of events is unavailable or unnecessary for providing an explanation. *In philosophy, this means that virtually any issue can be rephrased in informational terms.* (Floridi 2011: 16; italics mine)

Lyotard takes this supposed capacity of information to phrase anything to present the threat of *reductionism*, in which information becomes a 'common measure' enabling a universal translation. He writes:

> The major development of the last twenty years, expressed in the most vapid terms of political economy and historical periodization, has been the transformation of language into a productive commodity: phrases considered as messages to encode, decode, transmit, and order (by the bundle), to reproduce, conserve, and keep

available (memories), to combine and conclude (calculations), and to oppose (games, conflicts, cybernetics); and the establishment of a unit of measure that is also a price unit, in other words, information. (Lyotard 1986–7: 217)

Lyotard sees this reduction as bearing essentially on language: information is a way of treating language which emphasises certain of its qualities and capacities while ignoring others. The informational treatment of language, he believes, views it as an instrument of knowledge and communication. After describing the way new technologies (i.e. computers and media) process language, he explains:

> Language treated in this way is informational: it is made up of messages going from a sender to a receiver, both of whom are in possession of the same code (with or without translation). Information occurs only when the message responds to a question issued in the first place by the current addressee. The question is formulated in binary terms (yes or no, 1/0). The information is evaluated in terms of probability (between 1 and 0). It can be calculated. Its cost can be figured. *Science, technology, and economy find a common measure of knowledge, power, and price in information.* (PW: 16; italics mine)

Elsewhere, he reiterates this, indicating what he believes is at stake in information technologies: the wholesale reduction of the rich varieties of meaning of which language is capable to the relatively narrow idea of 'information'. Writing in the 1980s of the growth of information technologies and the general impact he believes they will have in the future, he writes:

> I believe that only phrases translatable into computer language will be taken into consideration. [...] We are already in a situation where the phrase must satisfy the demands of computer logic.
>
> That logic is relatively simple: one must be able to transcribe even a complex phrase in such a way that information units can be enumerated, in other words, according to the binary logic of Boolean algebra: yes/no. (Lyotard 1986–7: 210–11)

Accompanying this concern of the reduction of language to information is the reduction of events to 'data'. Lyotard understands this term in a specific way, as 'events that have been rendered significant by and for a reading code' (Lyotard 1994b: 189). Data are thus an event or series of events that have been processed, made ready for storage and transmission as information.

Lyotard's critique of information on this 'micro' level of the production of meaning in language and its (in)capacity to do justice to events is familiar from his better-known writings around the themes of the postmodern and the differend: the crux of his critique is that information is reductive because it provides a *universal measure* to which everything may be reduced, allowing generalised exchange. Everything is swept away in the tides of information flow. Information excludes incommensurability and the multiplicity of language games which he defends, and fails to do justice to the evanescent event which eludes capture in any particular discourse or representation, since it treats all meaning and events as adequately dealt with by the pragmatics of information processing. Voicing his objection to this informational model most clearly, Lyotard states: '*I believe that a scientific, artistic, or philosophical phrase is not susceptible to simple informational transmission*' (Lyotard 1986–7: 210–11; italics mine). On both grounds we have now seen – the 'macro' level of the Leibnizian hypothesis and the 'micro' level of the reduction of language to information and events to data – Lyotard characterises the idea of information as a contemporary, pervasive ideology.

Curiously, Lyotard was invited in 1982 to give a talk to some French computer scientists, and after outlining many of the critical points we have just noted, he suggests that research in 'New Technologies' (the published title of the talk) should be directed towards a 'postinformational' treatment of language:

> It would be necessary to direct efforts [...] to multiply the applications of the informational treatment of language, but also to support research on the *postinformational* treatment of language. [...] Informational treatment only takes into account phrases that describe a 'reality.' But language contains many other families of phrases that obey different regimes and require other methods of analysis. [...] the niche, so to speak, that French industries would have to occupy would be that of enlarging and making more complex the treatment of language (postinformational and postcommunicational) – for example, the analysis, the formalization, the commiting to memory of persuasive rhetorics, of 'musics,' of inscriptions of movement (kineographic techniques, such as kinetic holography), and so forth. (PW: 18; italics mine)

This 'postinformational' technological treatment of language would multiply phrase regimens and genres of discourse in order to preserve an 'ontological' dimension of language, to include artistic phrases, and to deploy paradox and paralogy, ideas which will be discussed later. But we may note two points here in conclusion to this section. First, since exactly what information is and how it should be understood remains a lively issue of debate in contemporary PI, Lyotard's terminological choice in calling for the development of a 'postinformation' might well seem premature. Nevertheless, it is arguably useful in specifying, within the broadly informational paradigm, an approach which tries to preserve the event. Second, Lyotard's construal of what is at stake in thinking information remains very much indexed on the linguistic turn: the choice he presents is between an informational or postinformational processing *of language*. However, following the more recent trend of specifying an informational turn after the linguistic turn, as outlined in the introduction to this chapter, I suggest that a critical updating of Lyotard's philosophy of information should centralise the concept of information itself, and concentrate on critically interrogating how this term might best be understood in relation to Lyotard's concerns. In what follows, I will move from the preceding summary of Lyotard's stated views on information to an outline of how such a 'critical updating' might take place.

Information Theory: Qualifying Lyotard's Critique

> Do not forget that a poem, even though it is composed in the language of information, is not used in the language-game of giving information.
> Ludwig Wittgenstein 1967: §160

I will now argue that Lyotard's critique of information needs to be qualified on the second point outlined above: the claim that information is reductive of meaning. I do not wish to refute this claim *in toto*, but to show that Lyotard appears mistaken in some of his claims, and to clarify his critique in relation to a more adequate understanding of theories of information. In short, the crux of my correction is that information may be understood in at least two main senses, and Lyotard conflates these, leading to some confusions and inaccuracies in his critique. These senses may be referred to as *data* and *semantics*. The first sense is associated with the theory of information invented by Claude E. Shannon, and publicised by Shannon and Warren Weaver in 1949 (Shannon and Weaver [1949] 1963). It is called simply information theory, or the mathematical theory of communication (MTC). As previously noted, the field of information is currently a broad, multiple, and contentious one. Shannon, widely recognised as the father of the general field of information theory, was very aware of the multiple meanings of 'information', and sceptical that any single theory would be able to sum them up:

> The word 'information' has been given different meanings by various writers in the general field of information theory. It is likely that at least a number of these will prove sufficiently useful in certain applications to deserve further study and permanent recognition. *It is hardly to be expected that a single concept of information would satisfactorily account for the numerous possible applications of this general field.* (Shannon 1993: 180, quoted in Floridi 2013; italics mine)

In his essay for a more general readership which accompanied the publication of Shannon's classic paper 'The Mathematical Theory of Communication', Weaver specified three main meanings of information in terms of problems to which he thought the term might apply (Shannon and Weaver [1949] 1963: 4). Floridi usefully summarises them as follows:

(1) technical problems concerning the quantification of information and dealt with by Shannon's theory
(2) semantic problems relating to meaning and truth; and
(3) what he called 'influential' problems concerning the impact and effectiveness of information on human behaviour, which he thought had to play an equally important role

(Floridi 2013)

Following Shannon and Weaver, a great number of other developments have taken place in theories of information. Nevertheless, MTC remains a central theory, and one on which Lyotard clearly draws, occasionally citing Shannon by name. This is the first sense of information we need to clarify. MTC is a theory of *data transmission*. It is a form of applied mathematics, and was developed to solve an engineering problem: how to transmit signals most efficiently from a sender to a receiver, through a medium. Shannon was employed by Bell Laboratories, and his work responded in large part to practical problems of telecommunication. In brief, and avoiding technicalities, the basic points of Shannon's theory relevant to our considerations may be described as follows.

MTC understands communication, or information transmission, in terms of probabilities. Information is only successfully communicated when the receiver receives something they did not already know. The receiver is in possession of a code which determines the probabilities of the signals being received – for example, when the signals being transmitted are English letters, statistical analysis allows the calculation of probabilities concerning which letters will be transmitted according to their frequency of occurrence in the English language. Shannon's theory measures the amount of information received as according with improbability, or what cannot be predicted. (If the signal received is entirely predictable, no information will have been received.) Understanding information in this way allows a calculation of *efficiency* in communication, since, for example, it allows parts of a message to be constructed on the basis of probabilities rather than having to be transmitted (the same principle allows what we call 'data compression'). Shannon calls the measure of information *entropy* (H), perhaps not least because John von Neumann helpfully advised him as follows:

> You should call it entropy for two reasons: first, the function is already in use in thermodynamics under the same name; second, and more importantly, most people don't know what entropy really is, and if you use the word *entropy* in an argument you will win every time. (In Golan 2002, quoted in Floridi 2013)

More technically, information is entropy because Shannon understands it as a *disorder* or unpredictability introduced into the system (the receiver), and entropy is the principle of disorder in thermodynamics (though as many commentators have pointed out, the analogy needs not to be pushed too far).

What needs to be emphasised is that MTC is a theory which deals with the engineering problem of the physical transmission of signals, and may be understood as concerning only *data* and not *semantic* information. *Contra* Lyotard, in information theory 'data' are not best understood as 'events that have been rendered significant by and for a reading code', but rather 'relata', bare distinctions which can act as symbols (such as 1s and 0s) which are capable of being encoded and decoded to carry semantic meaning (see Floridi 2008). What is transmitted as information in MTC is data, *not* the semantic information, which is the interpreted data rendered meaningful. Such meanings are never reducible to 1s and 0s, but are part of the virtual store of language and meaning which, along with the code, allow the data to be interpreted as meaningful. Shannon himself was clear and insistent on such a distinction, and as Weaver specifies: 'The word *information*, in this theory [MTC], is used in a special sense that must not be confused with its ordinary usage. In particular, *information* must not be confused with meaning' (Shannon and

Weaver [1949] 1963: 8). From the perspective of MTC, we can be sceptical of some of Lyotard's remarks about information. In particular, his claim that information reduces meaning to the binary language of 1s and 0s.

Interestingly, Heidegger makes the same mistake as Lyotard when discussing information in his text 'Traditional Language and Technological Language':

> The sole character of language remaining in information is the abstract form of writing that is transcribed into the formulae of a logic calculus. [...] The structure and performance of large-scale calculative planning rests on the technological-calculative principles of this transformation of language as saying into language as a mere report of signal transmissions. What is decisive for our reflection lies in the fact that it is from the technological possibilities of the machine that the instruction is set out as to how language can and shall still be language. The kind and character of language are determined according to the technological possibilities of the formal signal transmissions which execute a sequence of continual yes-no decisions with the highest possible speed. [...] The kind of language is determined by the technology. [...] linguistic tasks are also in advance and fundamentally bound up with the machine, which requires above all the clarity of signs. That is why a poem does not, on principle, let itself be programmed.
>
> With the unconditional reign of modern technology there is an increase in the power – the demand as well as the performance – of the technological language that was devised for the widest possible spread of information. Because this [power] is scattered in systems of formalized reports and signals, the technological language is the severest and most menacing attack on what is peculiar to language: *saying* as showing and as the letting-appear of what is present and what is absent, of reality in the widest sense. (Heidegger 1998: 140–1)

The mistake that Lyotard and Heidegger both make is to conflate 'information' understood as semantic information with the sense of 'information' implied by MTC, that is, the transmission of data. A possible reason for this mistake is that a conflation of 'amount of information' and 'amount of meaning' was made by Norbert Wiener in his popular book on cybernetics, *The Human Use of Human Beings* (1949), a book from which Heidegger quotes in the above-mentioned article, and which Lyotard references in *The Postmodern Condition*. This conflation has been noted by others (for example Beavers 2012), but Heidegger and Lyotard seem to take it at face value in insisting that poetry, or philosophical or artistic phrases, cannot be 'programmed' – by which they seem to understand, cannot be phrased in the form of simple questions to which a yes/no answer (1 or 0) could be given. But in MTC this kind of phrasing (translation, or, better, 'transcoding') is appropriate only to questions concerning *data*, not the semantic meaning which the *interpreted* data would convey (i.e. the transmission of a letter can be formulated in a string of questions requiring only a yes/no response, or the equivalent of this Boolean algebra in terms of electrical switching, on/off (another of Shannon's innovations) – for example, in binary code the letter 'L' (upper case) is 01001100 – but this is a level entirely different to that of the semantics of the transmitted word or phrase of which the letter forms a part.)

Considered from the point of view of MTC, any graphic or plastic trace can be encoded, transmitted, and reproduced. There may well be limits to this, so that, for example, a smudge in paint made with brush or hand cannot be reproduced in such a way that it captures in reproduction what the eye captures in direct vision. But it is not clear that our digital information systems are in any way inferior in this than the medium of books and print: the technical conversion through 1s and 0s is not immediately reductive of semantic or plastic meaning in the way philosophers such as Lyotard and Heidegger believe it to be. At least, if we restrict ourselves to the graphic traces which are letters, *contra* Lyotard's hesitations, any poetic or philosophical phrase can go through digital processing without doing any damage to its semantic meaning. Conversion to strings of 1s and 0s is no more reductive – and in fact probably much less so – than the natural English language's demand that expression use only twenty-six alphabetic letters. (Consider, for example, that poetry or philosophy may be typed into a word processor, stored on a USB, transferred to another computer and presented to an audience with a data projector – an informational transmission which has not in any way obviously reduced the semantic content of the phrases.)

However, despite this, Lyotard's (and Heidegger's) concerns with the reductive effects of information arguably remain highly relevant in relation to *semantic* theories of information, which, almost as soon as Shannon had proposed MTC, and despite his scepticism, began to be developed (see Bar-Hillel and Carnap [1953] 1964). In fact, it is the semantic theories of information which are taken by Floridi as the new *philosophia prima* and are key to the informational turn in philosophy. While in this area there are particularly multiple and contested theories, I will follow Floridi's general introduction to the topic in order to indicate what is at stake in Lyotard's critique, and its relevance. According to Floridi, *true semantic content* is the most common sense in which information seems to be understood (Floridi 2011: ch. 5, 2013, citing for example Quine 1970). He notes that

> [p]hilosophical analyses usually adopt a propositional orientation and an epistemic outlook, endorsing, often implicitly, the prevalence or centrality of factual information [...]. They tend to base their analyses on cases such as 'Paris is the capital of France' or 'The Bodleian Library is in Oxford'. (Floridi 2013)

Floridi proposes that semantic information can be understood as 'meaningful data', and, suggesting that this is based on an industry standard working model in various areas of information science, specifies a *General Definition of Information* (GDI) in terms of *data + meaning*:

> The General Definition of Information (GDI):
>
> σ is an instance of information, understood as semantic content, if and only if:
>
> (GDI.1) σ consists of one or more *data*;
> (GDI.2) the data in σ are *well-formed*;
> (GDI.3) the well-formed data in σ are *meaningful*.
>
> (Floridi 2013)

Floridi then explains that

> [i]n (GDI.2), 'well-formed' means that the data are clustered together correctly, according to the rules (*syntax*) that govern the chosen system, code or language being analysed. Syntax here must be understood broadly (not just linguistically), as what determines the form, construction, composition or structuring of something (engineers, film directors, painters, chess players and gardeners speak of syntax in this broad sense). (Floridi 2013)

Semantic information may be instructional (such as directives in a user's manual) or factual. Factual information may be ascribed truth values, and Floridi develops and defends a definition of *factual semantic information as well-formed, meaningful and truthful data* (Floridi 2005, 2011: ch. 5).

In short, MTC is not reductive in the way Lyotard thinks, but semantic theories of information (he does not indicate a knowledge of the difference) may well be. This is so because they tend to reinscribe – and quite possibly in a more pervasive and hegemonic way – a view of language as primarily propositional and factual, rather than 'ontological' (see below) which was already a point of debate between prominent analytic and continental philosophers, such as Carnap and Heidegger, in the midst of the linguistic turn.

The Informational Event

> The programming industry, as the operator of memory's industrialization, exploits the possibilities of memory's synthesis as opened out by analogic, numeric, and biologic technologies. Through on-line communication, data processing in real time, and genetic manipulation linking the somatic and the germinal, the structure of the event in all its forms is radically modified.
>
> Bernard Stiegler 2009a: 9

Despite the critiques outlined above, Lyotard does not see a reduction of meaning as *essential* to information technology as such. He writes:

> We are not alienated by the telephone or television as means (media). And we will not be by language machines. [...] for the human to be replaced by a complex and aleatory assemblage of (nondenumerable) operators transforming messages (*Stroudzé*) is not an alienation. Messages themselves are only metastable, catastrophe-prone states of information. (Lyotard 1986–7: 217–18)

We can approach Lyotard's relation to information but orienting ourselves according to his approach to language. Despite appearances, Lyotard's book *The Differend* is not a philosophy of language, but a sophistical retorsion or immanent critique which intervenes in the 'linguistic turn' in philosophy (as Keith Crome (2004) has demonstrated).[12] It says, 'Yes, language is ubiquitous, everything can be converted into language, and yet, even here, in the heart of language, is the event.' The question I would like to pose here then is this: can this sophistical strategy be applied within information theory? Can we think the event within an information-theoretic context? *Can there be an informational event?*

While we needed to be careful above to separate MTC from semantic theories of information in order to see where Lyotard goes wrong, in fact most contemporary semantic theories take MTC as an essential model and limit for any and all theories of information.

In what follows then, given the general and programmatic aims of this chapter, we need not be so careful to distinguish them, and may talk about 'information theory' in a very general sense. When we then begin to examine information theory in a little more detail than Lyotard does (as we have done above), it at first seems that its terms and concepts in fact lend themselves to a Lyotardian thinking of the event. Information is described in terms of *difference, unpredictability*, and *entropy*, all terms that Lyotard uses in connection with the event. In an oft-quoted phrase, Gregory Bateson (2000: 459) defined a bit of information as 'a difference which makes a difference', which *prima facie* might be acceptable as a short-hand description of how Lyotard and other French thinkers understand the event. Information is defined by Shannon, Wiener, and others as necessarily involving the reception of something unpredictable. If the thing received is predictable, then its reception is redundant; it is already known. As we have seen, it is for this reason Shannon called the measure of information *entropy*. Is this not the openness to the unexpected Lyotard defends?

However, this initial appearance is largely misleading, and it would be deeply wrong to see information theory as it is usually understood as being adequate to the event in a Lyotardian sense. This is because of where the *accent* lies in the relations between entropy and negentropy, unpredictability and predictability, disorder and order, in the information system. The only value an initial disorder (a newly received and improbable signal) has from an information-theoretic perspective is to establish an order – that is, to constitute a message when decoded. Ideally, we are always in possession of an established code. Entropy quickly gets absorbed into negentropy, the event into decoded meaning. The significant point about Lyotard's idea of the event, as opposed to the informational/communicational idea of the signal as entropy, is that an 'event' in the Lyotardian sense cannot be incorporated into the existing system or discourse without changing it (TP: 46). It would, I suggest, need to defy the established code, in some sense.[13]

Having put this initial promise to one side, how might we think the event in an informational context? Lyotard himself gestures, rather sketchily, towards the way, by mapping the 'pragmatic instances' of language outlined in *The Differend* onto the terminology of information and communication theory in writings for the exhibition he directed, *Les Immatériaux*. In *The Differend*, the event is understood as the occurrence of a phrase. It is an event because it cannot be predicted, and marks a fundamental change in the string of phrases it links on to. Each phrase presents a phrase universe, which has four instances: addressor, addressee, sense, and referent. The 'meaning' of the phrase is only given when the relations between these instances are fixed, and this fixing only takes place with the occurrence of another phrase, which 'situates' the first. In 'Les Immatériaux', Lyotard presents an analogous pragmatics of communication (based on Lasswell, Wiener, and Jacobson), which also bears a strong similarity to Shannon's MTC. The analogies are as follows:

    Addressor = Sender
    Addressee = Receiver
    Sense   = Code
    Referent   = Referent
                 [Support]

In addition to the four instances of language outlined in *The Differend*, this 'set-up' (*dispositif*) – also called by Lyotard an 'operational structure' – contains a *support* (*material*, constituting a *medium*, which contains differential features which may be used as discrete elements to form signs – that is, *data*).

In *The Differend*, the contingency of the phrase universe is given by the fact that it is only 'fixed' when the phrase is linked on to by another phrase. This ensures that no future phrase is absolutely determined, and remains an unpredictable event. In the informational terms of *Les Immatériaux*, the whole informational set-up functions according to a principle of '*interaction*', which means that 'each pole of the structure is only relevant with respect to its relations with other poles', and 'a modification in the function of one of the poles leads to a destructuring and restructuring of the whole: in which case it becomes a new message' (Lyotard 1985a: 50). This remains a sketch (Lyotard does not develop it further), but it constitutes a starting point from which the thinking of the event within the linguistic turn proposed in *The Differend* might be extended in terms of the informational turn.

In *The Differend*, Lyotard insists that phrases which are not 'well formed' may also be meaningful, and this would be a point on which to engage critically the semantic theory of information, which insists that data must be 'well formed' before being considered meaningful. The point of debate concerns the scope of meaning, and the kinds of uses of language or information accepted as meaningful. Lyotard distinguishes language understood as 'a means of communication of facts about reality' from what he calls 'ontological language', described as those modes of language which do not aim solely to describe exhaustively the objects to which they refer. Among these language modes, one can mention, for various reasons, free conversation, reflexive judgement and meditation, free association (in the psychoanalytical sense), the poetic and literature, music, the visual arts, everyday language. What matters in these modes is clearly the fact that all should generate occurrences before knowing the rules of this generativity, and that some of them even have no concern for determining those rules. (IN: 72)

The question this raises, then, is this: are there *modes of information* which could be considered ontological in this sense? Lyotard's insightful suggestion here is to attempt to consider 'ontological language' without recourse to the phenomenological and hermeneutic traditions to which earlier thinkers (such as Heidegger) had recourse, but to consider it in nonhuman, purely formal terms as having the capacity to 'generate occurrences before knowing the rules of this generativity'.

Lyotard clarifies this formal understanding of ontological language through the concepts of *paradox* and *paralogy*. In the essay 'Rules and Paradoxes' (1986–7), he notes that there is an ancient question about language, which was a matter of debate between the sophists and Aristotle: is language, by means of determinate operators, capable of producing phrases that are absolutely strange? He defines the terms he uses here, as he understands them, as follows. *Paradoxes* are phrases that are absolutely strange; *phrases* are articulations of separate (discrete) elements; *paralogies* are determinate operators which produce paradoxes; and *operators* are the rules that a scientific or artistic work obeys (see Lyotard 1986–7: 211–12). Lyotard himself takes the side of the sophists, and positions paradox and paralogy as a formal way of understanding what is at stake in 'ontological language'.[14] Elsewhere, he explains this stake as 'the search for the limit between the tolerable and the intolerable by way of moves lacking any given model' (Lyotard 1983: 124).

So, how can information technologies and philosophies of information incorporate paradoxes and paralogies? An indication is given by a significant paradox which already disturbs semantic theories of information: the Bar-Hillel–Carnap paradox, proposed in 1953 by Yehoshua Bar-Hillel and Rudolph Carnap. Briefly put, the paradox is this: the more nonsensical a message, the more information it would seem to contain. Therefore, *a contradiction would contain the most information*. This follows from the quantification of information in terms of statistical improbability established by MTC, but it only appears as a paradox when the semantic dimension (and thus truth value) is added. Typically, in the tradition of Russell and other epistemologist logicians, most have seen the Bar-Hillel–Carnap paradox as a problem to be solved by smoothing its paradoxical grind, undoing its tension.[15] However, we should expect a Lyotardian approach (thinking of his remarks on Russell's paradox and his love of the sophists[16]) to exploit such a paradox for all it is worth in demonstrating the possibility of the event within an information-theoretic context.

Moreover, there would seem to be an inverse of the Bar-Hillel–Carnap paradox which would imply that the great Monad which has complete information and predictability contains *no* information. So on the one hand – in the 'uphill' direction of the Leibnizian Monad, the paradox can be used to argue against the ideal of 'complete information' – that is, a system which has removed all unpredictability. If God knows everything, He knows nothing. As Lyotard writes: 'For a monad supposed to be perfect, like God, there are in the end no bits of information at all. God has nothing to learn' (IN: 65). If such an ideal attempts to ground itself in information theory as a kind of self-sufficient justification, this paradox can be used to show that no such grounding is possible. The logic of performativity defeats itself, and we face a blockage which forces us to reflect on the values which drive the system, which undergird instrumental rationality: it forces us to reflect not just on means, but on ends. In the other direction, 'downhill', the paradox invites us to accept and welcome messages which are not 'well formed', as Lyotard would say, messages which themselves seem paradoxical: messages which have aesthetic, ethical, and existential value, not 'outside' the informational system, but irreducible to a well-regulated, smooth decoding.

Eschewing a humanist response to the 'problem' of information, Lyotard seeks an 'inhumanist' or 'posthumanist', minimal response in the rules and paradoxes proper to information theory itself. Familiarising ourselves with such theory better than Lyotard himself did will allow us to extend his critique, to make it more rigorous and robust. But we must also realise, as Lyotard did, that so-called 'postinformational' uses of information technologies – such as in the digital arts – are in many respects a better form of resistance than theory itself. Lyotard writes:

> faced with the attempt to reduce language to the commercial unit of information, which is supposed to be able to translate all phrases, I believe that – in the absence of narratives of legitimation – there is only one possibility left us: to fight for that work of incommunicability, in

other words, for the work of the articulation of the possibility of new phrases.

This struggle is principally led by artists. The important thing in art is the production of works which bring into question the rules constituting a work as such. (Lyotard 1986–7: 213–14)

This invites us to fantasise about artists creating informational devices which would not contribute to the Monad, which would not be primarily communicational or epistemic, but would grind and hiss, generating extraneous noise and unpredictable effects, notional heterodoxies and material paradoxes. In fact, this has been going on since the technologies and the theories of information first became possible, but what is needed is for philosophers to attempt to receive their messages, and decode them in their own terms; to allow art to have an aesthetic critique on the epistemic model which has dominated theories and philosophies of information, and to take measure of the overhaul of meaning and value in the informational turn.

Conclusion

> Man instead of God: a theology is perpetuated in the creationist aesthetic.
> Lyotard MTI: 229

I would like briefly to conclude with a comparison of Lyotard's and Floridi's philosophies of information in order to show what is at stake in elaborating Lyotard's position. Floridi works primarily in the analytic tradition, and the majority of his work has focused on epistemological, ethical, and metaphilosophical issues framed in the terms of this tradition. However, at times he positions PI as post-analytic/continental divide, and engages with continental thought, particularly nineteenth-century German philosophy.[17] Along these lines he situates PI historically and metaphysically as follows:

> The history of contemporary philosophy may be written in terms of the emergence of humanity as the demiurgic Ego, which overcomes the death of god by gradually accepting its metaphysical destiny of fully replacing god as the creator and steward of reality, and hence as the ultimate source of meaning and responsibility. [...] ... one of the forces that lie behind the demiurgic turn is the Baconian–Galilean project of grasping and manipulating the alphabet of the universe. And this ambitious project has begun to find its fulfilment in the computational revolution and the resulting informational turn that have affected so profoundly our knowledge of reality and the

way we conceptualize it and ourselves within it. [...] Seen from a
demiurgic perspective, PI can then be presented as the study of the
informational activities that make possible the construction, con-
ceptualization, semanticization and finally the moral stewardship
of reality, both natural and artificial, both physical and anthropological. Indeed, we can look at PI as a complete *demiurgology* ...
(Floridi 2011: 23)

This quote suggests that Floridi positions PI as coextensive with the
centralisation of Man and the Subject after the death of God. By
contrast, Lyotard, in accord with much twentieth-century continental thought, follows Nietzsche further than the death of God, to the
death of Man, a death for which he sees information technology as
partially culpable.

In fact, there seems to be a tension in Floridi's work insofar as the
concepts and positions he is developing are increasingly becoming
'posthuman' in the sense of decentralising the traditional humanist notions of rationality and agency. He construes human beings as
'inforgs', informational organisms which inhabit a world of complex
informational processes (the 'infosphere'), along with other informational agents, some of which are machines which also process
information in an autonomous fashion (Floridi 2014: 94). By considering ourselves as one kind of information processor among others,
the human is displaced from the centre of the world of meaning and
activity. Moreover, the 'fourth revolution' of the title of his recent
book (Floridi 2014) situates the 'informational turn' precisely as a
further blow to human narcissism after those identified by Freud –
the Copernican, Darwinian, and Freudian (87–100). Indeed, he specifies that the fourth revolution necessitates

reassessing humanity's fundamental nature and role in the universe.
The deepest philosophical issue brought about by ICTs concerns not
so much how they extend or empower us, or what they enable us to
do, but more profoundly how they lead us to reinterpret who we are
and how we should interact with each other. (Floridi 2014: 166)

However, as the previously quoted passage above indicates, Floridi
does not seem to have followed this logic – as Lyotard does – to the
displacement of Man as the supposed successor to God in our metaphysical and moral universe. An appreciation of Lyotard's work in
the context of PI would allow a deepening insight into the displacement of the human by new technologies, which was staged at *Les
Immatériaux* in 1985 with more radicality than Floridi has quite yet

achieved.[18] The specificity of this radicality, for Nietzsche, Lyotard, and the problematic of nihilism as thought in the continental philosophical tradition, is that like God, the idea of 'the human' can act as a ground for a system of values, as it does for various humanisms. The displacement of this ground by information technologies raises questions regarding not just how values should now be implemented, but what our values should be, and the anxiety that we have lost any grounding for values as such. This anxiety, and the need to think what matters in a renewed way, torn from the orbit of 'the human', is what Lyotard tries to confront through this reflections on 'the event'.

A Lyotardian approach to PI is one which would attempt to think information in a context which is *not* epistemological; which would take into account aesthetics and ethics; and to think these on the 'micrological' level of information as a model of *meaning* rather than simply taking epistemology as the only appropriate consideration for this level, and thinking of aesthetic, ethical, existential, etc. concerns as only secondary considerations to be examined on the 'macro' level. Moreover, the implications of this are wider than technical considerations, insofar as what we understand information to be on a cultural level impacts our conceptions of ourselves and the values which structure our societies and drive our lives. My proposal is thus that this model needs to be opened up from the *epistemological* and *instrumental* concerns which largely govern our modelling of information, to include *aesthetic*, *ethical*, and *existential* considerations. I have tried to demonstrate here how Lyotard's work, while remaining fragmentary and suggestive, can be reconstructed to form a matrix for generating such a project. What I propose is to give Lyotard's retorsional turn within the linguistic turn yet one more turn; to use Lyotard to help us update critical, reflective thought as the linguistic turn turns into the informational turn.

Notes

1. Thanks are due to Andrew J. Iliadis for helpful comments on this chapter.
2. See for example Davis and Womack 2001; Horton-Parker 2007; Bryant et al. 2011; Littlefield and Johnson 2012; Grusin 2015.
3. As Antony Hudek has noted, in writings associated with *Les Immatériaux* Lyotard misspells Harold Lasswell's name with one 's' (Hudek 2009: n. 16). Moreover, in the essay 'The Works and Writings of Daniel Buren: An Introduction to the Philosophy of Contemporary Art', he

quotes Lasswell's well-known statement of the problem of communication – *Who (says) What (to) Whom (in) What Channel (with) What Effect?* – incorrectly dating it to 1939, and ascribing it to the Office of Radio Research at Princeton University. 'Lasswell' seems to be incorrectly called 'Lowell' here (Lyotard 1981a: 58). In the later version of this text which appears in *What to Paint?*, the organisation is now called the Mass Communication Centre at Princeton, and Lasswell is misspelled either as 'Loswell' or 'Losswell' (there is a note in the recent bilingual edition attempting to clarify this, but unfortunately the spellings in the French and English versions differ, reproducing the confusion yet again! See WP, pages 321 and 322, notes 94 and 3 respectively). Elsewhere, Lyotard spells his name 'Laswell' (Lyotard 1985: 49). In fact, although they are thought of as developing similar problems in the history of communications theory, Lasswell was not involved with the project at Princeton, and the statement Lyotard quotes comes from his paper 'The Structure and Function of Communication in Society' (Lasswell 1948).

4. See also Lyotard and Théofilakis 1985.

5. More recently, Leibniz has been claimed as a kind of precursor to the Algorithmic Theory of Information by Gregory Chaitin (2004), and – along with Plato and Kant – to the philosophy of information by Anthony F. Beavers (2012).

6. In his introduction to the English translation of *Matter and Memory*, Bergson explains: 'Matter, in our view, is an aggregate of "images." And by "image" we mean a certain existence which is more than that which the idealist calls a *representation*, but less than that which the realist calls a *thing*, – an existence placed half-way between the "thing" and the "representation"' (1911: vii–viii). And: 'Descartes, no doubt, had put matter too far from us when he made it one with geometrical extensity. But, in order to bring it nearer to us, there was no need to go to the point of making it one with our own mind' (ix).

7. However, Lyotard notes that this link depends on the twin caveat that Bergson's views be extracted from his own *pragmatism* and *vitalism*, which Lyotard sees as too tied to forms of humanism that technoscience itself is undermining (see IN: 44–5).

8. Lyotard refers to Stiegler's work in several essays collected in *The Inhuman*. The only direct citation is the preparatory note for the conference *Nouvelles technologies et mutation des savoirs* organised by Stiegler. Lyotard implicitly references research undertaken by Stiegler at the Collège Internationale de Philosophie on the philosophical stakes of new technologies (IN: 44, 148). This research produced three reports, entitled 'Les Nouvelles technologies. Aspects des enjeux philosophiques' (April 1985); 'Culture et technologies de communication' (with Thierry Chaput, July 1985); and 'Epoches et jeux de l'oubli: économies de la mémoire et de l'imagination' (September 1985). The results of these reports were published in summary in the essay 'Technologies de la mémoire et de l'imagination' (Stiegler 1986).

9. A more extensive analysis of Stiegler's thought, across a broader range of his writings, is undertaken in Chapter 3.
10. This 'general physics' is taken up for more extensive discussion in Chapter 3.
11. See for example the critical discussion of this tendency in Germain 2009.
12. For further discussion of this interpretation, see Chapter 4.
13. N. Katherine Hayles in fact argues that Shannon's information theory, constructed in terms of the signal/noise opposition, contains an inbuilt bias for stability and against change: 'Privileging signal over noise, Shannon's theory implied that the goal was a pre-existing state toward which the mechanism would move by making a series of distinctions between correct and incorrect choices. The goal was stable, and the mechanism would achieve stability when it reached the goal. This construction easily led to the implication that the goal, formulated in general and abstract terms, was less a specific site than stability itself. Thus the construction of information as a signal/noise distinction and the privileging of homeostasis produced and were produced by each other' (1999: 63–4).
14. This marks a significant and interesting contrast with Heidegger, who understands the important distinction as being between 'natural' language (understood in a specifically ontological and historical register) and formal language. Heidegger sees the formalisation of language as characteristic of information, and a threat to its 'ontological' dimension. See Heidegger 1993.
15. See for example Floridi 2011: ch. 5.
16. See 'The Strength of the Weak' in TP.
17. But also occasionally French philosophy. Notably, in a recent interview Floridi has drawn attention to the importance of Lyotard's *The Postmodern Condition* for its insights regarding the socio-political aspects of technology. See Floridi 2015.
18. This is taken up and discussed further in Chapter 7.

Economy, Ecology, Organology: On Technics and Desire

We need first to understand that the human form—including human desire and all its external representations—may be changing radically, and thus may be re-visioned [...] five hundred years of humanism may be coming to an end as humanism transforms itself into something we must helplessly call posthumanism.

Ihab Hassan 1977: 212

One important trajectory of Lyotard's thinking of the inhuman condition is a critical engagement with the theoretical developments in the twentieth century which have displaced the distinctions between nature, the human, and technology. These displacements have been made by new intellectual paradigms which have cut across old conceptual and disciplinary barriers. As we saw in the introduction, these developments give a leading meaning to the term 'posthuman', since they indicate an eclipse of the figure of the human as central to thought and value. Some of the major developments in question here have been charted by N. Katherine Hayles (1999) through three waves of cybernetics: 'classical' cybernetics, second-order cybernetics, and Artificial Life. In each of these, the human is displaced by being considered just one case (if indeed a remarkable one) of a complex system. Lyotard uses the term 'general physics' (of which cybernetics is a part) as a broader way of designating a kind of materialist monism he sees as having emerged from twentieth-century sciences. Another general term Lyotard and others sometimes use to designate these sciences is 'systems theory'; this term highlights the focus on generalities between different systems and the search for common principles of explanation and understanding between them.

The displacement of the human by systems theory instigates a crisis of values, since the human can no longer be taken as an evaluative measure. As we saw in Chapter 1, what this means according to Lyotard is that 'development' is no longer understood as a process acting for the human good, but rather becomes autonomous insofar as it is systemic complexity as such which takes on value and becomes the protagonist of the 'post-metanarrative'. We saw there that the principles of entropy and negentropy, which designate the movements of systems towards disorder or order, become evaluative concepts in this narrative of complexification, with the negentropic system as the protagonist and entropy as the antagonist. What I wish to explore in this chapter is an inflection of this approach which locates values in *desire*, understood energetically as a force which flows in and transforms systems, and the relation of this way of thinking value to technics. This is a posthuman or inhuman way of thinking values. For Lyotard, such values are what animate and motivate our projects after the decline of metanarratives. We find such an approach to both technics and desire in the works of Lyotard, and also, more recently, in the work of Bernard Stiegler.

The comparison of Lyotard with Stiegler is a fortuitous one which allows a thinking-together of Lyotard's own earlier and later works, as well as a critical comparison of two significantly different approaches to desire and technics. While Lyotard's earlier work was centrally concerned with desire thought as energetic libido, this concern largely disappeared as his attention turned to technics in the 1980s. Stiegler's earlier work was focused on technics, yet this concern has remained even as he has turned increasing attention in recent years towards the libidinal economy of desire. Stiegler's work provides a model, lacking in Lyotard's own work, for how to think desire and technics together. Yet the values each applies to technics and desire are radically different. Highly charged potentials for a critical encounter between Lyotard and Stiegler lie, largely unactualised, in their works, and it is just such an encounter I want to realise here. Lyotard refers to Stiegler's work in several of the essays collected in *The Inhuman*, and these constitute some of the earliest published engagements with the now-renowned philosopher's work. Stiegler, for his part, has frequently (if briefly) referenced Lyotard in his writings, and has recently returned to a more extensive engagement with Lyotard's early critique of his work (in Stiegler 2014, 2015b). However, much that is at stake regarding the differences (and as we shall see, even the *differend*) between Lyotard and Stiegler remains to be thought.

Revaluing the Drives: Lyotard's Nietzschean Freud

I want to begin by approaching Lyotard's work on libidinal economy via the readings of Nietzsche and Freud underlying it in order to uncover the evaluative categories within it. This is important because, as we shall see, Stiegler's more recent formulation of a libidinal economy is sharply at odds with Lyotard with respect to how they read Freud. This will require then not just a recap of Lyotard's own general description of the libidinal economy, but an uncovering of the Nietzschean influence which underlies his reading of Freud in the early 1970s.

The term 'libidinal economy', as it is used by both Lyotard and Stiegler, of course has its origin in Freudian metapsychology. For Freud, this term designates the flows and transformations of libidinal energy in the psychical apparatus (which importantly includes both the mind and body). Adapting principles of hydrodynamics and thermodynamics to psychology, Freud presents the psychic life of the human person as describable in terms of flows of energy and basic principles which regulate this flow. Following Deleuze and Guattari's (1983) lead, Lyotard elevates the concept of libido to the level of a monistic ontological principle, and extends the libidinal economy to all of reality. He argues that this economy is not restricted to the human person, as libidinal energies may be invested ('cathected') in any and all aspects of the world: 'words, books, food, images, looks, parts of the body, tools and machines, animals, sounds and gestures' (LRG: 205), among other things.

This then allows a libidinal economic model of society:

> One can imagine any society as an ensemble of persons ruled by a system whose function would be to regulate the entry, the distribution, and the elimination of the *energy* that this ensemble spends in order to exist. [...] The institution [...] would in general be any stable formation [...] transforming related energy into bound energy within a given field of the circulation of objects (the linguistic field, the matrimonial field, the economic field, etc.). (PW: 63)

Lyotard effectively describes reality (both social and psychic) as a system in which libidinal energies are invested in more or less well-regulated ways, and which punctuate and destabilise established structures with the occurrence of 'intensities', the name for 'events' in the libidinal philosophy. Within this system, Lyotard describes the flows of energy according to the principles which Freud identifies as governing the drives – Eros and the death drive – but 'revalues' the drives by reading Freud through Nietzsche, giving value to the death drive (read as the Dionysian and as a repetition of affects akin to the eternal return) as the motive force for artistic creativity, political transformation, and everything which he terms 'event'.

We may understand Lyotard's revisions of Freud in the *Libidinal Economy* period as a *revaluation of the values* underlying the Freudian economy of the drives, guided by Nietzsche.[1] In short, it consists in a displacement from the privileging of desire as wish (*Wunsch*) and the libido as Eros, governed by the pleasure principle and the reality principle, to a privileging of desire as force and the libido as the death drive, governed by the Nirvana principle. This is framed and supported by a Freudian rendering of the Nietzschean problem of nihilism, the devaluation of the value of life.

Both Freud and Nietzsche give a roughly naturalistic, and in many respects deflationary, account of human beings and their condition, in which consciousness is a kind of epiphenomenon whose function is primarily to act as part of the organism's defences. Both see the majority of mental life as consisting in unconscious, instinctual drives. Freud sees the psychic apparatus as bombarded with energetic excitations from sources which are both endogenous (internal – the instincts, which in impacting on the unconscious form the drives) and exogenous (external – perceptions of the external world). In order to survive and function, the organism needs to regulate this energy so it is not overwhelmed by it, and Freud's hypothesis is that the key regulator is the pleasure principle, associated with the principle of constancy: 'the mental apparatus endeavours to keep the quantity of excitation present in it as low as possible or at least to keep it constant' (SE XVIII: 9). For Freud, an increase in the quantity of excitation is felt as pain (tension or anxiety), while a decrease in excitation is felt as pleasure. The functioning of the psychic apparatus, and of all human behaviour, in the interests of self-preservation, is to *reduce tension* – to seek pleasure and avoid pain.

In infancy, the organism is subject to regulation primarily by the pleasure principle, but in learning to adapt to the contingencies of its environment – the fact that impulses cannot always be immediately discharged – the pleasure principle becomes supplanted by *the reality principle*. In Freud's words,

> [u]nder the influence of the ego's instincts of self-preservation, the pleasure principle is replaced by the *reality principle*. This latter principle does not abandon the intention of ultimately obtaining pleasure, but it nevertheless demands and carries into effect the postponement of satisfaction ... (SE XVIII: 10)

Thus, the reality principle is also guided by the *telos* of reducing tension or maintaining it at a low level, but introduces the strategy of *deferral* in order ultimately better to attain its ends. A further key strategy in the service of the reduction of tension is *phantasy*, the fulfilment of wishful impulses through an imagined substitute for the real thing.

For Freud – simplifying greatly – neurosis is caused by something going wrong in childhood psychosexual development, and a cure (the conversion of troubling neurosis into 'ordinary unhappiness') may be found by having the patient remember the repressed problem, and discharging the energies 'trapped' there into normal channels. Overall and in general, the healthy functioning organism will be able to regulate its libidinal economy in accord with the pleasure and reality principles, maintaining a quiescent state at a relatively low level of energy (that is, having the capacity to harmlessly discharge excess excitations of energy). In this sense, Freud's understanding of 'the good life' – the most meaningful and valuable life possible for a human being – seems to be a kind of Epicurean one, in which humans are not motivated by love of the good, but by the desire for pleasure ('ego instincts', self-preservation), and the best form of pleasure is quiescence, not excitation (retroactively, the Epicurean Sage appears as someone who has mastered the application of the reality principle to his own drives).

Extrapolating back from Lyotard's revisions of Freud, we can see how Nietzsche paints a somewhat different picture of the organism and what constitutes for it a 'good life'. Like Freud (and Darwin), Nietzsche sees the human being as just another animal that has evolved on the planet earth, but with the dubious distinction of having developed a fragile and problematic system which causes it perhaps more problems than it solves. This system is consciousness. Like Freud, Nietzsche sees consciousness as a system of adaptation which processes energetic excitations, enhancing self-preservation. However, for Nietzsche consciousness presents peculiar problems, and he sometimes writes as though we would be better off without it. In his *Genealogy of Morality*, Nietzsche writes that human beings suffer the most not from suffering itself, but from the failure to find a *meaning* for suffering (Nietzsche 2006a: Essay 3, §28). The interpretation of life is thus a strategy of coping and preservation, but one which Nietzsche thinks has generally led to an overall devaluation of the value of life, which he calls *nihilism*. (Nihilism is of course a complex phenomenon with a long history, and we are restricting ourselves here to its first and most basic form, which Nietzsche sometimes specifies as *religious nihilism*.[2])

Nihilism manifests in the Western tradition primarily through the 'Christian-moral' interpretation of the world, and through *ressentiment*, bad conscience, and the ascetic ideal, each of which may be understood as a kind of 'perversion' of the bodily drives. Now, Nietzsche is clear that religious nihilism has its own value, which is to *preserve* life, but it does so by preserving the organism at a very low level of will to power. It lives, but in constant hostility towards itself and its environment, denying the validity of its natural impulses and diverting them into futile expenditures. The mechanism of preservation operative here is one of *lack* and *deferral*: the world lacks value in itself, and the attainment of value is deferred until the afterlife.

The analogies which Lyotard makes between Nietzsche's religious nihilism and Freud's pleasure principle and reality principle now become apparent. Like religious nihilism, these Freudian principles function to preserve the life of the organism, but they do so by keeping it at a low level of energy, and key mechanisms for keeping it in this state are deferral (the reality principle) and lack (phantasy). Where Nietzsche presents his analysis of the human condition as a critical genealogy, Freud presents it as a neutral, 'scientific' anthropology. However, following Nietzsche's lead, Lyotard sees Freud's account as constructed, implicitly, on the basis of value judgements inherited from the Christian-moral tradition, which he seeks to revalue, within the Freudian framework (in essence, keep the concepts, but change the values attached to them, and their economic relations). Like Nietzsche, Lyotard then seeks a solution to the problem of nihilism from within Freudian psychoanalytic theory, in the interests of a greater capacity to affirm life (guided by a different philosophical conception of 'the good life').

Against the dominance of the pleasure principle and the reality principle, Lyotard advocates the raising of tension (greater tolerance for anxiety) and privileges excitations which produce a very high or very low level of intensity, towards an overall energetic transformation. He writes:

Analyse Freud's theory of representation: The elaboration of fantasy, of the dream, as originating in a *lack* or *depression*, and the charging of the mental apparatus. The implication should be: *to raise or maintain the intensity in order to obtain as high an energetic metamorphosis as possible*. [...] In such a process does affirmation reside ... (Lyotard 1978: 49; italics mine)

The aim that Lyotard thinks *should* follow from Freud's description, rather than the one that does in Freud's own approach, is to promote change, and thus to move away from the nihilistic and depressive lack and deferral, towards an affirmation of life. No doubt this destabilises the organism, and perhaps appears simply dangerous. Yet a key point in this revaluation is Nietzsche's emphasis that a high level of will to power is associated with a lack of concern for self-preservation. In such an organism, libido or will to power expands without regard for the preservation of the organism, even if it means its destruction. A revaluation of values indeed.

Lyotard further develops his conception of libidinal economy by making a couple of key identifications or analogies between Freudian and Nietzschean concepts: between Freud's *libido* and Nietzsche's *will to power*, and between Freud's *death drive* and Nietzsche's *eternal return*. While Freud, as he insists in *Beyond the Pleasure Principle*, was always a dualist, Lyotard develops a monism from Freudian theory by identifying the libido with Nietzsche's will to power. Nietzsche attempts to overturn the metaphysics associated with Platonism and the Christian-moral interpretation of the world by replacing dualistic belief in a suprasensory world with a monistic affirmation of the world as will to power. Nietzsche's theory of the will to power is an ontology and metaphysics of becoming, and the world itself is nothing but will to power. On Heidegger's interpretation, the 'complex forms of relative duration of life within becoming' are 'dominating centres' or 'ruling configurations' shaped within the will to power. Art, the state, religion, science, and society are forms of these ruling configurations, and these configurations attempt to preserve and enhance themselves (Schrift 1990: 74).

Lyotard directly identifies the libidinal theory of desire in Freud with Nietzsche's will to power: 'The word *desire* has two meanings in Freud's work: there is the sense of wish (*Wunsch*) and that of force or energy (Nietzsche's *Wille*)' (TP: 13). He then argues that libido is split between two regimes, or ways in which affects or intensities repeat themselves – Eros, which contributes to the harmonious functioning of the organism, and the death drive (or Thanatos), which contributes to its disorder. For Lyotard, libido is purely positive, governed by the 'laws of thought' operative in the unconscious, which, Freud tells us, know no negation, and is subject to a great mobility of cathexis (see Freud's 1915 paper 'The Unconscious' in SE XIV). Lyotard argues that until the discovery of the death drive, Freud could only posit desire as wish (desire seeking to fulfil itself) as primary. However, Lyotard himself insists that we should understand desire as wish as a secondary modification of desire as libido.[3] It manifests a representation of what is felt to be lacked:

> The quanta of energy (which is the same as desire, insofar as it is force) that cannot be discharged in a specific action with respect to

reality become represented on a scene opened up within the psychical apparatus (or is it within the subject?) – a scene opened by this impossibility, this lack. (TP: 13)

Second, Lyotard's identification of the death drive with the eternal return draws on Klossowski's interpretation of the latter as a repetition of *difference* (which was also an influence on, and in some ways resembles, Deleuze's) (see Klossowski 2005; Deleuze 1983). For Nietzsche, the thought of the eternal return is both the most nihilistic thought ('the heaviest burden'), or, if it can be borne, the highest achievement of the affirmation of life. Lyotard makes a similar assessment of the death drive, asserting that *it is only from the perspective of Eros* that the death drive appears destructive. In itself, it must be envisioned as pure positivity. He writes:

> In reality, the death instinct (intensity or drift) should be envisioned as positivity. The slow or lightning-quick displacement of investments is precisely positivity in so far as it escapes the rules of language and is without reason. What is positive in this sense is what is beyond regulated deviations, gaps or borders, or hierarchies ... (TP: 15)

For Lyotard, the death drive as eternal return of difference is an affirmation of aleatory intensities; fluctuations of the libido which defy the principle of constancy and the nihilistic, depressive form of life Lyotard seems to be suggesting it maintains.

If there is a core value in Lyotard's Nietzschean revaluation of Freud, it is the value placed on *intensity*[4] as an affirmation of life, and if there is an ethic which emerges from this reading, it is to encourage the emergence of intensities in energetic systems against the nihilistic tendency to keep them in a constant, depressed state. Such intensities encourage metamorphosis and change in systems. It is essential to realise here that Lyotard's libidinal economy is not aimed at the *liberation* of desire, as have radical psychoanalytic theorists from the surrealists to Marcuse (the latter is discussed below). He explicitly opposes such as possibility, asserting that libidinal energies must always be contained in systems (and conversely, that systems always contain libidinal energies capable of producing intensities). This mutual implication of systems and libidinal energies is what Lyotard calls *dissimulation*.[5] The aim of his libidinal economy, then, is to provoke intensities which will operate within and act to transform systems; he sees such transformation as an affirmation of life which combats nihilistic depression. Significantly, for the reading we are developing here, the intensity of desire in its capacity to provoke change in systems is associated by Lyotard with the death drive, itself associated with the second law of thermodynamics, entropy (see Saul 1958).

From Libidinal Economy to the Ecology of the Secluded

Having now detailed Lyotard's approach to the evaluation of the circulation of *desire* in systems, I wish to move to his treatment of technics. As noted at the outset, Lyotard moves away from libidinal economy as he moves towards a consideration of technics, in the late 1970s. In the previous chapter we saw how Lyotard develops a critique of the 'system' of capitalism and technoscience through the 'Leibnizian hypothesis', which postulates the continual stocking of information with the goal of absolute knowledge and control, determined by the principle of negentropy. Lyotard's move away from libidinal philosophy can be seen at least in part as motivated by a recognition that such a philosophy is a kind of metaphysics, accompanied by his own increasingly critical stance towards metaphysics in general (see 'Avis de déluge' in DP). Part of this stance towards metaphysics involves Lyotard's following of Heidegger (1977) in seeing the 'system' of contemporary technoscience (and along with it, Lyotard insists, capitalism) as the realisation of metaphysics.

While Lyotard's later works often seem to move in horizons very distant from the orbit of the libidinal philosophy, we can see a similar revaluation of the values of the drives expressed through a critical engagement with philosophical interpretations of the thermodynamic terms which inspired Freud's metapsychology; in particular, entropy and negentropy. These terms are taken up in a discussion of economy and ecology in the short essay 'Oikos' (in PW), a consideration of which allows us to see the relations of technics and desire which are implied by Lyotard's thought.

'Oikos' was presented at a conference on ecology in Germany in 1989 in which Niklas Luhmann also participated, and at points Lyotard engages critically with Luhmann's idea of 'ecological communication'.[6] This is significant for my concerns here, as Luhmann's 'Systems Theory' is arguably the most important attempt to apply principles of 'second-order' cybernetics to society. As I noted at the outset, following Hayles (1999) we may see cybernetics, in its various phases, as a key player in the development of technics in the twentieth century, leading to the posthuman crisis of values we are addressing here. Lyotard's criticisms of Luhmann indicate well his attitude towards the application of technical models such as cybernetics to social systems, and the political and ethical implications of such. Let us briefly rehearse Lyotard's argument.

First, Lyotard notes that the opposition man/nature belongs to the speculative tradition (Marx/Hegel), while the opposition inside/outside belongs to the tradition of *the metaphysics of the subject*. But there is another metaphysical tradition in which neither of these distinctions is relevant: *the metaphysics of energy*. What counts in this tradition is the opposition between *matter* and *form*. Leibniz is an extreme expression of this philosophical tradition, while, Lyotard asserts, cybernetics is its most recent form. This tradition suppresses the outside/inside border in favour of different degrees of complexity. For Leibniz there is only a difference in complexity (capacity to process information) between monads (see Chapter 2). In general, for the metaphysics of energy '[e]very entity (*alles Seiende*, if you prefer), may be thought in mechanical, dynamic, or economic terms, hence in terms of relationships of force and efficiency' (PW: 98). Lyotard calls this a 'general physics', of which he sees Luhmann's systems theory as an avatar.

Luhmann presents a generalised model of systems under the name of ecology in his book *Ecological Communication* (1989a). Significantly, for Luhmann ecology is not restricted to biological or natural systems, but is a general theory of all systems as they relate to their environment. In the glossary to *Ecological Communication*, ecology is defined as follows:

> in this context the totality of scientific investigations that concern themselves, on whatever level of system formation, with the consequences of the differentiation of system and environment for the system's environment. The concept does not presuppose any specific kind of system (ecosystem). (Luhmann 1989a: 144)

Luhmann develops what is explicitly a cybernetic understanding of the relationship between a system and its environment in terms of a difference in *complexity*. The 'environment' includes everything that is not the system, so is of greater complexity. This means that

> systems are constantly confronted with new and different environmental states. To deal with these they have to bring their own complexity into a relation of correspondence with that of their environments. Systems do this through establishing system structures that reduce the complexity of their environments and thereby obviate point-for-point correlations between their own changes and changes in their environments. (Luhmann 1989a: ix)

This 'reduction of complexity' suggests that environmental complexity is a problem for systems, and that they deal with it by increasing their own complexity.

To explain how this takes place, Luhmann draws on the concept of *autopoiesis* introduced by Humberto Maturana and Francisco Varela in their *De Máquinas y Seres Vivos* (1972; translated in *Autopoiesis and Cognition*, 1980). As Luhmann presents it, this term refers to 'the unique capacity of living systems to maintain their autonomy and unity through their very own operations' (Luhmann 1989a: x).[7] This allows Luhmann to conceptualise the system's relationship to its environment as *dynamic*: the system is both organisationally closed and structurally open. Luhmann effectively takes this idea of autopoiesis from biology and applies it to *social* systems. Moreover, within the generalised theory of systems he calls 'ecology', Luhmann specifies social systems as being defined by the presence of *communication*. Communication defines the organisational closure of social systems, and for society, whatever is not communication is *environment*.

As Luhmann further elaborates, social systems constitute themselves self-referentially. That is, they refer to something beyond themselves, then back to themselves, taking a detour through the external (Luhmann 1989a: 145). He defines social systems as being primarily constituted, not by persons and actions, but by communications, which form systems in this self-referential way by defining themselves against an environment understood as a restriction on communications. The environment presents dangers for the system, and environmental factors are felt within the system, which tries to compensate for them, as what Luhmann calls *resonance*: 'the communicative reactions or disturbances that society's environment produces within society itself' (xiii). Resonance is always *improbable*, with the result that in general society produces *too little resonance* in relation to its environmental dangers. In sum, then, Luhmann produces a theory of social systems under the rubric of ecology which accents the value of the *increasing complexity in ordered social systems*, since it is this complexity which allows the system to cope with the greater complexity of its environment.

At this point, we may well begin to recognise aspects of Lyotard's critical themes of general physics, complexity, and the 'monad in expansion' in Luhmann's systems theory. Lyotard in fact characterises and critiques it in the following way:

> systems theory is not a philosophical system but a description of reality, a 'so-called reality' ['*die sogenannte Wirklichkeit*'] that has become entirely describable in terms of general physics, which stretches from

astrophysics to particle physics (electronics, information technology, and cybernetics are only aspects of this general physics) and of course also in economic terms. In this description, the alive or the human appear as particular cases, very interesting cases of complex material systems. This means that, from this perspective, conflict (and ultimately war) does not arise between human and nature; rather, the struggle is between more developed systems and something else that is necessarily less developed and that the physicists know as entropy, the second principle of thermodynamics. (TP: 98–9)

For once in agreement with Jürgen Habermas (1971), Lyotard sees Luhmann's work as ideological. To see why, we may approach Lyotard's critique by first noting the crucial distinction between *economy* and *ecology* he develops in the 'Oikos' essay. He stipulates meanings of the terms as follows:

Economy is the *nomos*, that is, the regulation of the circulation of forces and information or messages [...] it is a question of regulation, that is to say, of the ability to preserve, conserve, store, and use the past, past events, the effects that past events have had on the system or the apparatus, and to use this information in order to adjust for efficiency, optimal performance. [...] The economy functions precisely insofar as people and instances observe rules that are something like what is called a 'memory' in cybernetics, a sort of set of rules. (TP: 99–100)

Lyotard understands *ecology* not as a relation to the environment, but as characterised by an *Oikeion* (belonging) which is an 'otherness' not outside or beyond, in the *Umwelt*, but in the core of the apparatus (like the unconscious in the mind). He writes:

I think that when Freud speaks of a 'psychic economy,' he would have done better to speak of a 'psychic ecology,' for the term 'libidinal economy' (in the Freudian sense, not mine), presupposes that something necessarily escapes publicity, *Öffentlichkeit*, that something resists openness and hence communication. (TP: 105)

For Lyotard, ecology concerns what he calls in this essay *the secluded*, that which is private, concerned with the home, and is precisely withdrawn and distinguished from the public realm of the economy. Ecology – the *Logos* of the *Oikeion* – concerns that which is a remainder, in the sense of not being placed in circulation and exchange. By contrast, economy – the *Nomos* (law) of the *Oikeion* – concerns the rules which regulate such circulation and exchange.

With economy, Lyotard continues to elaborate, something is understood in terms of *function*. By contrast, he stipulates that we should understand 'ecology' in terms of *dysfunction*. As he understands it, a *function* is simply a rule for operating, and he associates 'economy' with Kant's determinate judgement (which follows a rule), and 'ecology' with Kant's reflective judgement (which proceeds without a rule). In the terms used by both thermodynamics and information theory, and which he places at the core of 'general physics', economy proceeds by *negentropy*, whereas ecology proceeds by *entropy*. And here we see the analogy with the principles developed in Lyotard's earlier libidinal economy: in terms of the Freudian regimes of the drives (themselves based on the thermodynamic model), economy can be said to be governed by the regime of *Eros*, and ecology by *Thanatos* (the death drive).

According to Lyotard, the contemporary environment is determined by economy in the above sense; that is: 'we are in an *Umwelt* that is the realization of metaphysics as a general physics under the name of cybernetics' (TP: 101). He explains that '[i]n the *Umwelt* I am describing, all politics is certainly nothing other than a program of decisions to encourage development. All politics is only [...] a program of administrative decision making, of managing the system' (101). Lyotard's fear with respect to the current economic system of development, which for him is functionally identical to a generalised physics which privileges negentropy, is that '[f]rom the point of view of development [...] the Third World is nothing but a source of entropy for the *autopoesis* [*sic*.] of the great monad' (99) – and would be better eliminated so as not to be an inefficient energy drain on the system (the same critical point made with respect to the 'postmodern fable' – see Chapter 1).

These points allow us to see how Lyotard's critique of negentropic technics and defence of entropy are related to his earlier critique of nihilistic, depressive systems and celebration of intense libidinal events. In the libidinal philosophy, we saw that Lyotard revalues the Freudian drives, rejecting the ideal of quiescent energies and stable systems in preference to the production of intensities and systemic transformations. Given their inspiration in thermodynamic concepts, these drives map onto Lyotard's later discussions of entropy and negentropy in cybernetic systems. For him, entropy is a trope for *otherness*, understood as both that which we must welcome if we are to be open to the creative forces of thought and art, and to which we have an ethical obligation in the forms of cultural, racial, sexual, and other kinds of difference. Lyotard sees technics to a large extent through the lens of Heidegger's thesis on the realisation of metaphysics in 'general physics', and the tendency of the technoscientific and capitalist system to eradicate all otherness through programmed efficiency. Yet, as I will argue below and in later chapters, the 'Leibnizian hypothesis' does not fully determine Lyotard's view of technics, especially with respect to art, where he sees in technics the possibility for the 'second inhuman' (of infancy) to resist the 'first inhuman' (of 'the system'). We now move to a consideration of the work of the younger philosopher Bernard Stiegler.

From Libidinal Economy to the Ecology of the Spirit

Bernard Stiegler is an important contemporary philosopher who, since the mid-1980s, has been dealing with many of the same important themes as Lyotard, including those which structure this volume: nihilism, information, and art. Significantly for the themes of this chapter, Stiegler made his name as one of the most important contemporary philosophers of technics, and he has more recently turned his attention to his own thinking of libidinal economy, a way of thinking the circulation of desire in our new information society. Given this course in the development of his thinking, an opposite order of presentation to that we took with Lyotard is in order – first we will consider Stiegler's thesis on technics, then his thesis on desire.

Stiegler's most significant original thesis, concisely stated, is that '[*t*]*ekhnē* produces time' (Stiegler 2009a: 18). Deeply influenced by Derrida's critique of metaphysics, particularly as it pertains to writing, Stiegler develops an argument for 'originary technicity'. According to Derrida, the 'metaphysics of presence' which has structured the Western philosophical tradition has posited an origin of meaning (for example, in consciousness) which is simple and self-identical, and posited the inscription of this meaning in writing as secondary, derivative, and corrupted in relation to the original meaning (introducing 'difference' into 'identity'). Plato's argument about writing denigrating memory in the *Phaedrus* is the *locus classicus* of this view. Against this, Derrida develops the well-known argument that the characteristics of writing which have been opposed to the pure identity of meaning as 'presence' – spatial differing and temporal deferring (*différance*) – are in fact necessary conditions for the production of meaning as such.[8] Derrida's deconstruction may from this perspective be understood as an extended argument against the supposed simple identity of a pure origin, a 'presence', of meaning.

Applying and extending this idea, Stiegler argues for a '*différance* of *différance*' (Stiegler 1998: 177–8) which conditions *différance* itself, which he identifies as technics. Drawing on André Leroi-Gourhan's anthropological theory of the evolution of the human through tool use,[9] Stiegler argues that what we think of as the interiority of consciousness is founded on an exteriority, first and foremost of objects which can act as memory supports. According to Stiegler, then, the differing and deferring of *différance* are themselves grounded in technics – understood first and foremost as *mnemotechnics*, external memory supports – which produce time. Without such external supports, Stiegler argues, consciousness would not be capable of the protensions and retentions that Husserl identifies as the temporal process through which consciousness of the present is synthesised. While Derrida critiques the 'metaphysics of presence' by emphasising the temporal syntheses of internal time consciousness that Husserl's phenomenological analysis identifies (see Husserl 1991; Derrida 1973), Stiegler goes further to insist that these temporal syntheses are themselves only possible because of the external inscriptions which allow memory traces to be formed. Stiegler thus transforms Derrida's (quasi-)transcendental play of *différance* into a play of external, material inscriptions, posited as necessary conditions for the constitution of phenomenological temporality – and hence consciousness – as such. He calls these objective memory traces *tertiary* retentions, supplementing Husserl's specification of the *primary* retentions of the immediate past constitutive of our conscious awareness of the present moment, and the *secondary* retentions forming longer-term memories.

These tertiary retentions are artificial supports for memory, which enable the historical transmission of memories beyond genetic memory and individual cognitive memory. As such, they ground *culture*. Modes of tertiary retention have 'evolved' from the oral traditions of preliterate cultures, to writing, to the Internet. Stiegler argues that the relation of the human to technics is 'originary', such that to claim a human essence prior to technics would be 'metaphysical' in the pejorative, Derridean sense. As we have just seen, Stiegler, following Leroi-Gourhan, asserts that the evolution of the human being has been essentially bound up with tool use, and he sees human consciousness and culture as produced in intimate relation with technicity. As such, his philosophy may be understood as focusing around a deconstruction of the metaphysical opposition of the human and the technical, an opposition he sees as deeply structuring the history of Western thought and which he argues manifests as a widespread repression of technics.[10]

Stiegler extends this thesis on the originary technicity of the human to develop a theory of how individuals and social structures are formed in relation to technologies. Significantly, he draws on and extends the work of Gilbert Simondon (1989) on *individuation*, to argue that individuals, societies, and technologies come to be what they are through processes of mutually conditioning relations. Stiegler describes these processes as a whole as a 'general organology', composed of three primary levels: the psychosomatic, the technical, and the socio-ethnic (Stiegler 2013: 35). 'General organology' is Stiegler's own kind of systems theory; it emphasises the relations between these different levels, and the idea that despite their differences, each is subject to essentially the same kinds of processes of individuation. Perhaps most significantly, Stiegler's theory proposes that individuals and societies become what they are through their interactions with technologies.

Despite Stiegler's thesis of originary technicity, he develops a theory of nihilism around contemporary technics. He believes that we are now in a significantly new situation, because the technical developments which used to take place more or less unconsciously and very slowly have now passed into a system of extremely rapid technological innovation. He explains that '[e]ach time these technical systems mutate, they create what Bertrand Gille calls *disadjustments between the technical system and the society*' (Stiegler with Neyrat 2012: 11–12). Stiegler analyses these technical mutations and their effects through a great variety of concepts, and drawing on many different theoretical sources. One of the more important and repeated of these sources is Sylvain Auroux's concept of *grammatisation*, which Stiegler defines as 'the process by which all the fluxes or flows [*flux*] through which symbolic (that is, also, existential) acts are linked, can be discretized, formalized and reproduced' (Stiegler 2011: 172 n. 4). In short, grammatisations are discretisations of continuous processes; they describe the systems of inscription which Stiegler sees as constitutive of meaning as such. The most significant forms of grammatisation which have developed in human history include alphabetic writing, the printing press, and computerisation.

Disadjustments between the social and technical systems are produced, Stiegler conjectures, when the symbolic systems constitutive of human cultures rapidly alter because they are subject to new forms of grammatisation. Such has occurred with the new information technologies. Echoing Husserl, Heidegger, Adorno and Horkheimer, and others, Stiegler describes these 'disadjustments' wrought by the new technologies as largely erosive of meaning, disorienting in terms of our habitual relations to time and space, and as *instituting* a state of 'symbolic misery' (or perhaps better, 'symbolic poverty')[11] in the contemporary world. We can understand this claim in terms of

Stiegler's earlier thesis: if meaning is itself constituted through technics (exteriorised traces), then the changes wrought to such systems of traces (writing, television, computer programming, and so on) will have a deeply conditioning effect on meaning as such (since there is no 'prior meaning', thought to consist in internal consciousness or anything else, which would escape this conditioning power).

In more recent works, Stiegler has turned to psychoanalytic theory to analyse his profoundly bleak view of the contemporary situation.[12] In an even more dire sense than Lyotard or other recent continental philosophers, Stiegler sees our age as one afflicted by a threatening nihilism. His diagnosis of this situation has seen him develop his own theory of libidinal economy, quite different to Lyotard's. The crux of this theory is the predominance of the model of *consumption* in contemporary capitalism. Stiegler sees this as a mutation in capitalism which has wrought a profound change in the libidinal economy as such, as it affects both individuals and society as a whole. This analysis is profoundly linked to his theses on general organology and the disadjustments produced by current technologies, since information technologies in particular have made consumer capitalism possible through what he calls 'psychopower', the strategic targeting of consumers.[13] On the individual level, Stiegler argues that the advertising and marketing industries train the desire of individuals to expect and demand immediate satisfaction through the consumption of products. In his terminology, this 'short-circuits' desire, preventing it from being *deferred* and *invested* in long-term aims, goals, and projects, or 'long circuits'. For Stiegler, it is these long circuits of desire which allow individuals to pass through paths of development or individuation, and to be invested in and attached to people, values, and goals which make life worth living. This short-circuiting of desire creates an individual unable to love themselves or others, unable to have the feeling that they truly exist, or that life is worth living.[14]

Perhaps unsurprisingly, Stiegler sees an originary technicity at the 'origin' of desire itself, and asserts that Freud was in error in failing to think the artifactuality of desire (Stiegler 2014a: 49). He again draws inspiration from Derrida in this interpretation, and extends Derrida's arguments concerning the *différance* of writing with his concept of technics as exteriorised, objectified *différance*. He writes: 'As was clearly shown by Derrida in *The Post Card*, the reality principle *is* the pleasure principle, but as its différance – that is, its writing, which according to my own analysis also means its *technesis*' (56).[15]

This thesis is explained in the context of a critical discussion of Herbert Marcuse's *Eros and Civilization* (1962), in the course of which Stiegler develops his own theory of libidinal economy. He opposes Marcuse's proposal that in contemporary capitalist societies, the pleasure principle is dominated and repressed by the reality principle, and that it must be liberated. To the contrary, Stiegler argues that there is no desire at all without repression. He writes:

> There is no sublimation, nor any individuation, no concretizing or fixing of libidinal energy on this or that object, without the occurrence of a process of repression – if only as the circuit of différance that extends a pleasure and realises a desire. (Stiegler 2014a: 56)

We can see in this thesis regarding desire – that there is no desire without repression, and that the pleasure principle is 'always already' the reality principle – an analogue of the idea of *différance* as originary complexification of a supposedly more simple and prior term.

Stiegler then argues, against any notion of a natural or already existing libido, that libidinal energy must be *produced*:

> [t]he 'mutability of instincts', through which animality becomes humanity, is the *passage of desire*, which *begins* by *deferring the satisfaction* of the drive, or in other words by saving it up, *economizing* it. Libido is libidinal energy, and this energy is produced by an economy, the economy of différance, through which the drive becomes an energy invested in objects ... (Stiegler 2014a: 57)

Significantly, then, Stiegler distinguishes libidinal energy, able to be constructively invested in objects, from 'drive-based' energy, which he sees as purely destructive. Stiegler argues that desire as libidinal energy is produced through the *composition* of the two tendencies of the drives, Eros and the death drive. If these tendencies *decompose*, they regress to purely drive-based energies, unable to be sublimated and invested into objects of desire, and thus become purely destructive. It is in this way that Stiegler believes that there is in contemporary consumer capitalism a *fall* in the level of libidinal energy, because consumerism decomposes the tendencies, diverting them into short-term satisfactions and destroying their capacity for long-term investment. That is, Stiegler believes that while consumer capitalism exploits the libidinal economy, it also destroys it. Stiegler sees this decline in the overall level of libidinal energy in society as a modality of the contemporary 'energy crisis' (along with diminishing fossil fuels) about which we need to be globally concerned (see Stiegler 2013: 90–1).

Up to a point, Stiegler's analysis of the libidinal economy reflects many aspects of Lyotard's. In the following passage, for example, we see much in common with Lyotard's principle of 'dissimulation':

> Libido can and must socialise itself insofar as it is always already diverted, having always already begun to be tamed. This being the case, libido would also be, through that, always already on the way to a reversion to wildness, as a kind of 'perversion', and ultimately as a power of transgression that may 'rebound' upon the process itself, causing the rebirth of the phoenix. (Stiegler 2014a: 68)

Thus, both Lyotard and Stiegler posit an ambivalence of the libido, and the necessity of both the tendencies of Eros and the death drive as essential regimes of desire. The key points of difference between Lyotard's and Stiegler's readings of the libidinal economy, however, seem to be the following. As we have just seen, Stiegler sees these as together forming a process of 'composition' which *produces* desire and allows it to be sublimated, that is, bound through investments in objects of desire. He sees the unbinding of the drives, conditioned by consumer capitalism, as destructive of desire itself, leading to an overall fall in libidinal energy, and the nihilism of the contemporary era. By contrast, Lyotard sees nihilism primarily in *excessive* sublimation, the work of the binding of libidinal energy, and he sees the affirmative response to this nihilism as consisting in processes which *deregulate* the drives (which might involve either binding or unbinding, depending on the context, the particular system). Notably, while Stiegler sees the *deferral* of desire and its investment in objects as necessary for healthy processes of individuation, and the immediate gratifications of desire as belonging to a destructive unbinding of the drives, Lyotard sees such a deferral (Stiegler's 'long circuits') as the very mechanism of nihilism, and the production of intensities involving unbound libidinal energies (Stiegler's 'short circuits') as life-affirmative.

Furthermore, in contrast to Stiegler, who stresses the binding and sublimation of libido for all healthy investments and creative processes, Lyotard stresses the necessity of unbound libido for thought and creative activity, the capacity for libido to be invested in an *unforeseeable* manner. He explains:

> Though he does not write anything definitive on the subject, Freud insists on the fact that the notion itself of 'sublimation' precisely presupposes that there is the order of the primary drive, the energetic that remains unbound. Here he speaks both of unbound energy and

of the fact that this energetics is put to work in literary, artistic, musical creation, and, second, this remainder, although utilizable because it is yearning for investment (en mal d'investissement), is nevertheless a remainder that is unfixed. (Lyotard 1999)

Moreover, rather than see desire as a higher product of the drives, Lyotard emphasises libido *as* drive, specifying this drive as the motive force of art, thought, and political engagement:

> though one does not know what this 'X' [libidinal energy] is, nevertheless it drives, thereby prompting the name 'drive' (pulsion, Trieb). It drives the psyche to write, to paint, to become involved with politics, etc. (Lyotard 1999)

Stiegler's concerns with contemporary nihilism extend to the broadest level of what are widely recognised as contemporary global crises, those concerning the financial economy and the environment in particular. He emphasises the environmental, as well as economic, scope of what he includes in his 'general organology' by using the term 'ecology', invoking a 'libidinal ecology' (in addition to a libidinal economy), and what he calls an 'ecology of the spirit'. 'Spirit' is to be understood here not in a metaphysical or spiritualist sense, but in a very general sense that has been handed down through the Western tradition, as a short-hand term for something like the highest aspirations of human beings.[16] Stiegler takes up the term directly from authors on nihilism that he engages, such as Heidegger, and, perhaps most significantly, Paul Valéry (see Stiegler 2013). For Stiegler, 'Spirit' indicates in a general sense the production of healthy processes of individuation, and he speaks of it terms almost synonymous with libido (such that the fall in libido he identifies is equated with a fall in Spirit). Ecology here evokes the Greek root *oikos*, or home, and implies *taking care*, in terms of caring for other humans, as well as for the environment, and at all levels of the general organology. (Stiegler in fact notes (2013: 88) that this 'taking care' is also the original meaning of 'economy'.)

We can see, then, that Stiegler develops a radically inventive philosophy which breaks down previous metaphysical oppositions, particularly those between the human and the technical, and posits a systemic model which thinks values according to 'tendencies' at work in such systems, particularly the flows of desire and how they are produced and processed by technics. In a way which cannot but bring to mind Lyotard's treatment of technics examined above, at times Stiegler describes these 'tendencies' using the thermodynamic terms entropy and negentropy. In his most recent work (at the time of this writing), volume one of *The Automatic Society*, this accent seems to be coming to the fore, as the general tendencies of social and individual reality are described as aspects of a cosmic dynamic. Stiegler asserts here that 'the theory of entropy redefines the question of value' (Stiegler 2015a: 132) and that 'the *question* of entropy and negentropy among human beings [is] the *crucial problem* of the everyday life of human beings and of life in general, and, finally, of the universe in totality for every form of life' (133). This discussion of the energetic tendencies at the cosmic level then sets the agenda for what Stiegler believes needs to be done to confront the crisis of contemporary nihilism in all its forms:

> Reading Marx and Nietzsche together in the service of a new critique of political economy, *where the eco-nomy has become a cosmic factor on a local scale (a dimension of the cosmos)* and therefore an *eco-logy*, must lead to a process of *transvaluation*, such that both *economic values* and those *moral devaluations* that result when nihilism is set loose as consumerism are *'transvaluated' through a new value of all values, that is, by negentropy* – or negative entropy, or anti-entropy. (Stiegler 2015a: 131–2)

It is apparent that Stiegler has begun to adopt language very reminiscent of the 'post-metanarrative' of the development of negentropic order in the cosmos that Lyotard strenuously critiqued (as we saw above, and in more detail in the previous two chapters), and has developed an idea of a transvaluation of values very different to the revaluation of values Lyotard applies to Freud. We will return to these points in a summary comparison of Lyotard and Stiegler below. But first, let us turn our attention to Lyotard's and Stiegler's own explicit critical engagements with each other's thought.

Regimes of Memory

Lyotard engages Stiegler's thesis regarding the originary technicity of memory directly and critically in the essay '*Logos* and *Techne*, or Telegraphy' (in IN), originally presented in 1986 at the conference *Nouvelles technologies et mutation des savoirs* (New Technologies and the Mutation of Knowledge), organised by Stiegler. Decades later, Stiegler has recently returned to this essay, and Lyotard's wider philosophy, to re-engage the debate (Stiegler 2014: ch. 4, 2015b). Lyotard questions Stiegler's thesis that meaning is essentially objective and technological, requiring the inscription of spatialised traces on a material support which constitutes memory, giving it persistence through time and making it communally available. He does this by developing the idea of three types of 'memory-effects of technological inscription', drawn from discussions of memory (temporal synthesis) in Freud (specifically, the essay 'Remembering, Repeating, and Working-Through' in SE XII). In effect, Lyotard challenges Stiegler's thesis around the third kind of memory he (Lyotard) specifies, and I will argue that this leads to a *differend* between them regarding how each understand *meaning as such*. This differend encapsulates the essential difference between Lyotard's and Stiegler's approaches to meaning, and hence how they see the problem of nihilism – what is at stake in it, and how we might respond to it. Recognising this differend allows us better to appreciate the many points of divergence between the two thinkers, and to be in a position to draw our own conclusions regarding them.

The three types of technological inscription and their corresponding types of temporal synthesis (which together I will gloss as 'regimes of memory') that Lyotard specifies are as follows:

1. Breaching (habit)
2. Scanning (remembering)
3. Passing (anamnesis)

Breaching (*frayage*) is a 'putting into series of elements' (IN: 48) which facilitates habit, understood as an arrangement of a (nervous, muscular, etc.) system which allows repeated behaviours to be performed more efficiently. In the form of traditions and customs, habits apply to cultures as well as to individuals. Lyotard associates them with the relationships and interactions of selected elements in what structuralist theory calls 'structures' in general. Breaching is then a distinction and selection of elements and a placing of them in ordered series, such that habitual patterns and behaviours become possible.

Scanning (*balayage*) is what is typically called 'remembering', and involves the constitution of the past understood as such. This involves the identification and classification of what is remembered (IN: 51). Lyotard associates remembering with language, understood already as a kind of metalanguage insofar as it involves a recursivity which allows the operation of memory to refer back to itself. Scanning allows a move to a 'higher level' than the immediate reactions of breaching which facilitate behaviour, and allow the formation of complex cognitive processes, including voluntary remembering.

Passing (*passage*), which Lyotard associates with what he calls 'anamnesis', is the most elusive and most important of the regimes of memory he specifies. He associates it with a kind of writing which is not simply the linguistic inscription of scanning, but what the French, within a certain avant-garde tradition, call *écriture*. Lyotard specifies that the term 'passing' refers to Freud's *Durcharbeitung*, and to the 'through' part of the English translation of this term, 'working through'. It proceeds without a rule, or according to a deregulation; it has no set-up (*dispositif*) except the absence of a set-up. Most crucially, Lyotard explains that with this regime of memory, '[t]he point would be to recall what could not have been forgotten because it was not inscribed' (IN: 54).

Lyotard relates this form of memory with anamnesis, in his distinct understanding of the term. Inspired by Freud (but reading him with a distinct inflection), anamnesis as Lyotard understands it is the 'remembering' of an event which cannot be fully or accurately remembered because it was not 'properly' registered or inscribed when it first occurred. In the '*Logos* and *Techne*' essay, Lyotard borrows a metaphor from Zen master Dōgen's classic work, the *Shōbōgenzō*: the memory involved in anamnesis is like the reflection in a mirror which was broken by the reflection (IN: 55). Anamnesis is thus the attempt to remember something which *broke* the apparatus which would have recorded it. The image from Dōgen is perhaps an appropriate one, given the materialist metaphysic which Lyotard explicitly and strategically adopts in this essay. Yet it is also instructive to note that there is another materialist metaphor which expresses much the same idea, yet in a somewhat different way, in *Heidegger and "the jews"*. There Lyotard explains primary repression (which he notes, in '*Logos* and *Techne*', expresses a similar problematic with regard to memory) as being like a dispersed state of a thermal system, a cloud which enters an organism (the so-called 'first blow', the initial event which provoked a traumatic response), and remains there for an indefinite time before condensing and causing an effect (the 'second blow', the deferred reaction to the trauma) (HJ: 15–16).[17]

For Lyotard, passing is the regime of memory which expresses the relation to what he understands as the event, which motivates art and literature, and which cannot be adequately captured in any structure or representation. Lyotard sees this third regime of memory as something like a *resistance* to the first two syntheses, those of breaching and scanning. His analysis proposes what he believes must be possible for technologies, if they are to be capable of doing justice to what he believes are necessary conditions for philosophical thought and artistic activity. Though he does not spell it out specifically, Lyotard's analysis challenges Stiegler's thesis, that meaning is generated through processes which are inherently objective and technical, because it points to a kind of remembering of which new technologies – or indeed, *any* kind of technics, understood on Stiegler's model of objective, material inscription – are not obviously capable. This is because anamnesis in Lyotard's sense of the term is a model of memory that strives to remember that which, precisely, has *not* been inscribed.

In Stiegler's revisitation of Lyotard's contribution to his 1986 conference in his book *States of Shock* (first published in French in 2012), he summarises what he sees as the key point of Lyotard's intervention: it is an argument for the distinction between telegraphy (technological writing or digitisation) and 'literary or philosophical' writing (the French '*écriture*'). According to Stiegler's gloss, Lyotard asserts that '[t]his writing is irreducible to any telegraphy whatsoever, that is, to any technicization or technologization of language whatsoever' (Stiegler 2014b: 97). In short, Stiegler sees Lyotard as opposing technics to language, telegraphy to writing. Where Lyotard raises the *question*, at the end of his paper, of whether the new technologies might be capable of passing and anamnesis, and signals this as a possibility and a hope, Stiegler insists that he did not really believe this vague hope, and even that it was only inserted by Lyotard to please Stiegler himself (!) (98).

Stiegler argues that Lyotard's supposedly clear distinction between technics and writing is able only to propose a *resistance* to the technoscientific and capitalist system, and that it is incapable of an *invention* of the new within this system, which Stiegler sees as essential for genuine political engagement within the contemporary context. He goes on to identify in Lyotard the 'political flabbiness' and '*systemic dilution of responsibility*' (Stiegler 2014b: 100) he sees as characteristic of the poststructuralist generation, rather than to engage in a more detailed discussion of the differences of perspective he and Lyotard seem to have around the issue of inscription.

However, clearer focus is given to a key issue at stake in Stiegler's critical response to Lyotard – an issue which hinges on the distinction between writing and technics he emphasises in *States of Shock* – in his contribution to the thirty-year retrospective symposium on *Les Immatériaux* held at Lüneburg (Stiegler 2015b). Here, he asserts that for all the admiration and fascination he held for what was staged at the 1985 exhibition, *Lyotard's thinking around technics remains metaphysical* (152–3). In this essay, 'The Shadow of the Sublime', he seeks to show this with reference to his interpretation of the schemata that Kant develops in his first *Critique*. Notably, Stiegler associates tertiary retentions – that is, mnemotechnics – with what he suggests must be a 'fourth synthesis' added to Kant's first three (the synthesis of apprehension in intuition, of reproduction in the imagination, and of recognition in the concept) (see Kant 1929: A97–A105). This fourth synthesis is

> that of the *transcendental imagination as the power of exteriorization that founds tertiary retention and is founded on it, and that constitutes as such organological power and knowledge* (that is, the power and knowledge that arranges living, technical and social organs into a noetico-pharmacological becoming). (Stiegler 2015b: 153)

Significantly, Stiegler asserts that this fourth synthesis is the *condition* for any memory, and that Lyotard's three types of synthesis (breaching, scanning, passing) are unable to think this.

Why then does Stiegler believe that Lyotard's thinking of technics remains metaphysical? Because as he sees it, Lyotard distinguishes the *logos* from the seizure by *techne*, seeing the former as an original meaning corrupted by the latter. This follows, he thinks, from what he sees as the distinction Lyotard makes between *writing* and *techne* ('telegraphy'), and his insistence that the latter cannot do justice to *anamnesis*, the form of memory associated with writing as he (Lyotard) understands it. Stiegler sheds light on his characterisation of Lyotard's thinking of technics as metaphysical when he writes that '*logos* [has been] deemed since the advent of metaphysics (that is, since Plato) to proceed from or originate in those immaterials that are the spiritual, the suprasensible, the intelligible, and so on' (Stiegler 2015b: 154). According to him, Lyotard seems to think language machines (computers) – the 'immaterials' – too much on the model of *logos* besieged by the corrupting forces of *techne*. According to Stiegler, Lyotard was unable to think technics as anything other than a '*deceptive machine*' (155). Like Husserl, Heidegger, Freud, and the other major thinkers in the Western tradition he has analysed, then, Stiegler sees in Lyotard (both in *Les Immatériaux*, and in his critique of Stiegler in '*Logos* and *Techne*') a metaphysical thinking of technics which 'represses' it by seeing it as secondary, derivative, and corrupting in relation to a 'primary meaning'.

In 'The Shadow of the Sublime' Stiegler asserts that '*Lyotard leaves in the shadows the question of the schematism*' (Stiegler 2015b: 153–4), yet he himself leaves in the shadows (that is, fails to acknowledge or comment on) Lyotard's own analyses of the Kantian schemata.[18]

I cannot enter here into anything like the detail that Lyotard's and Stiegler's respective analyses of the schemata deserve. However, the following passage, taken from Lyotard's article 'Argumentation and Presentation: The Foundation Crisis' (2013) indicates well the key point around which Lyotard and Stiegler disagree:

> The privilege of the aesthetic feeling [...] is that in it judgement is exercised in the regime that is the least subordinated to the understanding and to the end goal of knowledge. In it, reflexivity is, so to speak, pure and as close as possible to receptivity, that is to say, to presentation 'before' the mind wishes to seize hold of the object and constitute itself over against it as legislative subjectivity. In this aesthetic reflexivity is heralded what Heidegger opposes to knowledge and, more precisely, to the *Gestell* [enframing] of technoscience, under the name of poetry – *Dichtung*.
> *Reception is a pure feeling before it becomes the schematic registration of data that can be processed with concepts.* (Lyotard 2013: 128; italics mine)

In short, Lyotard takes something like the opposite direction to Stiegler in his reading of the Kantian schemata, seeking to locate in Kant's aesthetics a 'pure givenness' prior to the syntheses constituting the schemata, or involving only the most minimal of such syntheses. As with all Lyotard's work, he tries to locate the event in terms of something which 'touches' the mind before it has the power to constitute, represent, or recognise it (see chapter 2, 'Touches' in P). While Lyotard is fundamentally in agreement with thinkers such as Derrida and Stiegler who assert that such 'pure givenness' – an understanding of the event as an 'instant' prior to temporal synthesis – is conceptually incoherent, his point is precisely to insist that rather than being received *conceptually*, it produces a *feeling*. It is such a feeling that Lyotard insists indicates something not coherently inscribed in terms of memory traces, and which anamnesis, on his understanding, tries to remember.[19] By contrast, as we have seen, Stiegler proceeds in the opposite direction with Kant, positing that a 'higher level' fourth synthesis, corresponding to objectively inscribed external memory traces, is a necessary condition for the first.

Arguably, Stiegler fails to see what I believe is a *differend* between Lyotard and himself. In short, the differend is this: Lyotard sees meaning in the event 'prior' to inscription, while Stiegler sees meaning as 'always already' inscribed. I am tempted to call this difference a differend (rather than a litigation) because there would seem to be no common measure, no rational rule of judgement, which might adjudicate between Lyotard's and Stiegler's positions. The differend between Lyotard and Stiegler could not be turned into a litigation over the correct reading of Freud, for example, since both self-consciously present heterodox readings (Stiegler asserts that Freud did not correctly understand the originary technicity of desire, while Lyotard subjects the drives to a Nietzschean revaluation). And the same goes for their readings of Kant. More generally, this is a differend because the question of whether or not the event as Lyotard understands it is or is not significant seems not to be something that could be established through argumentation. It is a matter of *feeling*, not of concepts – 'the differend itself', as Lyotard calls the affect-phrase, the minimal feeling of pleasure and/or pain without any other sense[20] – and something which calls for judgement, not argumentation.

Regardless of what one thinks regarding this differend over meaning, there is an important sense in which Lyotard's thinking of technics *does* remain metaphysical: in the specific sense he gives to this term, and explicitly acknowledges, in asserting that a materialist perspective, and a philosophy of *energy*, remain metaphysical. Indeed, at the beginning of the 'Logos and *Techne*' essay, he states that he is adopting 'a terminology that could be called materialist, and therefore metaphysical' (IN: 48). Yet Lyotard inhabits these metaphysical, materialist analyses *ironically*, seeking to undermine what for him remains most troublingly metaphysical about them: the claim to ground an ethical or political discourse (an *ought*) in a physical or metaphysical claim about the nature of reality (an *is*). As intimated previously, it is difficult to see how Stiegler's own discourse escapes metaphysics in *this* sense, as he increasingly seeks to discuss values in the very terms in which Lyotard critiqued them around the time of *The Inhuman*: as 'negentropology',[21] a thinking in terms of the drama of energy in the universe. It is this kind of metaphysics which Lyotard sees as supporting the system of 'development'. From this Lyotardian perspective, Stiegler's negentropology would appear as a kind of transcendental illusion, with attendant potential political and ethical problems. Indeed, from Lyotard's perspective – as is evident from his critical analyses of Luhmann's Systems Theory and of 'general physics' – the temptation after the death of God and decline of metanarratives to see values in terms of energetic tendencies is one towards which we should be sceptical, and engage only in a strategic and ironic manner. In a confrontation of Lyotard's and Stiegler's positions, then, we may see not only a differend between them concerning the nature of how meaning should be understood, but different understandings of how philosophy may be most problematically 'metaphysical'.

Implications

We have seen that Lyotard and Stiegler share many concerns regarding technics and desire as they shape the contemporary condition. Yet the two philosophers differ on the issues of metaphysics, of the values that should be attached to systems of desire, and the broad political question of 'what is to be done' (James 2012: 77). In short, and simplifying, while Stiegler privileges Eros, the binding of the drives, and negentropy, Lyotard privileges Thanatos, the unbinding of the drives, and entropy.[22] As we have seen, this difference of ascription of values in energetic systems corresponds with a difference between Lyotard and Stiegler in terms of how they understand desire. I have argued that the crux of their differences is the differend between them concerning the constitution of meaning. Stiegler, following and extending the logic of Derridean *différance*, sees meaning as always already technical, constituted and conditioned not just by the spacings and temporalisations, the differings and deferrals, of linguistic structure, but by the material, external supports of these structures (in other words, *technics*). By contrast, Lyotard locates the 'origin' (which of course needs to be placed in scare quotes) of meaning in 'presence', what touches the body or mind before any structuration, including the most minimal syntheses.

With regard to the constitution of meaning and value as such – as exemplified in Lyotard's and Stiegler's differing views of desire and technics – we can see that the *differend* between them causes Stiegler to adopt what is in a way a far bleaker vision of nihilism than does Lyotard. If Lyotard tends to adopt the view that structures and processes of individuation can take care of themselves, that is because he does not see these processes as the places in which meaning and value primarily reside. Rather, it is in the *remainder* from these processes. For all Lyotard's concern with the hegemonic tendencies of contemporary technoscience, he posits that something resists, and will perhaps inevitably resist in some form – a 'something' which, as we have seen, he analyses through a variety of concepts, including libidinal intensity, the secluded, the event, and the uninscribed that anamnesis tries to remember. Understanding it in terms of 'general physics', a realised metaphysics, for Lyotard technics is a construction, organisation, or giving form which always leaves a left-over or remainder, something which has not been incorporated into 'good form', even if this 'something' could never be identified in any pure state, prior to technics. And significantly, for Lyotard, this remainder is precisely what energises the structural organisation, even while threatening to destabilise it, and is thus understood as a locus of 'what makes life worth living' (to adopt Stiegler's 2013 title). By contrast, since Stiegler sees meaning as always already constructed by external inscriptions, he sees nothing which might 'remain' from this process, and act as a resistance to it. Thus for Stiegler, everything hinges on technics and the processes of individuation they condition. That is why he *has* to insist on technics, and *has* to insist on invention – since for him, there is nothing that can resist *but* invention, technics, part and parcel of the processes of individuation to which technics give rise. Even desire, for him, is 'constructed', and any part of it which is not properly constructed cannot be thought as having the potential for positive resistance (as it does for Lyotard), but can only be destructive.

This chapter has been largely exploratory in nature, and I have only been able to 'actualise' a few of the potential points of engagement between Lyotard and Stiegler, those around the issues of technics and desire. Moreover, these points deserve much deeper investigation than I have been able to give them here. Hopefully, however, this preliminary encounter I have staged begins to throw light on some of the critical issues at stake regarding one significant way of responding to the humanistic crisis of values in the posthuman or inhuman condition: the attempt to think values in terms of economies and ecologies of desire in generalised systems. In the following chapters I move on to considering further issues in Lyotard's thinking of nihilism, information, and art, and to chart conceptual resources in Lyotard's work that Stiegler overlooks. While, as we have seen here and in the previous chapters, Lyotard's thinking of technics is largely negative and critical, he nevertheless finds potentials for resistance to the metaphysical determination of technics (the 'Leibnizian hypothesis') *within* technics, with a positive aesthetic appropriation of new technologies, in the aesthetic of the sublime. As we shall see, Lyotard's sublime is an analysis of contemporary social conditions which outlines the stakes of a paradoxical new situation, related to technics – the 'crisis of perception' of time and space, of traditional notions of matter – calling for experimentations with parahyletisms (paradoxes of matter), parachronisms (paradoxes of time), and paralogies (paradoxes of reason). It is to such themes that we turn in the remaining chapters of this book, in order to see how Lyotard develops his own response to nihilism in relation to information and art.

Notes

1. In an interview, while preferring to cite Freud and Bataille as inspirations for *Libidinal Economy*, Lyotard specifies that insofar as Nietzsche was an influence, it must be attributed to Klossowski's *Nietzsche and the Vicious Circle* (2005): 'a text which impressed me greatly' (Lyotard 1994a: 81).
2. For further discussion of nihilism, and the specification of a religious form of nihilism, see Chapter 4.
3. For details of Lyotard's argument on this point, see the discussion of Freud's example of the '*fort-da*' game in Chapter 4.
4. 'Intensity' is a term also found in Klossowski's interpretation of Nietzsche, but Lyotard identifies his inspiration for its use as Bataille's *Inner Experience* (Bataille 2014). See Lyotard 1994a: 81.
5. For further discussion of dissimulation within the libidinal economy, see Chapter 4.
6. Luhmann's paper was titled 'Ökologische Kommunikation – Ein Theorie-Entscheidungsspiel'. Both are published in Fischer 1989.
7. In more detail, here is how Luhmann defines it in the glossary which accompanies the work: '*Autopoiesis:* Refers to (autopoietic) systems that reproduce all the elementary components out of which they arise by means of a network of these elements themselves and in this way distinguish themselves from an environment – whether this takes the form of life, consciousness or (in the case of social systems) communication. Autopoiesis is the mode of reproduction of these systems' (1989a: 143).
8. See the essay 'Differance' in Derrida 1973.
9. Stiegler takes his bearings here from Derrida's own brief discussion of Leroi-Gourhan in *Of Grammatology*. See Stiegler 1998: 136–7.
10. This is a précis, *grosso modo*, of some of the main themes developed in Stiegler's first, and arguably still most philosophically significant book, *Technics and Time 1: The Fault of Epimetheus* (1998).
11. See the two volumes of Stiegler's series *De la misère symbolique*, translated under the title 'Symbolic Misery' (2014d, 2015c). The French *misère* could also be rendered as 'poverty'.
12. Stiegler's first significant discussion of psychoanalytic theory, centring around his original concept of 'primordial narcissism', takes place in 'To Love, to Love Me, to Love Us' in Stiegler 2009b. His idea of libidinal economy is then developed in the three volumes of *Disbelief and Discredit* (Stiegler 2011, 2012, 2014a). Stiegler's most recent discussions of psychoanalytic theory have taken another significant turn, towards Donald Winnicott's object relations theory (see Stiegler 2013).
13. This concept is most extensively developed – in relation to Michel Foucault's analysis of biopower – in Stiegler 2010.
14. See 'To Love, to Love Me, to Love Us' in Stiegler 2009b.

15. Stiegler further indicates how his views on technics and *différance* inform his reading of libidinal economy in the following passage: 'In this genealogy [of general organology], it is technics that, itself constituting a process of individuation, comes constantly to reconfigure psychic individuation, which falls on the side of the pleasure principle, and collective individuation, on the side of the reality principle – and it does so by rearticulating the transductive relation in which they are constituted. This means that one does not precede the other – the pleasure principle does not precede the reality principle. The reality principle, *as circuit*, is on the contrary the *realization* of the pleasure principle, to the extent that it is the horizon of *transindividuation* of psychic individuation, governing the pleasure principle as its *différance* – a différance that passes through the circuit of collective individuation or, obviously, may fail to do so' (2014a: 45).

16. In his 'Translator's Preface' to Stiegler's *The Re-Enchantment of the World*, Trevor Arthur comments on the inadequacy of the English 'spirit' to encompass the range of meanings embedded in Stiegler's use of the French *esprit*: 'in the fullness of its concept, *esprit* expresses a synthesis of the psychic and social, as well as intellectual and historical life of man, being tied up in the vicissitudes of processes of individuation in which one becomes who he is, and in processes of transindividuation whereby we become who we are. Hence *esprit* pertains, too, to the epochal nature of becoming in which memory and intelligence conjoin in the moment of reflection faced with the world, lighting the way forward from out of the depths of its inwardness. It is precisely this capacity of *esprit* to express vivacious reflection, searching rumination, and the passion of sublimation that renders it so valuable – as such it constitutes perhaps *the* essential value of human being' (Stiegler 2014c: viii–ix).

17. For insightful discussions of these three kinds of memory that Lyotard specifies, see Harris 2001 and Hui 2015.

18. Developed in a number of texts. See in particular P; LAS; Lyotard 2013.

19. I also discuss Lyotard's analysis of Kant's schematism in Chapter 6, §13.

20. See 'The Affect-phrase: From a Supplement to *The Differend*' in LRG, which was originally published under the title 'L'Inarticulé, ou le différend même' ('The Inarticulate, or the Differend Itself') (Lyotard 1990).

21. 'Anthropocene and Negentropology' was the title of the paper Stiegler delivered at the first international conference devoted to his work, *General Organology: The Co-Individuation of Minds, Bodies, Social Organisations and* Techne, held at the University of Kent, 20–22 November 2014.

22. I have further developed this contrast between Lyotard and Stiegler around the values accruing to these thermodynamic terms in my essay 'Circuits of Desire: Lyotard and Stiegler' (Woodward, forthcoming).

Chapter 4

Nihilism and the Sublime: The Crisis of Perception

Although it is often only addressed obliquely, nihilism arguably remains one of the central problems of contemporary continental philosophy. Lyotard has engaged deeply with this central philosophical problem, but his positive responses to nihilism remain largely unappreciated. The notable exception to this is James Williams, whose important book *Lyotard and the Political* (2000a) situates nihilism as one of Lyotard's central concerns. Williams's book defends Lyotard's much-maligned *Libidinal Economy*, arguing – against Lyotard's own later assessment – that the book develops an effective response to nihilism. However, Williams finds Lyotard's later, 'Kantian' philosophy lacking any adequate response. My aim in this chapter is to demonstrate that in Lyotard's later writings, the sublime acts as a response to nihilism in ways that have not been sufficiently appreciated by Williams, or by Lyotard scholars in general.[1]

The attempt to demonstrate that the sublime acts as a response to nihilism in Lyotard's thought is significantly complicated by the fact that he seems to *identify* nihilism with the sublime. This identification takes place both explicitly and implicitly in his writings. Explicitly, he states that Nietzschean nihilism is a later development of the aesthetic of the sublime, and that they are fundamentally the same idea. Implicitly, this identification is evident in Lyotard's use of some of the same examples and analogies to illustrate nihilism and the sublime: both are linked to *signs*, and both are elaborated with reference to the '*fort-da*' game in Freud's *Beyond the Pleasure Principle* (SE XVIII). This identification of nihilism and the sublime in Lyotard's works has also been largely overlooked by scholars, and I aim to demonstrate this identification here because it is integral to appreciating the *nature* of his response to nihilism. I argue that in his later works, the sublime acts *both* as a trope of nihilism, and as a *positive response* to nihilism.[2] This double deployment of the sublime is not an inconsistency or contradiction, but an instance of his use of the sophistical strategy of *retorsion*, the attempt to turn an opponent's argument back against them. In effect, Lyotard uses the sublime both as a diagnostic category to characterise the nihilism of contemporary cultural conditions, and as an idea which suggests a possible resistance to nihilism *from within* those very conditions. Moreover, this strategy can be understood as being motivated by Lyotard's concern for justice, defined as a respect for difference. Lyotard's engagement with nihilism shifts through the course of his career. This chapter will chart this shift, as an understanding of his earlier approaches to nihilism helps to illuminate the apparently paradoxical position adopted in his later work.

The Abyss Between Meaning and Existence

For Nietzsche, nihilism is an ambiguous and complex phenomenon which manifests as several main types.[3] First, *religious nihilism* (which Nietzsche associates primarily with Christianity and Platonism) provides an interpretation of life which imbues it with meaning and value, but only to a severely impoverished degree. The impulse of religious nihilism is to confer a negative judgement on life itself, finding it inadequate because of the existence of suffering. The religious nihilist compensates for the lack of value of *this* world by supposing that there is a better world elsewhere, in a transcendent realm we might attain in the afterlife. The 'immanent world' of our earthly existence is then only supposed to have value as a bridge to the 'transcendent world'. Moreover, aspects of life in this world – such as sensuous pleasure or strong emotion – are believed to prevent us from achieving the transcendent source of value, and so are shunned (Nietzsche calls this 'the ascetic ideal'). Described in Platonic terms, religious nihilism makes a distinction between *the intelligible* and *the sensible*, elevating the intelligible and associating it with transcendence, while denigrating the sensible and restricting it to the immanent realm.

Nietzsche sees much of Western history as marked by religious nihilism, but proposes that a new and deeper form of nihilism is inaugurated with modernity. Briefly put, Nietzsche sees modern science as undermining religious belief, but as unable to replace the religious interpretation of existence with a new interpretation which would give meaning and value to human life. This development, which Nietzsche indexes with the shorthand expression 'the death of God', institutes a *radical nihilism*. Nietzsche sees here the danger of the complete collapse of any and all meaningful worldviews. There are at least two discernible responses to radical nihilism in Nietzsche's works. In his early writings, he proposes to reinstitute a meaningful culture through an 'artist's metaphysics' based in Schopenhauer's philosophy and Wagner's music-drama. In his mature thought, Nietzsche rejects such a reinstatement of religious or metaphysical interpretations of existence, and instead proposes to push nihilism to its extreme consequences. He proposes a 'self-overcoming' of nihilism, in which the nihilistic impulse will destroy all categories thought to provide meaning and value, and arrive at a 'blank slate' from which to create new categories of valuation which will give a new and superior sense of meaning to existence. This last stage is one of *complete nihilism*; for Nietzsche it is a necessary preparation for a 'revaluation of all values'.

As I noted in the introduction to this book, it is well known that for Nietzsche *art* plays an important role in responding to nihilism. How exactly this is the case is a complex and contested issue, but we may note, with Keith Ansell Pearson, the following:[4]

> Art is valued by Nietzsche for two main reasons; firstly, because it enables human beings to endure life in the face of the terror and absurdity of existence; and secondly, it acts as the great *stimulus* of life, encouraging human beings not to recoil from the horror of existence, but to seek its furtherance and perpetual self-overcoming. (Ansell Pearson 1994: 159)

In short, while religious nihilism devalues life because of suffering and projects a transcendent world in compensation, art as Nietzsche conceives it is able to affirm life by transforming it into an aesthetic phenomenon. Art plays a decisive role in both responses to nihilism mentioned above: it can give meaning to culture by providing a focus for religious and metaphysical worldviews, and it can act as a model for the creation of new values. We will return to these themes below when we consider how the aesthetic experience of the sublime acts as a response to nihilism for Lyotard.

Nihilism is a theme that concerned Lyotard over a wide span of his career. As is well known, he was a militant Marxist in the 1950s and 1960s, and his early engagement with nihilism takes place within a Marxian theoretical framework.[5] In an essay dating from this period, 'Dead Letter' (1962), the problem of meaning in life is given preeminent value. He writes here:

> The unthought question in the grind of the technical world, the question that the absurdity of the extermination camps first brought into

> the open – What meaning is there in existing? – is a question that resounds for everyone, Monday morning and Saturday night, that reveals the emptiness of 'civilization' in all of its industrial flashiness. [...] it is in reality the only serious, vital, everyday question. (PW: 38–9)

In this essay Lyotard raises the question of meaning bluntly in order to point to the failings of university teaching and capitalist culture. Defining 'culture' as 'existence accepted as meaningful', he posits a divide between existence and meaning in capitalism: 'We are essentially cut off from [meaning]. In our society sign and signification, activity and culture, living and understanding, are dissociated' (PW: 34).

According to this analysis, the problems of existence lie in the mechanised and alienated world of the factory and the worker, while the realm of thought and meaning – the university and what has come to be called 'culture' – fails to address these problems. He thus finds fault with the intellectual and with the university curriculum: 'When the mind and life are divorced, the intellectual is the one who cultivates the mind, who cultivates the meaning of life without life itself' (PW: 35). Lamenting this abyss between meaning and existence, Lyotard endorses a closing or bridging of the abyss which would result in a 'unified' experience of culture as meaningful existence. While his prescriptions for closing the gap remain sketchy, he gestures towards the possibility of life being given meaning through the embodiment of values in activities. He advocates putting 'an end to the exile of activities as estranged from their sense' (39), restoring the identity of speech and meaning, and reconstituting community. This 1962 essay can be understood as elaborating the familiar Marxian themes of alienation and the dream of its overcoming through concrete changes in class relations and the structures of political economy. However, the approach to the problem of the meaning of life here – the problem understood as an abyss between meaning and existence which might or might not be solved through the return to an original unity – is one that Lyotard retains long after his theoretical departure from Marxism.

While Lyotard does not do so explicitly in this early essay, we may draw an analogy between his concerns here and Nietzschean nihilism: the abyss between meaning and existence can be understood as the abyss between the intelligible (meaning) and the sensible (existence). This abyss between meaning and existence is construed in a number of different ways throughout the course of Lyotard's work: first in the Marxian sense of alienation, then in the 'great Zero' of his 'libidinal' philosophy, and then in the idea of the 'immanent sublime' which appears in the Kantian phase of his work. In each of these modalities, the basic structural features of this abyss remain the same: meaning is divided from existence, and existence devalued in relation to meaning. As we shall see, these features are characteristic of both nihilism and the sublime. As we shall also see, Lyotard ends up insisting that this abyss between meaning and existence cannot and should not be closed, but arguing that we may nevertheless find ways of resisting the abyss's potential to devalue life. However, Lyotard's path to this position is far from straightforward, and moves first of all through the extensive elaboration and response to the problem of nihilism in his libidinal philosophy of the early 1970s.

Libidinal Economy 'contra' Nihilism

By the time of writing his second major book *Libidinal Economy* (1974), Lyotard had lost his faith in Marxism, and with it the hope that the abyss between meaning and existence might be overcome by putting an end to alienation.[6] In this and subsequent works, he encounters nihilism in new and innovative forms, and searches for ways of resisting nihilism beyond any hope of its final overcoming.[7] As analysed in detail in the previous chapter, the book develops a reading of Freud inspired by Nietzsche in order to show how nihilism may be understood in 'libidinal economic' terms. Lyotard fills out his analysis of nihilism in *Libidinal Economy* through critical discussions of semiotics and of Freud's example of the child's *'fort-da'* game in *Beyond the Pleasure Principle*. Since these same two examples are presented in his later works in association with the sublime, it is worth elaborating them in order to establish the identification between nihilism and the sublime which is central to my thesis here.

In *Libidinal Economy* Lyotard identifies semiotics as a form of nihilism. He notes that for the semiotician, any *thing* may be treated as a sign, and treating something as a sign negates the value of the thing itself by treating it as a *replacement* for something else (that which it is a sign *of*). This replacement may be understood according to two different theories of the sign, and Lyotard understands both as nihilistic. On the first model of the sign, the sign replaces what it signifies (that is, it 'stands in' for an absent meaning). The material given of the sign is taken as a replacement or stand-in for the concept it signifies. Lyotard writes that '[t]his is, to put it as brutally as possible, the Platonism of the theory of Ideas, for example: the sign at the same time screens and calls up what it announces and conceals' (LE: 43). Given Nietzsche's analysis of Platonism as nihilism, Lyotard's meaning here is clear: the sign replaces a meaning which is itself absent, just as Platonism sees the sensible as signalling a transcendent intelligible. Translated into Nietzschean terms, semiotics finds what is apprehended as present guilty of not being meaningful in itself, and posits an absent meaning which gives the sign a derivative value.

On the second model, the sign may be understood in terms of its place in a wider network or structure of signs, in which case the meaning of any particular sign is deferred throughout the structure, from one sign's reference to another in an 'interminable metonymy' (LE: 43), never achieving an origin or end. Each signified is in turn a signifier for another signified. On this model, meaning itself is infinitely deferred, and can never be grasped as present. In Lyotard's words, this model of the sign means 'that signification itself is constituted by signs alone, that it carries on endlessly, that we never have anything but references, that signification is always deferred, meaning is never present in flesh and blood' (43). Moreover, he argues that for thinkers like Freud and Lacan, the signification of all signs – that is, their capacity to be meaningful – is grounded in an absent 'great signifier', which he calls the 'great Zero'. This 'Zero', like God, is the source of all meaning, but cannot itself be grasped as meaningful. In Lyotard's libidinal philosophy, 'the great Zero' acts as a general term for the abyss between meaning and existence which constitutes nihilism.

Taking both of these theories of the sign into account, Lyotard's critique of semiotics may be summarised by two factors he believes characterise the semiotic sign as nihilistic: the *absence* and *deferral* of meaning. The semiotic sign is thus a modulation of the abyss between meaning and existence for Lyotard, where existence is the material given of the sign, and meaning is its conceptual signification. In the passage quoted above from the early essay 'Dead Letter', he blames social conditions for the separation of sign and signification. In *Libidinal Economy*, he sees this separation as intrinsic to the structure of the sign itself. In terms of the understanding of nihilism outlined above – the separation of meaning and existence – we can see that for Lyotard, semiotics presents a theory of meaning which always implies a separation from what is supposedly meaningful. Treated as a text, as a network of signs, existence is never meaningful *in itself*. We can see here the parallel he draws with Nietzsche's theory of nihilism, in which life is found guilty of lacking meaning, and so meaning is projected as lying in some transcendent realm, beyond our reach.[8]

Lyotard further elaborates nihilism in *Libidinal Economy* through a reading of Freud's analysis of his grandson's '*fort-da*' game in *Beyond the Pleasure Principle*. This reading is aimed to show that desire understood as *lack* is not primary (as Freud presents it[9]) but secondary, the product of a transformation of desire understood as positive force or *libido*. This is important for Lyotard, because he wants to show that desire as lack is a manifestation of nihilism, while positive libido is a life-affirmative alternative. Implicitly following Nietzsche, Lyotard shows how nihilism arises from the forces of life turning against themselves. He uses the '*fort-da*' game to illustrate how desire as lack arises only with the 'secondary processes' of the conscious mind. Lyotard's reading proceeds via a critical reinterpretation of Freud's own presentation of this example. Freud interprets the '*fort-da*' game as the child's 'staging' of its separation from its mother, the wooden reel representing the mother, who was sometimes absent (*fort*, i.e. 'gone'), but would then return (*da*, i.e. 'there'). In effect, Freud uses the theory of desire as lack to explain the meaning of the child's game as a representational activity aimed at dealing with the suffering induced by the mother's absence. Lyotard, however, accuses Freud of presupposing what he is attempting to explain. Freud's explanation implies that the feeling of lack (associated with the mother's absence) precedes representation. However, Lyotard argues that this feeling of lack would not be possible if the child were not already able to represent the mother *as* absent. According to Lyotard, representation precedes the feeling of lack, and not the other way around.

Lyotard argues that the '*fort-da*' game may be seen as a 'theatre of representation'. In *Libidinal Economy* he argues that all rational theory understood as representation has the same basic structure and function as what Nietzsche identifies as religious nihilism, and he draws this out by illustrating representational theory with the image of a theatre. It is as if theory represents something on the stage of the theatre (the world of immanent existence), the meaning of which (i.e. the real or original thing represented) remains outside the theatre walls (in the world of transcendent meaning; Plato's *Eidos* or the Christian heaven). The theatre illustrates the conscious mind, the ego. In Lyotard's analysis, the '*fort-da*' game is simply the exterior mirror of the interior theatre. The ego is a theatre of representation insofar as it distinguishes between interiority and exteriority, presence and absence, itself and its mother, and is able to 'stage' the absence of the mother because of these distinctions. The '*fort-da*' game gives us a clear image of this theatre, with the edge of the child's cot forming the stage and the wooden reel the present/absent object of representation.[10] In challenging Freud's interpretation of the '*fort-da*' game, Lyotard uses it to illustrate the basic structure of nihilism as representation, and in so doing further elaborates the great Zero, the abyss between meaning and existence. This Nietzschean reading of Freud is what underlies Lyotard's scepticism towards reason and concern with the limits of representation in his libidinal philosophy.

Lyotard develops a response to nihilism in *Libidinal Economy* that is focused around desire understood as *libido*; that is, as a positive, energetic force. Libido acts as a counter-force to nihilism for at least two reasons in Lyotard's libidinal philosophy. First, it affirms those aspects of existence that nihilism denies: desire, the body, sensual enjoyment, erotic pleasure, materiality; in short, the sensible. Second, Lyotard emphasises Freud's statement in his 1915 paper 'The Unconscious' that the primary processes of mental functioning – those most closely associated with the libido – know nothing of negation.[11] As such, Lyotard finds in the libido a response to nihilism on purely 'logical' grounds: it founds a form of mental functioning prior and other to negation, which is a necessary condition for the very possibility of nihilism (since, put simply, nihilism requires a distinction between meaning and existence, and the negation of existence in relation to meaning). For both these reasons, Lyotard understands the purely positive libido as a force of life-affirmation, and, as discussed in the previous chapter, he associates it with Nietzsche's will to power (TP: 13).

In the last chapter we also noted Lyotard's concept of 'dissimulation'. Given its crucial role in the argument about nihilism in *Libidinal Economy*, it is worth reiterating this key idea. Dissimulation is the rejection of any idea of a liberation of 'pure desire' which would definitively overcome nihilism. Lyotard insists that desire is always manifest in relation to structures (understood, broadly speaking, in the structuralist sense, as composed of discrete elements and their relations), both giving rise to them, and disrupting their stability. Dissimulation refers to the way that structures always hide desire, and desire is always manifest in a structured form (for example, the theatre of representation is itself an energetic formation, a transformation of libido). In *Libidinal Economy*, Lyotard advocates a response to nihilism through encouraging the freeing and intensification of desires dissimulated within structures, which tend to dampen their intensity. However, such desire is never found in a 'pure' state, but through its creation, destruction, and transformation of structured states.

Libidinal Economy dismisses any hope of decisively overcoming nihilism, and instead offers a strategy of intensifying life-affirmative desire *within* structures which will inevitably dampen its intensity to some degree. This indicates a refusal to posit an 'other' or 'outside' of nihilism, or an end of alienation, a tendency we shall see radicalised in Lyotard's later work. Nevertheless, in *Libidinal Economy* and related work of this period the libido acts *'contra'* nihilism insofar as it bears different properties or (anti)structural features: nihilism implies negation, while the libido is purely positive. As we shall see, the resistance to nihilism Lyotard finds in the sublime is more profoundly identified with nihilism itself.

The Crisis of Perception

In the 1980s, Lyotard's theoretical references shift from Marx, Freud, and Nietzsche to Kant, Levinas, and Wittgenstein. Lyotard describes this turn in terms of a renewed concern with *justice*, and with the theme of *judgement* that emerges from this concern. *Libidinal Economy* was not well received, and Lyotard harshly criticised it himself on the grounds that it was ethically irresponsible. The release of libidinal forces it advocates takes place 'beyond good and evil', respecting only the criterion of intensity.[12] In an interview Lyotard explains that his next major book 'Le Différend remedies the shortcomings of *Economie libidinale*; it is an attempt to say the same things but without unloading problems so important as justice' (Lyotard 1988: 300–1). In this period of his work Lyotard retains a scepticism towards purely theoretical reason and a concern to draw the limits of representation, but turned now towards the end of justice. In the philosophy of phrases developed in *The Differend*, Lyotard defines justice in terms of the 'space' in which phrases meet (rather than being given by any particular phrase regimen or genre of discourse), and injustice is understood as the silencing of a phrase which demands to be heard (which is what he calls a 'differend'). In more general terms, Lyotard understands justice as the expression of differences free from the 'terror' of being excluded or silenced.

Kant becomes an important resource for Lyotard in this period because of the distinction he draws between the different faculties: in particular, pure reason (the faculty of theoretical knowledge) and practical reason (the faculty of desire or the will, which is concerned with action and with ethics). In this phase of his work, Lyotard wishes to underline this distinction because he is sceptical about the power of pure reason to establish principles adequate to ensure ethics and justice. Lyotard argues that there will always be events and differences which will be excluded from any particular representation or system of theoretical knowledge. For him, Kant's separation of the faculties serves to protect against the 'transcendental illusion' that pure reason can be all-encompassing. Reflective judgement is a form of thinking which ventures between the faculties without being determined by the rules of either: it judges 'without criteria'. For Lyotard, judgement becomes a privileged model of philosophical thought because it is unbound by predetermined rules and regulations, and operates with openness and creativity. As such, it can serve the demands of justice because of its capacity to be sensitive to the differences to which purely theoretical representations often blind us.

Lyotard also has frequent recourse to the aesthetic of the sublime in his writings in the 1980s and 1990s. The aesthetic of the sublime has traditionally been invoked to explain the experience of things which move us, but which cannot be explained according to traditional theories of the beautiful. The notion of the sublime dates from antiquity,[13] but it received particular interest in the later seventeenth century when travellers began to cross the Alps and were confronted with vast and dangerous natural vistas, which they found moving in a way that they could not explain as beautiful (Westphal 1998: 37). Kant's analysis of the sublime, which is decisive for Lyotard, has been particularly influential. In contrast to the aesthetic of the beautiful, which involves a feeling of pleasure, according to Kant the aesthetic of the sublime involves a mixed feeling of pleasure *and pain*. He explains the sublime feeling as occurring when we are exposed to sensory data which cannot be synthesised with a form by the imagination, and so cannot be matched with a concept (even in an indeterminate fashion, as with the beautiful). The pain of the sublime is felt as the inability of the imagination to present a form for sensations. Because of this formlessness of sensation, the understanding cannot match a concept with such sensation. However, another faculty, that of *practical reason*, presents an Idea which accords with the formless sensation, and the success of reason is felt as pleasure.

An Idea, for Kant, is a special kind of concept which seems to point towards a transcendent realm, moving beyond the possibility of any empirical verification – it does not relate to anything which can be the object of experience ('here is a case of it'). For Kant, the most important Ideas are God, freedom, and the immortality of the soul. In the aesthetic of the sublime, the Idea presented is that of the infinite or absolutely great, or that of freedom. Sensory matter without form acts as a sign or 'negative presentation' of the Idea; it alludes to the infinite in the very failure of the imagination to present a formed object, and to the Idea of freedom in the fact that our reason has the capacity to transcend empirical conditions and the empirical will (such as our instinct for flight in the face of a dangerous situation). Lyotard deploys the aesthetic of the sublime in various ways in his writings, not all of which are necessarily consistent.[14] However, the sublime typically appears with a positive valence in his work, and is posited as offering creative possibilities beyond the impasses of modern thought and postmodern social conditions.

Lyotard also closely associates the sublime with nihilism in a number of places. For example, in the essay 'Answer to the Question: What Is the Postmodern?', he writes:

> Modernity, whenever it appears, does not occur without a shattering of belief, without a discovery of the *lack of reality* in reality – a discovery linked to the invention of other realities.
>
> What would this 'lack of reality' mean if we were to free it from a purely historicizing interpretation? The phrase is clearly related to what Nietzsche calls nihilism. Yet I see a modulation of it well before Nietzschean perspectivism, in the Kantian theme of the sublime. (PE: 19)

Again, in the short piece 'Complexity and the Sublime', the sublime is associated with nihilism through Nietzsche's expression of the latter as 'the death of God': 'The retreat of regulation and rules is the cause of the feeling of the sublime [...] It is also the death of God ([...] this is of course exactly Nietzsche's position)' (Lyotard 1986: 511).

A further example may be found in the essay 'Anima Minima':

> In two centuries [between Vermeer and Van Gogh], and whatever the case might be with the theme of the sublime, the nihilist problematics from which it proceeds is diffused into every treatment, literary and artistic, of the sensible. Nihilism does not just end the efficiency of the great narratives of emancipation, it does not just lead to the loss of values and the death of God, which render metaphysics impossible. It casts suspicion on the data of aesthetics. (PF: 245)

In these brief but highly suggestive passages, Lyotard indicates that the sublime is an *earlier modulation* of nihilism, that the sublime is *caused* by the death of God (which is also the cause of contemporary nihilism), and that the theme of the sublime *proceeds from nihilist problematics*. These passages further suggest that both nihilism and the sublime are integrally related to a 'lack of reality' and a 'retreat of rules and regulations'.

More obliquely but no less significantly, Lyotard makes a further association between nihilism and the sublime by linking the Kantian problematic of the sublime with the Heideggerian analysis of nihilism in terms of the retreat of Being.[15] He writes:

> In a certain way the question of the sublime is closely linked to what Heidegger calls the retreat of Being: retreat of donation. For Heidegger, the welcome accorded something sensory, in other words some meaning embodied in the here-and-now before any concept, no longer has place and moment. This retreat signifies our current fate. (IN: 113)

The precise relationship between nihilism and the sublime remains elusive in these passages, but they are clearly strongly associated, perhaps to the point of identification. And yet, there is also the suggestion of a difference between them: they proceed from the same problematic, but are different modulations of that problematic. I wish to show how both poles of this ambiguity are developed in Lyotard's thought.

Briefly put, Lyotard can associate Nietzschean nihilism and the Kantian sublime to the point of identification because they can be seen as having the same form and implying the same content. Both concepts are structured according to a distinction and tension between related sets of terms: sensible and intelligible, existence and meaning, finitude and infinitude, immanent material and transcendent Idea. In Nietzsche's formulation of nihilism, as we have seen, transcendent meaning negates immanent existence. In Kant's formulation of the aesthetic of the sublime, transcendent Ideas are found in tension with an immanent material which defies good form. Sublime feeling arises when the objects of perception overwhelm our capacities to synthesise the raw data of sensation into intuitions (sensory objects presented in time and space); the faculty of imagination thus fails to present intuitions and match them with concepts as it does in the case of ordinary experience. However, the faculty of reason presents an Idea of *limitlessness* which is provoked by the 'badly-formed' sensation.[16] As with nihilism, the sensible world is called into question in relation to a supposedly superior intellectual category, but a category which itself cannot be verified by accordance with objects of experience. Both nihilism and the sublime thus rupture the integrity of experience, instituting a divide between the sensible and the intelligible, and casting doubt on the reality of the world.

The analogy Lyotard makes between Heideggerian nihilism and the Kantian sublime proceeds along similar lines: with the sublime, experience fails to be presented in the forms of space and time; with the Heideggerian retreat of Being, the world is no longer revealed to us in a way which is phenomenologically prior to conceptual analysis. In the language of *Being and Time*, the world no longer appears to us primarily in a hermeneutic manner, but an apophantic one. Or, in the language of his later works, beings are now revealed as stocked resources [*Bestand*] through techno-scientific enframing [*Ge-Stell*]. What Lyotard highlights is how this shift in the way beings are revealed impacts on perception, through a distortion of the forms of time and space, of our sense of moment and place.[17] It is this link with perception that allows Lyotard to make the analogy between the Heideggerian meditation on nihilism and the Kantian sublime. For Lyotard, both nihilism and the sublime may be understood in terms of a 'crisis of perception' in which space and time are destabilised and the reality of the sensible world is called into question: an abyss opens between the sensible and the intelligible.

Lyotard develops this analogy between nihilism and the sublime in one of his earliest (1981) treatments of the sublime aesthetic, 'Sublime Aesthetic of the Contract Killer' (in A). While the principal subject of this essay is the painter Jacques Monory, Lyotard argues that 'Monory's oeuvre testifies to a discrepancy between presence and infinity, between existence and meaning' (A: 157), and he interweaves his interpretation of Monory with a striking analysis of contemporary nihilism. In contrast to his position in 'Dead Letter', in this later essay – in which the issue of the meaning of life is once again raised explicitly – Lyotard seems to insist on the intractability of the abyss between meaning and existence. The essay begins with a metaphoric description of nihilism, in which the lengthening shadows that indicate the onset of winter illustrate the origin of our nihilistic tendencies: 'The abyss between what can appear and what can be thought was opened at the outset by the coming of winter' (157).

Winter here symbolises the negative judgement made on the sensible world of appearance (existence). Thought separates itself from the sensible world in the hope that a better, more meaningful world might lie elsewhere. The coming of winter thus signals the onset of suffering and the disappointment with life which, on Nietzsche's analysis, causes us to negate it. Lyotard writes that 'the paucity of reality is revealed, and suffering in the face of winter starts moaning and covers the experience of finitude with curses' (A: 157).

In this essay Lyotard advances the striking thesis that in the contemporary world, the sublime has become an 'immanent sublime'. Kantian Ideas – concepts which extend beyond the possibility of presentation in empirical objects of our experience – are no longer solely or primarily the province of transcendent metaphysical speculations such as God, the immortal soul, or freedom of the will. He argues that such Ideas have become immanent through the mapping of the world, with the aid of scientific techniques and new technologies, in ways which defy the possibility of our experience. In particular, Lyotard notes the discovery of macroscopic and microscopic worlds with telescopes, microscopes, and other sensitive equipment, and the capacity of computers to store amounts of information that exceed the competence of any individual to master. He then attributes Ideas with a 'murderous power' because of the way they reduce the significance of the data of our direct sensory experience: 'Nothing ever in sense-able things can equal the infinity of Ideas' (A: 157). In the context of our new, scientifically and technologically expanded worldview, 'reality' can no longer be considered as given in perception. Indeed, the world of perception is itself 'derealised' in comparison with the world that science and technology have revealed. Thus, in one of Lyotard's first deployments of the sublime, it functions as a concept through which to analyse the nihilism of the contemporary world.

In addition to these relatively explicit identifications of nihilism and the sublime, Lyotard's writings contain implicit suggestions of a strong association between the two ideas. We saw in the previous section how, in his 'libidinal phase', Lyotard identified nihilism in the structure of the sign, and in the construction of desire as lack through representation, illustrated with Freud's '*fort-da*' game. Further indication of the identification of nihilism and the sublime may be found in Lyotard's analysis of the sublime as a sign, and his revisitation of the '*fort-da*' game in an elaboration of sublime feeling. Lyotard characterises the sublime work of art as a sign in the book *Karel Appel*:

> the sublime thing is withdrawn beyond or below all capacity to form the presentable, to make appear – it is like a pure idea that exceeds the imagination, defies it without remedy, and closes its horizon of visibility.
>
> Thinking is conscious of breaking its moorings in the sensory, it feels the trembling of its objects on the edge of a night. Certainly the object that is the occasion of this distress and of this exile *is there*, but at the same time it *is not there*. Grandeur or force, Kant calls it 'raw nature', '*die rohe Natur*'. As a phenomenon, the strange event is certainly figured, but in inspiring the idea of an absolute, it does not belong to presentation. It is the *sign* of the unpresentable. (KA: 77–9)

Here, the aesthetic object itself – the sensible material of the artwork – acts as a sign for the supersensible (the Idea), and is threatened with nonexistence ('trembling . . . on the edge of a night'). The sublime object is the *sign of* presence, and its meaning (the Idea) is not present in it: it thus plays 'the game of de-presence, the very game of semiotic nihilism' (LE: 46–7). Here with the sublime, we are very close to Lyotard's own vitriolic description of the 'bad, nihilist' sign in *Libidinal Economy*, where he accuses the semioticians: 'See what you have done: the material is immediately annihilated. Where there is a message, there is no material' (44). The material, sensuous element of the sign is not meaningful in itself, and in that sense it is negated, while it signifies its meaning as a transcendent 'presence' which is not itself present in, or immanent to, the material. With the sublime understood as a sign, then, we appear to be back to the basic structure of religious nihilism.

Lyotard briefly returns to the *'fort-da'* game in one of his last significant essays on the sublime, 'Anima Minima' (published in 1993). His discussion of the game in this context underscores in many respects the representational nihilism it is used to illustrate in *Libidinal Economy*, but turned to quite a different end. Lyotard's aim in the paper is to extend certain qualities of the sublime aesthetic sentiment to all aesthetic sentiments (PF: 242). These qualities are directly related to nihilism. Lyotard claims (in a passage quoted above) that a kind of nihilism is identifiable in all aesthetic experience. To repeat:

> Nihilism does not just end the efficiency of the great narratives of emancipation, it does not just lead to the loss of values and the death of God, which render metaphysics impossible. It casts suspicion on the data of aesthetics. (PF: 245)

He elaborates what he means here with reference to the *'fort-da'* game. He rehearses Freud's example uncritically this time, saying that of course the reel represents the absent mother, but then goes on to give the following interpretation:

> The child makes the object disappear over the edge by mumbling *'fort'* and celebrates its return with a *'da.'* What is played out is the mutation of sight into vision and appearance into apparition. Apparition is appearance stamped with the seal of its disappearance. Art puts death's insignia on the sensible. It ravishes sensation from the night and impresses the seal of darkness upon it. (PF: 246)

Lyotard is suggesting here that there is a nihilism inherent in aesthetics insofar as the apprehension of the sensible which gives rise to aesthetic sentiment (*what I see, hear, etc. is beautiful, or is sublime*) is something other than the mere apprehension of sense data (of the kind which might, for example, and according to Kant's metaphysics, be matched with concepts and form objects of knowledge). For Lyotard, aesthetic apprehension involves a destabilisation or calling into question of the 'everyday' apprehension of sensible material; aesthetic experience turns our perception away from an ordinary apprehension of the world with its habitual identification of objects, and towards a 'something else' which invites aesthetic sentiment. Lyotard calls this 'something else' *presence*. He also sometimes calls it 'the unpresentable', 'nothing', or 'the immaterial'.

In Lyotard's late writings, aesthetics thus involves a kind of nihilism insofar as the aesthetic sentiment negates or calls into question the data of perception and sensation, indicating something beyond what is merely given in or as sensation. Lyotard suggests that this *presence* is itself what *gives* the given, what *presents* the presented; it is a *condition* for what is sensed that cannot itself *be* sensed.[18] In more prosaic terms, we might suggest that what Lyotard means by 'presence' is that which is felt, but which cannot be reduced to anything given in the aesthetic object itself.[19] Lyotard thus conceives aesthetics – the sublime in particular, but ultimately aesthetics in general – as inherently paradoxical, insofar as it concerns both the sensible and the negation of the sensible. In other writings Lyotard indicates this theme with paradoxical terms such as 'presenting the unpresentable', 'anaesthetic aesthetics', and 'immaterial matter'. In the essay 'Anima Minima', this paradox is illustrated with the '*fort-da*' game: it indicates the nihilism – the negation of the sensible – at the core of the sublime aesthetic.

Survivors, or Experimenters?

I have now sketched in some detail the reasons, both explicit and implicit, for thinking that Lyotard associates nihilism and the sublime so closely that we may seem justified in thinking that for him they are essentially the same thing. I will now argue that Lyotard presents the sublime not only as a modality of nihilism, but as a response to it. I will then attempt to explain Lyotard's use of the sublime in this ambiguous way by contextualising it in the wider movement of his thought.

Lyotard's deployment of the sublime as a response to nihilism has both important continuities, and important discontinuities, with Nietzsche's response. Like Nietzsche, Lyotard proposes that art, and the aesthetic experience to which it gives rise, acts as an important counter to nihilism. However, the kind of art Lyotard endorses, and the political and cultural dimensions of the aesthetic experience to which it gives rise, differ significantly to that advocated by Nietzsche. Lyotard breaks with Nietzsche on both responses to nihilism outlined above: on the reconstitution of a unified culture, and on the hope of overcoming nihilism by pushing it to its extreme. In relation to the first of Nietzsche's proposed responses to nihilism, Keith Ansell Pearson explains that

> [i]t is important to appreciate that the 'art' Nietzsche speaks of and esteems is *public* art, that is, art such as Greek tragic drama, which gathers together a people or community and discloses to them the 'truth' of their existence. One could say, therefore, that in this sense the experience afforded by art *is* political. (Ansell Pearson 1994: 5)

It is possible that Lyotard may have supported this idea of art at the time he wrote 'Dead Letter'. From the late 1960s onwards, however, he consistently opposed such a conception of art. This opposition first becomes evident in the political aesthetics he sketched around the themes of his first major book, *Discourse, Figure*. In 'Notes on the Critical Function of the Work of Art', for example, he argues that the political vocation of art is to 'unmask all attempts to reconstitute a pseudo-religion'; that is, to criticise all attempts to reunify culture through some substitute for religion (DW: 72). This opposition to a unified culture continues in his later works on the sublime and the differend, where Lyotard opposes such a conception of culture on precisely the grounds which distinguish him most strongly from Nietzsche – the grounds of *justice*. While Nietzsche believed that the demands of justice needed to be sacrificed for the sake of a healthy culture,[20] Lyotard is unwilling to make such a sacrifice, and instead seeks to find a way to negotiate the needs of justice and the needs of culture ('existence accepted as meaningful'). Lyotard's shifting approach to the problem of nihilism – from his early endorsement of a closing of the abyss between meaning and existence to his later insistence on the intractability of this abyss – may likewise be understood as a factor of his changed conception of justice. He begins to see any proposal for closing the abyss as potentially terroristic, because to construe existence as meaningful in a determinate way is to exclude those who disagree with such a meaning, or are not recognised as significant in its terms.

The aesthetic significance of Lyotard's concern with the politics of culture and community emerges in his engagement with Kant, particularly in *Lessons on the Analytic of the Sublime* (LAS). Here, we see a preference for sublime art and sublime aesthetic experience over the experience of the beautiful on explicitly political grounds. Kant draws an interesting link between aesthetic experience and community through an analysis of the *communicability* of aesthetic experience.[21] In an original reading of Kant, Lyotard argues that the conditions for a unified and homogenous community (the kind he thinks contains the threat of terrorism) are given in the kind of communicability required for the aesthetic of the beautiful, while the aesthetic of the sublime breaks with such a community. He analyses this both through the changing experience of art, and – in more technical terms – through the transcendental conditions of the different types of aesthetic experience outlined by Kant in the *Critique of Judgement*.

Lyotard argues that modern or avant-garde art (that is, experimental art since the end of the nineteenth century) has not been governed by the beautiful, but by the sublime. As he puts it, 'I think the aesthetic of the sublime is where modern art (including literature) finds its impetus and where the logic of the avant-garde finds its axioms' (PE: 19). Conversely, he associates 'traditional' art with the aesthetic of the beautiful. Lyotard argues that such art was governed by a relative consensus regarding rules of composition, examples of which are the Neoplatonic hierarchy of colour values, and the compositional rules of perspective discovered in the Quattrocento (IN: 119). Such aesthetic rules, in combination with religious and mythic exemplars being considered the 'proper' subject material for art, 'helped to encourage the identification of new political communities: the city, the State, the nation, by giving them the destiny of seeing everything and of making the world transparent (clear and distinct) to monocular vision' (IN: 119). Thus, beautiful art had a socially and culturally integrating function.

For Kant, there is a link between the aesthetic of the beautiful and community as such. In responding to the problem of how to explain the status of judgements of taste – which do not seem to be objective or open to demonstration, like knowledge claims, but which nevertheless differ from mere personal preferences – Kant argues that such judgements demand a consensus which is qualitatively different from that involved in rational argumentation. That is, when we judge something to be beautiful, we expect others to agree with us, without having to – or being able to – argue our point. Kant describes this as an *immediate* communicability of the feeling of the beautiful.[22] According to Lyotard, it is based on the presupposition of a shared 'community of feeling', and so it establishes the possibility of community on an aesthetic, pre-rational basis, and on the ideal of *consensus* (IN: 109–10).

It is precisely such a community based on consensus that Lyotard sees as a threat to justice. He develops a complex reading of Kant, against Kant's own intentions, to show that the aesthetic of the sublime breaks from this notion of community as consensus. Kant argues that while there is an immediate communication of the feeling of the beautiful, the communication of sublime feeling is mediated by a feeling for the moral law. In *Lessons on the Analytic of the Sublime*, Lyotard argues that '[t]he sublime feeling is neither moral universality nor aesthetic universalisation, but is, rather, the destruction of one by the other in the violence of their differend' (LAS: 239). Lyotard's reading is complex, but we may summarise its upshot as follows. While Kant seeks to show that the feeling of the sublime testifies to the power of reason and the moral law through the experience of the superiority of reason (the faculty of Ideas) over imagination (the faculty of the presentation of sensations), Lyotard insists on the irresolvable 'differend' between the two faculties. For him, the feeling of the sublime is the experience of incommensurability itself (Bennington 1988: 167). Such a feeling breaks with the ideal of consensus because it is an experience of *dissensus*: the faculties find themselves in disagreement regarding their experience. While such a possibility remains relatively undeveloped in Lyotard's works, the feeling of the sublime announces the possibility of a new model of community, one based on the sublime and dissensus rather than the beautiful and consensus.[23]

This deployment of the sublime aesthetic directly breaks with the project of a public art and a shared culture which Nietzsche sometimes endorses as a response to nihilism. This break takes place in the name of justice. Lyotard draws together the preservation of the difference between the Kantian faculties and the refusal to reconcile the intelligible and the sensible, both in the name of justice understood as a respect for difference, in the programmatic statement closing the essay 'Answer to the Question: What Is the Postmodern?':

> it is not up to us to *provide reality* but to invent allusions to what is conceivable but not presentable. And this task should not lead us to expect the slightest reconciliation between 'language games' – Kant, naming them the faculties, knew that they are separated by an abyss and that only a transcendental illusion (Hegel's) can hope to totalize them into a real unity. But he also knew that the price of this illusion is terror. We have paid dearly for our nostalgia for the all and the one, for a reconciliation of the concept and the sensible, for a transparent and communicable experience. Beneath the general demand for relaxation and appeasement, we hear murmurings of the desire to reinstitute terror and fulfil the fantasm of taking

> possession of reality. The answer is: war on totality. Let us attest to the unpresentable, let us activate the differends and save the honour of the name. (PE: 24–5)

Moreover, as we have already seen, Lyotard rejects the Nietzschean hope of overcoming nihilism by pushing it to its limits. As Lyotard understands it, such a project is bound up with revolutionary and utopian politics, and the Marxist idea of social change being produced by the contradictions of capitalism being pushed to their extremes. Lyotard lost his faith in Marxism in part because of his experience of disappointment with Algeria: for a long time he agitated for revolution, but after Algerian independence there was no significant social transformation in the Marxist sense, and new structures of exploitation simply replaced the old. In *Libidinal Economy* he argues that any form of social organisation will necessarily be exploitative and alienating to some degree, and rejects the revolutionary project. Moreover, he argues that Marxism is precisely a *faith*, and a form of religious nihilism. It is predicated on a 'reconciliation fantasy' in the form of a utopian idea of society, and Lyotard rejects it as nothing but a fantasy. Often, the idea of utopia remains nothing but an absent and deferred source of value, which devalues the present in relation to a futural projection.[24] However, the real danger of such fantasies is that they can motivate violent political actions, both through revolution, and through the exclusions and repressions which take place in the name of creating a utopian society. For these reasons, Lyotard rejects the idea of a definitive overcoming of nihilism, and opts instead for a strategic working within existing social conditions.

Despite Lyotard's disavowal of the Nietzschean project of overcoming nihilism in both senses discussed above, there are significant ways in which Lyotard's descriptions of the sublime resonate with Nietzsche's explanations of how art can act as a countermovement to nihilism. I wish to suggest three such ways. First, for all the annihilation of the sensible and the elevation of the intelligible in the aesthetic of the sublime, it is *still* an aesthetic, the occasion of a sensation and a *feeling*, and not just a cognition. For Nietzsche, art acts counter to nihilist religion and metaphysics because it engages the sensuous and sentimental aspects of our being and of life that the nihilists condemn. It thus engages the whole of our nature, and enables us to affirm the whole of life. It is distinctive of Lyotard's reading of the sublime to underline precisely its sensuous and sentimental aspects.[25]

One of the most original aspects of Lyotard's reading of the Kantian sublime is his insistence on the significance of the fact that the sublime is a *feeling*. While this is of course not denied by any of

Kant's interpreters, there is a tendency by some to interpret the sublime as functioning primarily to indicate the superiority of human *reason* over perceptible nature.[26] Characteristically, Lyotard rejects such a reading, emphasising instead the tension between reason and imagination – between the intelligible and the sensible – which is the occasion for the feeling of the sublime. In emphasising sublime *feeling*, Lyotard calls attention to the limits of reason. Moreover, at times Lyotard emphasises the *sensuous* side of the sublime, and the way that the sublime experience involves the suspension of the active powers of the mind in the confrontation with sensible materiality.[27] The sublime may be understood not as a devaluation of the sensible but as the very recuperation and triumph of its possibility when the objects of sensible perception are called into doubt. As such, it resists the devaluation of the sensible aspects of existence that nihilism threatens.[28]

Second, in place of the stability of the triumph of reason over sensation, Lyotard underlines Kant's suggestion that the sublime feeling is a constant *agitation*, and links this agitation to the stimulation of, and increased feeling for, life. This point remains suggestive in Lyotard's writings, and is not filled out in great detail. It is most clearly articulated in the first few pages of the essay 'Judiciousness in Dispute, or Kant after Marx' (Lyotard 1989). Referring to section 27 of the *Critique of Judgement*, Lyotard notes here the contrast with respect to the mind that Kant suggests between the feeling of the beautiful and that of the sublime. With the feeling of the beautiful, the mind is in a state of restful contemplation; with the feeling of the sublime, the mind feels itself moved. Lyotard quotes Kant: '[This sublime motion] may be compared to a vibration (*Erschütterung*); that is, to a quickly alternating attraction towards and repulsion from the same object' (Kant 1914: 120 [345], quoted in Lyotard 1989: 326–7). (Lyotard explains this agitated movement as consisting in the imagination's alternating repulsion from and attraction to reason, as the two faculties debate over the status of the sublime object in experience, alternately agreeing and disagreeing.) While the agitation proper to the sublime is the agitation of a transcendental subject and not of an empirical human individual, Lyotard further notes that a critical analogy may be made with Kant's anthropological texts, in which *health* in an empirical sense is also associated with an agitated movement. Lyotard describes the agitation discussed in these texts as 'an alternation, an exchange between two poles, a thrust inhibited by an obstacle, a movement to and fro, a race from one point to another and then back again, a visceral *vibrato*, an excitation of the life force' (Lyotard 1989: 326).

Lyotard finds further evidence for this association of the sublime and vitality in Kant's claim that the indirect pleasure and delight associated with the feeling of the sublime stem from 'a momentary checking (*Hemmung*) of the vital powers and a consequent stronger outflow of them' (Kant 1914: 102 [329], quoted in Lyotard 1989: 327). Lyotard's emphasis on agitation in the sublime and its association with health recalls the role Nietzsche gives to art in responding to nihilism by being a *stimulus* to life, by activating our vital powers and increasing our appetite for living. Lyotard's reading suggests that the sublime can provide precisely such a stimulus through the agitation of the faculties it produces.

These first two points – the emphasis on the sublime as sensation and feeling, and the agitation it produces as having an affinity with vitality and health – are drawn together in 'Anima Minima'. Here, Lyotard portrays *aesthesis* itself as a stimulation to life, and even as the origin of life: 'Sensation makes a break in an inert nonexistence. It alerts, it should be said, it *exists* it. What we call life proceeds from a violence exerted from the outside on a lethargy' (PF: 243). Life is presented here, as the title of the essay suggests, as a 'minimal animation', the result of sensible stimulation on something which has a capacity to receive sensations. (Lyotard often calls this capacity '*passibility*'.) Lyotard suggests, then, that life and health are associated with the agitation and animation which sensation exerts on something which has a capacity to receive it. The sublime, as an aesthetic of agitation, acts as a model for this sensible stimulation to life. In this respect, the sublime may be seen as resisting nihilism by activating and affirming the integral connections between agitation, sensation, and life.

Third, for Lyotard the aesthetic of the sublime acts as a stimulus to new possibilities for creative artistic experimentation. The sublime allows new possibilities for creative forms in the arts, forms which may be found through experimentation with materials under the conditions of the privation of the 'good forms' of time and space. Lyotard argues that new technologies provide materials for such artistic experimentation, an argument which is explored in detail in the next chapter. As is well known, and noted above, Lyotard also argues that the sublime aesthetic is what is at stake in the avant-garde art movements of the twentieth century, movements such as minimalism and abstraction. These developments are explored in Chapters 6 and 7.

The value of the creative sublime as a response to nihilism is emphasised by Lyotard's privileging of experimentation over 'mere survival'. This theme appears in several of his later works in the context of an analysis of changing social conditions. As we have seen, according to Lyotard the sublime has become an 'immanent sublime' as a result of the technological displacement of our sense of reality, from perceptual givens to infinite data. One of the decisive transformations of social conditions Lyotard believes technologies effect is the decline of the category of 'experience'. Experience, in this sense, is the 'life experience' gained over time, through which a person accumulates knowledge and forms character. In place of the human subject understood as 'experiencer', Lyotard contends, our cultural ideal is now the 'expert', who needs only to know the specific technical knowledges which allow her to perform her function in her field. The goal of the expert is not personal growth, but the operation and maintenance of the technical apparatuses which exceed the capacities of any user, to which the store of knowledge is entrusted.

Given these new conditions of existence, Lyotard sketches two possible fates for us: we may become 'mere' survivors, or we may become experimenters. He writes that 'the quantitative infinite of knowledges and powers [...] has eaten away at experiences and made us into survivors or experimenters ...' (A: 193). And further:

> For the abyss aroused by sublime feeling, is substituted the concrete mass of materials and hardware in self-regulating set-ups. What remains of 'us,' with our capacity for desiring and suffering, is that 'we' have to serve these set-ups. It is in this respect that 'we' are either survivors (but we can only know this from the outside) or experimenters. (A: 191)

Unsurprisingly, given Lyotard's frequent celebration of experimentation in the arts and in thought, being an experimenter is for him a happier fate than mere survival.[29] The challenge of such experimentation is to find new ways of activating the sensible and the agitated feeling of vitality. The value of the aesthetic of the sublime as a response to nihilism is thus that it opens up the possibility of experimentation within our new cultural conditions; it offers a way of activating life-affirmative feeling through experimentation with materials that are not well presented in the forms of time and space. Comparing contemporary culture and sublime art, Lyotard writes that '[t]heir only common motif is nihilism. But the cultural consists in concealing, the artistic in elaborating' (PF: 247; translation modified).

Creativity is an essential aspect of Nietzsche's response to nihilism, and an important reason he values art. For Nietzsche, there is no objectively given meaning to life as such. Therefore, creative acts of interpretation are needed to imbue life with meaning. The artist and the work of art are exemplary for Nietzsche precisely because they demonstrate the strength – the will to power – necessary to create meaning out of a meaningless existence. Lyotard's response to nihilism through the advocacy of experimentation and sublime art follows the same general contour, but has a greater historical and cultural specificity: it is not aimed at compensating for the meaninglessness of life in a general existential sense, but at artistically transforming the experience of postmodernity.

Lyotard's response to nihilism from within, through an elaboration of the sublime which is itself a modality of nihilism, may better be understood by considering it in the wider context of his thought. We have already seen how Lyotard's recourse to the sublime may be understood in terms of his rejection of revolutionary politics and a community based on consensus. A further dimension of understanding is given in the idea of 'retorsion'. One of the most potentially puzzling aspects of Lyotard's work as a whole is his shift from a polemical critique of the linguistic turn in philosophy and the humanities generally (in *Discourse, Figure* and *Libidinal Economy*)[30] to his apparent contribution to this turn by developing a philosophy of phrases (in *The Differend*). However, Keith Crome's study *Lyotard and Greek Thought: Sophistry* (2004) has highlighted a fact which is (arguably) readily apparent from a careful study of *The Differend*, namely that this book is not a positive contribution to the linguistic turn, but a critical reaction to it. Crome's study helps to explain the confusion here by tracing the influence of ancient Greek sophistry on Lyotard's thought, and in particular, his adoption of the sophistical strategy of retorsion. This is a technique whereby an opponent's argument is turned back against him through the employment of paradox and rhetoric.[31] As Crome argues, *The Differend* should not be understood as a book of philosophy which puts forward a positive philosophy of language, but as a *retort* to the linguistic turn in philosophy, which strategically adopts certain premises of this turn in order to show how they might lead to a different conclusion.[32] In *The Differend*, Lyotard's aim is to show how it is possible to resist a reduction of all events to language (and particularly to a philosophical metalanguage) from within the philosophy of language itself. This project is effectively a form of Kantian immanent critique, insofar as it seeks to draw the limits of the philosophy of language in order to protect what it is in danger of obscuring (on Lyotard's account, justice, the event, the sensible, and in general all differences which do not survive metalinguistic translation).

The point I wish to draw from this is that we may see the itinerary of Lyotard's thought as being moved by an increasing attraction to the strategy of retorsion and to the resources of immanent critique. In his Marxian phase and still to some extent in *Discourse, Figure* and the essays preceding *Libidinal Economy*, he posits the possibility of a transgression of existing social and conceptual structures and hopes for a revolution which will bring an end to alienation and (in effect) restore the identity of meaning and existence. In *Libidinal Economy*, the gesture of transgression and the end of alienation are rejected as naïve and contradictory. Nevertheless, the libido is still posited in some sense as an 'other' to nihilism, the possibility of an immediacy of feeling immanent to, but clearly different from, the absence and transcendence of nihilism. The privilege of the sublime in Lyotard's later works, I wish to argue, may be seen as a further deepening of his attraction to retorsion and immanent critique. Just as he moves to a position of accepting the premises of the linguistic turn in order to mount a retort to it, so he becomes fascinated with the possibilities harboured by the aesthetic of the sublime precisely because it *is* a modality of nihilism. The sublime offers a response to nihilism which accepts its premises but demonstrates the possibility of a different conclusion: the negation of the sensible by the intelligible and transcendent is not necessarily accompanied by a loss of the sensuous feeling of life, but rather may be attendant to its intensification.

Considered in terms of the themes and concerns treated above, Lyotard remains a deeply Nietzschean thinker long after explicit and sympathetic references to the German philosopher disappear from his works. This Nietzschean perspective on Lyotard illuminates his great value as a philosopher. The general problem, to which Lyotard's reflections on nihilism and the sublime might minimally be thought to begin to sketch a response, is how to constitute a culture rich in meaning, value, and significance, without imposing a hegemony which does injustice to difference. Lyotard wants both meaning and justice, but, unlike Nietzsche, he is absolutely unwilling to sacrifice the latter for the former. Lyotard's rejection of the hope of overcoming nihilism – of reconciling the sensible and the intelligible, of meaning and existence – is driven by this insistence. It prompts him to search for a model of community based on dissensus rather than consensus, as well as for possibilities for responding to nihilism from within a nihilistic culture. Lyotard finds both in the aesthetic of the sublime. If Nietzsche is right in supposing that life can only be justified aesthetically (Nietzsche 1993: 32), then the sublime is a form of aesthetic justification appropriate to contemporary cultural conditions, as well as to a community based on dissensus.

Notes

1. Williams in fact raises the possibility that the sublime might act as a response to nihilism, but dismisses it as ineffective. See Williams 2000a: 132. My strategy here is to offer an alternative interpretation of nihilism and the sublime in Lyotard, rather than argue against Williams's interpretation. I therefore forgo a discussion of it here, but see Chapter 6 for further details.
2. In his *Nihilism and the Sublime Postmodern*, Wil Slocombe (2006) notes the close relationship between nihilism and the sublime in Lyotard's work, but does not recognise how for him the aesthetic of the sublime also acts as a positive response to nihilism.
3. Like most everything in Nietzsche's work, his understanding of nihilism is open to multiple and contesting interpretations. Here I draw on White 1987.
4. For interpretations of Nietzsche's complex and changing views of art, see Young 1992 and Ridley 2007.
5. Lyotard was a member of the Marxist organisations Socialisme ou Barbarie (1954–64) and Pouvoir Ouvrier (1964–6).
6. For an account of this loss of faith, see Lyotard's 'A Memorial of Marxism: For Pierre Souyri', trans. Cecile Lindsay, in P.
7. Insofar as it emphasises the book's merits as an analysis of and response to nihilism, the reading of *Libidinal Economy* here follows that of Williams (2000a) and of my own in *Nihilism in Postmodernity* (Woodward 2009).
8. Lyotard writes: '[S]emiotics is nihilism. Religious science par excellence [...] It is a religious science because it is haunted by the hypothesis that someone speaks to us in these givens [i.e., signs] and, at the same time, that its language, its competence, or in any case its performative capacity transcends us [...] Thus the sign is enmeshed in nihilism, nihilism proceeds by signs; to continue to remain in semiotic thought is to languish in religious melancholy ...' (LE: 49).
9. For example, in the paper 'The Unconscious' Freud writes: 'The nucleus of the Ucs. [unconscious] consists of instinctual representatives which seek to discharge their cathexis; that is to say, it consists of wishful impulses' (SE XIV: 186). On this issue, see Bennington 1988: 16.
10. The quotation above continues as follows: 'Our question is: who suffers in pain? Freud's response is: the child, thus an already constituted subject, formed in the object-mother's gaze, in symmetry with her, already, then, there is the specular partition between them, already the auditorium-side and the stage-side, already the theatre; and the theatre the child constructs with the edge of his bed as the footlights, and the thread attached to the bobbin as curtain and scenery, governs entries and exits, this prosthesis-theatre is of the same type as that already hollowed out within him, it is the replica in "exteriority" of the hollow volume in which the two poles of his own body and that of his

mother, theatrical counterparts, non-existent poles, capture, secure in their field, dominate every event of the libidinal band' (LE: 23).

11. In section V, 'The Special Characteristics of the System Ucs. [Unconscious]', Freud writes: 'There are in this system no negation, no doubt, no degrees of certainty: all this is only introduced by the work of the censorship between the Ucs. and the Pcs. [preconscious]. Negation is a substitute, at a higher level, for repression. In the Ucs. there are only contents, cathected with greater or lesser strength' (SE XIV: 186).

12. For Lyotard's criticisms of *Libidinal Economy*, see JG: 3–6; P: 13–14.

13. See especially Longinus's *On the Sublime* (1985).

14. Keith Crome and James Williams suggest that the sublime develops through four modalities in Lyotard's work: aesthetic, political, ironic, and bodily (LRG: 18).

15. See 'Nihilism as Determined by the History of Being' in Heidegger 1987.

16. See CJ, sections 23–9 ('Analytic of the Sublime').

17. Heidegger gives an early illustration of this in section 23 of Being and Time, in terms of the effect of modern technologies such as the radio on *Dasein*'s spatiality: 'All the ways in which we speed things up, as we are more or less compelled to do today, push us on towards the conquest of remoteness. With the "radio," for example, *Dasein* has so expanded its everyday environment that it has accomplished a de-severance ["bringing-close" or "making the farness vanish"] of the "world" – a de-severance which, in its meaning for *Dasein*, cannot yet be visualized' (1962: 140 [105]). It is the more general effects of such technologies that Heidegger describes in later works in terms of *Ge-Stell* (see 'The Question Concerning Technology' in Heidegger 1977). Lyotard endorses and extends this Heideggerian theme, suggesting that Heidegger understood the apogee of technoscience as nuclear science, but that 'we have done much better in Gestell nowadays', and citing contemporary communication technologies and computer science (IN: 114).

18. As this point suggests – insofar as the wording evokes Heidegger's 'ontological difference' – there is an ontological dimension to Lyotard's analysis of the sublime. For an extended discussion of this, see Gasché 2001.

19. For Lyotard's most significant discussion of this idea, see 'Presence' in WP.

20. In the posthumously published essay 'The Greek State', for example, Nietzsche fears 'the cry of compassion tearing down the walls of culture', in which case 'the desire for justice, for the equalization of suffering, would swamp all other ideas' (quoted in Ansell Pearson 1994: 73).

21. See in particular CJ, sections 39 and 40.

22. Kant writes: 'I say that taste can with more justice be called a *sensus communis* than can sound understanding; and that the aesthetic, rather than the intellectual, judgement can bear the name of a public sense [...] We might even define taste as the faculty of estimating what makes our feeling in a given representation universally communicable without the mediation of a concept' (CJ: 153 [295]).

23. For an indication of such a possibility, see Vandenabeele 2007.
24. See in particular chapter 3 of *Libidinal Economy*, 'The Desire Named Marx'.
25. Kant announces this point at the beginning of the 'Analytic of the Beautiful': 'be the given representations even rational, but referred in a judgement solely to the Subject (to its feeling), they are always to that extent aesthetic' (CJ: 42). Lyotard clarifies this point in *Lessons on the Analytic of the Sublime*, explaining first why Kant calls the sublime an '*intellectual* feeling', but then why for him it still necessarily remains a *feeling*, that is, aesthetic (rather than cognitive): 'The part played by the imagination (or sensibility) in sublime judgement must consequently be reduced, "retracted"; the content of forms is weak in sublime presentation [...] This is why, for Kant, the sublime is said to be an "intellectual feeling" (*Geistesgefühl*), as opposed to taste' (LAS: 184). '[T]he sublime can be classified as aesthetic because *aesthesis*, sensation, here means not "the representation of a thing (through sense as a receptivity pertaining to the faculty of knowledge)", but "a modification of the feeling of pleasure or displeasure", a representation that refers "solely [*lediglich*] to the subject and is not available for any cognition, not even for that by which the subject *cognizes* itself" [...] This sensation is not information about the object, whether it be internal or external [...] What is informative, on the contrary, is the sensation furnished by the senses' (185).
26. See for example Crowther 1999.
27. See for example IN: 140.
28. To elaborate this point a little further, we may note that feeling is usually thought on the sensible side of the sensible/intelligible opposition. The feeling of the sublime is analysed by Kant as a feeling of both pleasure and pain, and pleasure and pain are both identified by Plato as lying on the side of the sensible and distracting the soul from remembering its true divine origin in the intelligible world of the forms. In the *Phaedo*, for example, he has Socrates say: '[E]very pleasure and every pain provides, as it were, another nail to rivet the soul to the body and to weld them together' (Plato 1977: 34).
29. Elsewhere, in the context of a discussion of childhood, survival is unambiguously given a negative value: 'we have to be children if we are to be capable of the most minimal creative activity. If we are sent to space after the explosion of the sun (I don't even know if it will be us), if something is sent to space without this extraordinary complexity that is precisely the paradox of childhood, I am afraid that this complexity is not complex enough. In this case, we could call this by the terrible name of mere survival, which is not very interesting. I am not interested in surviving, not interested at all. I am interested in remaining a child' (PW: 107).
30. For example, in *Libidinal Economy* he refers to the linguistic turn in French thought, associated with ' the closure of representation', as

'that sarcastic discovery, that sham dropping of the scales from our eyes, by those thinkers who come and tell us: what is outside is really inside, there is no outside, the exteriority of the theatre is just as much its interiority [...] this sad piece of news, this cacangelism which is only the other side of evangelism, this wretched news that the artefact-bearers running along their little wall behind the backs of slaves who are bound and seated at the bottom of their cave, do not even exist, or what amounts to the same: that they themselves are only shadows in the cave of the sunlit world, reduplication of sadness ...' (LE: 4).

31. A prominent example of this technique is one analysed by Lyotard in the first 'Notice' of *The Differend*, on the sophist Protagoras. Protagoras' student Euathlus has to pay him only if he has won a dispute at least once. Euathlus claims he has not won a dispute, and should not have to pay. Protagoras retorts that he does have to pay, for either he has won a past dispute, in which case he must pay, or he has not won a past dispute – in which case he wins the present dispute – and should therefore still pay. See D: 6–8.

32. Crome writes: 'If, and as Lyotard says in the introduction to The Differend, the context of the book is to be understood as "the 'linguistic turn" of Western philosophy [...], then that turn is itself put through another turn, a sophistical turn, a retorsion, by Lyotard' (2004: 147).

Chapter 5

Aesthēsis and Technē: New Technologies and Lyotard's Aesthetics

While commentators have often emphasised the political dimension of Lyotard's thought, there is just as strong a case to be made that his most central concern was with art and aesthetics. From his first major book *Discours, figure* (DF) to the posthumously published *Misère de la philosophie* (MP), Lyotard's work displays a deep engagement with both particular artists and movements (he wrote many exhibition catalogues and essays on artists) and the general problems of philosophical aesthetics. It is well known that Lyotard's thinking about art is characterised by the view that postmodern art 'presents the unpresentable', and should be understood in relation to an aesthetics of the sublime.[1] One of the less appreciated modalities of his aesthetics, however, is a consideration of the way that new technologies reconfigure the nature of aesthetic experience. Moreover, those commentators who have given attention to this aspect of Lyotard's aesthetics have tended to characterise it negatively, focusing on the problems he raises rather than the possibilities to which he alludes.[2]

As we have seen in previous chapters, according to Lyotard, the most significant new technologies are those which deal with language, communication, and information.[3] Such technologies are a central feature of Lyotard's analysis of the postmodern or inhuman condition; he argues that these technologies have decisively altered our experience of reality at the fundamental levels of time and space, and are complicit with capitalism in reducing life to bare efficiency. Furthermore, Lyotard examines the implications of the application of these new technologies to art. Working within a Kantian framework, he articulates a series of problems that seem to arise for the very possibility of aesthetic experience with the application of new technologies to the production of artworks.

134

Lyotard was a thinker more interested in opening up the possibilities of thought than in providing supposedly final answers, and his reflections on new technologies and aesthetics offer seemingly divergent angles of approach on a fascinating issue. This chapter draws together these diverse strands of Lyotard's exploration of the impact of new technologies (*technē*) on society, and indicates their contribution to new directions in art and aesthetics (*aesthēsis*). The first part outlines his analysis of the role of new technologies in postmodern society, while the second and third examine his theoretical writings on new technologies and art. Despite Lyotard's hesitations about art and technology, I argue that it is possible to clearly discern a path in his writings which characterises new technological art as invoking an aesthetic of the sublime, and which positions it as a crucial form of experimentation in the postmodern condition. The final part of the chapter critically examines the parameters of Lyotard's engagement with new technologies and aesthetics, outlining the limitations to his work indicated by more recent developments in information theory. Ultimately, this chapter seeks to locate Lyotard as an important and provocative early theorist of the 'digital' or 'new media' arts, whose own thought was limited by a restricted understanding of new technology, but who nevertheless provides a valuable orientation for thinking the place of such technology in philosophical aesthetics.

New Technologies and the Postmodern Condition

The advent and proliferation of new technologies play an important role in Lyotard's analysis of the decline of metanarratives and the constitution of a postmodern society. A consideration of this role will allow us to understand what motivates, and what is at stake in, his examination of the impact of these technologies on art and aesthetics. Lyotard develops the role of new technologies in postmodernity on two significant points: the 'criterion of performativity' which has replaced metanarratives, and the 'crisis of time and space'.

In *The Postmodern Condition*, Lyotard takes the field of his study as the status of knowledge in 'computerised societies'. Commissioned to write a report on the status of knowledge in the late 1970s,[4] Lyotard chooses 'computerisation' as the central issue affecting this status. He argues that the most significant recent developments in science and technology have all borne on language and communication:

> it is fair to say that for the last forty years the 'leading' sciences and
> technologies have had to do with language: phonology and theories

> of linguistics, problems of communication and cybernetics, modern theories of algebra and informatics, computers and their languages, problems of translation and the search for areas of compatibility among computer languages, problems of information storage and data banks, telematics and the perfection of intelligent terminals, paradoxology. (PC: 3–4)

The question at stake for Lyotard in this study is how knowledge, impacted by these communication technologies, is legitimated. In other words, what forms of knowledge are considered legitimate in the postmodern condition, and why?

Lyotard argues that while knowledge had for several centuries (since the European Enlightenment) been legitimated with respect to metanarratives of one form or another, in the postmodern condition this form of legitimation has become obsolete. While he points to various causes for our 'incredulity toward metanarratives', the argument which concerns us here bears on the development of technologies. Lyotard argues that in the Industrial Revolution science became closely coupled with technology, and the resulting 'technoscience' became coupled with capitalism. Science turned greater attention to the development of technologies rather than the investigation of nature. Such technologies in turn fuelled industry and developed the economy, enabling more money to be channelled into the development of technoscience itself (PC: 45). Lyotard argues that in the contemporary conjunction of technoscience and capitalism we can discern a criterion for the legitimation of knowledge which has become autonomous, and which need have no recourse to legitimation by a metanarrative. This criterion is what he calls 'performativity', and it may be simply stated in the following formula: minimum input, maximum output. Performativity – or what may be more familiarly termed 'efficiency' – functions as a criterion of legitimation by determining what is required to maximise profits and productivity. Performativity is a form of instrumental rationality, which concerns itself not with the ends of technoscientific and economic development, but only with the most efficient means of achieving it. Metanarratives have become incredulous to us, then, because our societies no longer need them in order to legitimate their developmental projects.

For Lyotard, the significance of the fact that the most important recent developments in technoscience have been in the areas of language and communication is that capitalism, and the criterion of performativity with it, has come to bear on meaning itself. While Lyotard is a thinker with a very diverse range of interests, he is perhaps best understood as a kind of antireductionist, who is always concerned to preserve, and to open up, possibilities for thought and feeling in those areas where they are threatened with narrowing, stupefaction, and stagnation. As we have seen in previous chapters, the term which best captures this concern, and which is widely recognised in the secondary literature as the most central to Lyotard's corpus, is 'the event'.[5]

As was discussed in Chapter 3, Lyotard's concern with linguistic and communicational technologies is that they reduce the possibility of events by subjecting language to a set of predetermined parameters. He suggests that all language will henceforth have to pass through the tyrannical reduction of computer languages: whatever cannot be translated into computer languages will be eliminated. This process of reduction is closely associated with communication, since it is the efficient communication or transmission of information which motivates its translation into computer languages. This coding and communication of language conforms to the criterion of performativity; if linguistic meaning cannot be coded and communicated, it cannot be understood to contribute to the efficient functioning and development of the technoscientific and capitalist system. According to Lyotard, however, artistic and philosophical phrases are not susceptible to simple informational transmission, and are in danger of obsolescence (Lyotard 1986–7: 211).

In addition to his concern with technologies which bear directly on language and communication, and as examined in the previous chapter under the heading of 'the crisis of perception', Lyotard is also concerned with scientific and technical developments which bear on time and space. Such developments, he argues, link with new technologies to unsettle our sense of reality and the very possibility of experience. Lyotard argues that the crisis of foundations which is frequently thought to beset the sciences in the twentieth century is the result of unsettling developments in those sciences which concern themselves precisely with time and space: 'arithmetic, in other words the science of number which is the science of time; [...] geometry, the science of space; [...] mechanics, the science of movement, which is to say the science of space and time' (IN: 116). Moreover, Lyotard draws attention to the fact that the 'crises' in mathematics, physics, geometry, and mechanics pertain to debates concerning whether conceptions of space and time 'are based on intuitive syntheses, or whether they are constructed out of concepts in an axiomatic, artifactual theory' (P: 42). In fact, Lyotard sees the crisis in terms of a shift from the intuitive, preconceptual synthesis of space and time associated with our *perceptions* to a primarily conceptual and calculated grasp of these. The project of applying rationality to all spheres of human life has extended itself, in postmodernity, to the rational calculation of time and space themselves. New technologies of communication and information contribute to this crisis of space and time by destabilising the perceptual bases of our sense of them. This destabilisation is linked with the saturation of contemporary societies by media technologies:

> [T]ime and space are approached in terms not of givens but of thoughts, the mere presentation of things driven away by the generalisation of the media and the closure of thought on itself, the images and sounds we confront having already been thought insofar as they have been calculated. (P: 42)

With this media saturation and real-time communication over vast distances, Lyotard's argument suggests, our habitual perceptions of time and space as locating things and events in a determinate *here* and *now* are being replaced with more abstract calculations. Since time and space are the fundamental parameters of what is given to us in perception, and are basic to our understanding of reality, Lyotard argues that in postmodernity reality is undergoing the disorienting process of 'derealisation'.[6] This crisis of time and space has direct import for the possibility of aesthetic experience, and it is to Lyotard's analysis of this problem that I now turn.

Kant After New Technologies

In 1985, at a conference entitled *Art et Communication*,[7] Lyotard presented a paper which critically interrogates the very possibility of art that employs new technologies of communication and information in its production and transmission. Taking Kant's aesthetic theory as his framework for this interrogation, Lyotard argues that communication technologies undermine the possibility of aesthetic experience on at least four major points that Kant takes as necessary conditions for such experience: *immediate communication without a concept*, *the formation of matter into sensible objects*, *the free play of imagination and understanding*, and *passibility* (the capacity to be affected). After a brief orientation to Kant's aesthetic project, I will outline Lyotard's concerns with new technologies in the arts on each of these points.

In *The Critique of Judgement* (CJ), Kant turns to the question of how judgements of the beautiful are to be understood, and employs many of the concepts and terms developed in the earlier *Critique of Pure Reason* (1929). In the first *Critique*, which develops a metaphysics of experience primarily concerned with how knowledge is possible, such a possibility depends upon the synthesis of concepts and 'intuitions', which together form an object. Intuitions are themselves a synthesis of sensations and forms; they present data from sensory input in a way which is ready to be categorised by concepts. Kant calls the faculty (that is, the particular power of the mind) responsible for presenting intuitions the *imagination*, and the faculty responsible for concepts the *understanding*. Moreover, in the Transcendental Aesthetic of the first *Critique* Kant argues that space and time are basic intuitions necessary for the presentation of any object, since objects must occupy space and time (a *here* and *now*) in order to be experienced (Kant 1929: 67–91).[8] In the third *Critique*, Kant applies this model of the constitution of the sensuous forms of objects to a different end, that of understanding how aesthetic *feeling*, rather than knowledge, is possible. Kant argues that judgements of the beautiful concern a feeling of pleasure which is subjective (that is, it cannot be said to constitute knowledge), but which nevertheless demands universal agreement. In order to explain how such judgements are possible, he posits that they must conform to various *a priori* criteria. It is precisely such criteria that Lyotard believes are undermined or eluded in the application of new technologies to works of art.

First, Kant argues that judgements of the beautiful imply an immediate communication of aesthetic feeling. That is, such judgements must be universally communicable without the mediation of a concept. Crucially, for Kant, if concepts are involved then aesthetic judgements would be a matter of knowledge, subject to proofs, demonstration, and argumentation – but it is clear that this is not the case with aesthetic judgements. The demand that others agree with our aesthetic judgements, however, suggests the idea that they be universally communicable. That is, the feeling of the beautiful should in principle be communicated to anyone placed in the same situation or before the same work of art. This is a form of communication which concerns *feelings* (i.e. the pleasure felt with a judgement that something is beautiful) and which is prior to any conceptual determination or communication. Moreover, it is an immediate communication which operates in principle, rather than an empirical form of communication which operates 'in fact'. This 'communication without communication' in the aesthetic feeling of the beautiful is what gives Lyotard's paper under consideration its title, and which announces the central question he wishes to dramatise: 'what about communication without concept at a time when, precisely, the 'products' of technologies applied to art cannot occur without the massive and hegemonic intervention of the concept?' (IN: 109). The hesitation Lyotard evinces with respect to art and communication technologies on this point, then, is that with such technologies concepts, and the actual communication of these concepts, are involved from the very beginning. With such technologies, Lyotard suggests, there is no longer space for the immediate communication of feeling because artworks themselves are already mediated, and communicated, through concepts.

Second, Lyotard argues that the application of the new technologies to art also disallows the synthesis of matter and form into sensible objects, a process which according to Kant should take place independently from, and free of, conceptual determination. For Kant, matter is what is *given* to us in pure sensation; it is a chaotic flow of manifold colours, sounds, and other sensory impressions. Various pre-conceptual syntheses are responsible for giving matter form, and these forms are what then give rise to the feeling of the beautiful. All of this must take place without matter and form being determined by concepts. Lyotard notes, however, that what Kant calls 'matter' has precisely to do with what we cannot calculate. In the more traditional arts, Lyotard names colour in painting and timbre in music as corresponding to those elements which escape formal definition and calculable specification (IN: 140–1). With the application of new technologies to the arts, however, it appears that the works are entirely calculated according to concepts from the beginning; there is no space for the imaginative synthesis of matter with form which is a necessary part of aesthetic experience in general and the experience of the beautiful in particular. Moreover – and this is a crucial point to which I will return later – matter is the aspect of the work of art where Lyotard locates events. Matter is that which is '*par excellence* diverse, unstable, and evanescent' (138), it is the element of *difference* in works of art which accounts for their richness and their capacity to arouse feeling. For Lyotard, the principle of identity implied in calculation (to calculate something it must be attributed with a quantifiable identity) stifles this element of difference and undermines the ability of the work of art to be, or give rise to, an event.

Third, Lyotard takes the calculative function of new technologies to mean that the forms of objects in works of art made using these technologies are determined by concepts. This undermines a further *a priori* condition of aesthetic judgement. According to Kant, the pleasure elicited by the feeling of the beautiful is constituted by the *free play* of forms and concepts; this pleasure is in fact the result of a feeling of harmony between the faculties of imagination and understanding. In the judgement of beautiful objects, the forms presented are not objects of knowledge, and the concepts applied to them are not determinate. Moreover, there is a kind of excess of the presentation of forms over the possibility of capturing any of those forms in determinate concepts (see Lyotard's discussion in KA: 63–5). Nevertheless, concepts can be applied to such forms in a kind of 'free play', where concepts are matched with forms in an indeterminate way. This *a priori* condition of the judgement of the beautiful, when applied to a work of art, means that the meaning of the work will never be something determinate – the forms it gives rise to will always be free from, and in excess of, any conceptual determination. With new technologies, however, Lyotard argues that the meaning of the work of art is conceptually determined in advance. When artwork is produced or presented using such technologies, all of its parameters are programmed, and while the viewer of the artwork will not necessarily know what the conceptual meaning of it is, the crucial point is that it is *in principle* fully knowable (IN: 111). Lyotard takes this to imply that the supposed artwork can be entirely reduced to conceptual determination, and is thus not capable of inducing an aesthetic experience of the beautiful.

Finally, using less specifically Kantian terminology, but remaining within the framework of Kant's aesthetic problematic, Lyotard argues that new technologies undermine what he calls *passibility*, the capacity to be affected. This capacity underlies the possibility of any aesthetic experience, and requires a form of passivity. Passibility may be understood as an openness to being affected by the occurrence of events, that is, a receptivity to being affected in ways which are not foreseen and not controlled. Passibility depends on a recession of the mind's attempt to grasp sensuous experiences in concepts. Lyotard writes:

> If we are in a state of passibility, it's that something is happening to us [...]What happens to us is not at all something we have first controlled, programmed, grasped by a concept [*Begriff*]. Or else, if what we are passible to has first been plotted conceptually, how can it *seize us*? How can it test us if we already know – of what, with what, for what, it is done? (IN: 111)

Lyotard suggests that passibility is being undermined by the *interactivity* which is often distinctive of art that employs new technologies. Such works of art call on the viewer/receiver to constitute themselves as an active subject; to respond to the artwork and take an active role in a process of communication with it. But in this process of interactivity, Lyotard argues, our capacity for *passibility* becomes lost – we are no longer able to achieve the degree of passivity necessary in order to be open to the occurrence of unexpected events. Insofar as passibility is a necessary condition for aesthetic experience, on this point too the possibility of such experience with the new technological arts is called into question.

Lyotard's hesitations concerning the possibility of art made and presented using new technologies outlined above may be summarised as follows. Employing an interpretation of Kantian aesthetics, he argues that aesthetic experience requires a sensible *presentation* of an object, prior to and free from its *representation* by a concept. Technologies of communication and information apply determinate concepts to sensible forms from the outset, undermining the possibility of aesthetic feeling. These arguments link back to Lyotard's concern with the 'crisis' of time and space in postmodernity, a theme also discussed in 'Something Like: "Communication ... without Communication"' (in IN). The presentation of sensible forms which Lyotard claims is lacking in art made with communication technologies requires the minimal intuitions of time and space in which to be given. As Lyotard notes, then, the question of 'new technologies and art' is also the question of 'art and postmodernity' (IN: 109). To summarise the points made above in the more general terms of Lyotard's concerns, we may say that the calculation, programming, and conceptual determination that he sees as distinctive of the new technologies stifle the emergence of events, which for him are what is vital about art.

The Technological Sublime

Lyotard's thought, in particular the paper 'Something Like: "Communication ... without Communication"', has been taken by some commentators to decide against the possibility of art being produced with new technologies (see Kluitenberg 2002; Gere 2006). This is not surprising, given the polemical rhetoric in which he sometimes engages (for example, he alludes to *communicationalist* and *interactional* ideologies) (IN: 108, 116, 117). However, despite the apparently severe problematisation of this possibility that this paper performs, its findings are not conclusive. Lyotard ends the paper with a series of questions, which seek to clarify what is at stake in the question of art and technology rather than to give any decisive answers. 'The true issue', he writes, 'is to know whether or not are maintained the actuality and immediacy of a feeling which appeals to the co-belonging to a "ground" presupposed by concept and calculation in their eluding of it' (IN: 117). In other words, Lyotard suggests here that there is a possibility that the cognitive functions of concepts and calculations imply a sensible given which is a necessary condition for their possibility, and which would be maintained in a minimal form despite the growing hegemony of the concept in the new technologies. This is a question Lyotard leaves unanswered.

More significantly, however, a close reading of this text suggests that the problematisation of aesthetic experience presented by communication technologies bears primarily on the aesthetic of the *beautiful* – the aesthetic of the *sublime*, on the other hand (in which Lyotard is in general far more interested), seems to emerge as significant precisely at the point at which new technologies make the aesthetic of the beautiful problematic. This reading is, moreover, confirmed by several other texts Lyotard wrote in the 1980s.[9] In 'Something Like: "Communication ... without Communication"', he writes: 'In singling out the sublime, Kant places the accent on something directly related to the problem of the failing of space and time. The free-floating forms which aroused the feeling of the beautiful come to be lacking' (IN: 113).

Rather than close the door to an art and aesthetics of new technologies, then, Lyotard offers a direction of thought in which the postmodern scene and the new technologies of communication in particular open onto an aesthetic of the sublime. The possibilities of this new situation are hinted at in the paper on art and communication, where he asks at one point:

> Is it the case that in this crisis, which bears on the conditions of space and time [...] – is it the case that in this work, which we take up under the aspect of communication, there is simply the loss of something (donation or presentation) without there being some gain? We are losing the earth (Husserl), which is to say the here-and-now, but are we gaining something and how are we gaining it? (IN: 116)

The more specific question relevant for our concerns here would be this: are we gaining new possibilities for art and aesthetic experience with the application of new technologies to these? A positive answer, again invoking the aesthetic of the sublime, is hinted at in the same paper when Lyotard writes that 'In Kant, passibility does not disappear with the sublime, but becomes a passibility *to lack*' (IN: 118). That is, the very absence of forms required for the feeling of the beautiful is precisely what inspires and allows the feeling of the sublime.

Lyotard's most positive suggestions regarding art and new technologies are made in the final pages of his book *Peregrinations*. Here, the crisis of space and time is presented as the very condition for an aesthetic of the sublime. Significantly, Lyotard draws a link between this crisis and the 'retreat of Being' according to Heidegger,[10] but then writes that

> in opposition to the Heideggerian idea of a decline, I would argue that this retreat takes a path that allows the artist to search for other forms by means of new technologies, if they are taken as *Technai*. I think that the question at stake in art today is whether a programmed synthesis allows the artist to invent new forms which were not possible with the immediate contact with so-called nature. [...] We must find new paths in order to approach new artistic clouds and new clouds of thoughts. (P: 42–3)

Since these new paths apparently lie along the lines of the aesthetic of the sublime, we must approach Lyotard's positive suggestions here via an examination of this second kind of aesthetic as it is presented by Kant, from whom Lyotard again takes his bearings.

If we consider some specific features of the aesthetic of the sublime, we can see that this aesthetic escapes the hesitations posed by Lyotard in relation to art and new technologies on several points. First, as Lyotard notes, the aesthetic of the sublime requires no immediate communication (IN: 113). According to Kant, such a communication, which makes the judgement that something is beautiful supposedly universal despite being subjective, is grounded in the presentation of forms by the imagination. Forms are, for Kant, the locus of what is communicable and shareable, and represent the power of the imagination to synthesise sensations. It is the function of such faculties which is shared by subjects, and which renders the feeling of the beautiful universally communicable despite being subjective.[11] The feeling of the sublime, however, 'is manifested when the presentation of free forms is lacking. It is compatible with the formless. It is even when the imagination which presents forms finds itself lacking that such a feeling appears' (138).

The relation of sublime feeling to formlessness means that this aesthetic eludes Lyotard's critique on a second point: if sublime feeling requires no formed object, then it does not require the intuitions of space and time in which to present an object. If new technologies inhibit the possibility of the sensible *presentation* of forms by passing directly to *representation*, then, this may rule out the possibility of a feeling of the beautiful, but it appears to be conducive to a feeling of the sublime.

Third, as I have already noted, sublime feeling is evoked by passibility to a *lack* of objects given in time and space. Passibility itself, the capacity to be affected, is therefore not necessarily ruled out by the lack of the synthesis of objects by the imagination. Once again, while this may rule out a feeling of the beautiful, it is an entryway to a feeling of the sublime. In sum, then, the aesthetic of the sublime seems to be possible in relation to art made with new technologies in spite of – or even because of – the factors which rule out an aesthetic of the beautiful in such a context.

There is at least one hesitation that Lyotard raises regarding art and technology, however, which nevertheless still seems to apply to an aesthetic of the sublime: the tendency of calculation to eradicate *matter*. In the essay 'After the Sublime, the State of Aesthetics' (in IN), Lyotard argues that the modern and postmodern arts have been moving resolutely away from an aesthetic of the beautiful towards an aesthetic of the sublime, and that this shift can be understood as a move away from form and towards matter. The matter of the work of art, then, is equated by Lyotard with formlessness, and this is what gives rise to sublime feeling. When the new technologies come to bear on works of art, however, the danger is that 'organic' form (free form, the result of syntheses of the imagination) is not replaced by formlessness, but by *calculated* forms, determined by concepts. The critical question then becomes whether and how it is possible for artworks involving 'programmed syntheses' to evade such forms and achieve a formlessness which might be the occasion for sublime feeling. This is a question I will take up in the conclusion to this chapter.

Lyotard argues that the tradition of avant-garde art in the twentieth century has borne witness, in sensibility, to the crisis of space and time encountered conceptually in the sciences (IN: 115; P: 42).[12] He draws a distinction between *modern* and *postmodern* art according to the extent of this crisis on which they work: in modern art, there are *only* the conditions of space and time; in postmodern art, there are *not even* the conditions of space and time (IN: 116). Lyotard sees postmodern society in terms of an ongoing process of complexification,[13] and suggests that the aesthetic of the sublime, with its 'split' between pleasure and pain, between formless sensations and Ideas of reason, is an analogous complexification in sensibility (P: 44). The reading of Lyotard I have offered here, then, points towards a direction in which art produced with the new technologies of information and communication – far from being disqualified *as* art – would be precisely the locus of the most significant postmodern, avant-garde art, which works on the crisis of sensibility and evokes sublime feelings.[14]

Art and Information

In the final section of this chapter, I wish to indicate some limitations of Lyotard's analysis of new technologies and their role in art and aesthetics, and gesture towards the lines of experimentation for the new media or digital arts which are suggested by the complex of problems and questions with which Lyotard has left us. We have seen how Lyotard links new technologies with the postmodern or inhuman condition on two points: the crisis of time and space, and the criterion of performativity. We have also seen how the aesthetic of the sublime shows the possibility of aesthetic feeling in conjunction with works of art made with new technologies despite the crisis of space and time. However, Lyotard's second point concerning new technologies persists as a problem for such arts despite the sublime: information forms a 'common measure'. As such, it performs a reduction on meaning itself, eliminating everything that cannot be converted into, and communicated as, information. In relation to the problems of art and aesthetics, this concern bears on the very possibility of aesthetic experience, which for Lyotard necessarily involves events, which cannot be quantified, codified, or in any way calculated or programmed in advance.

However – as discussed in detail in Chapter 2 – it is clear to us today that Lyotard was working with a restricted understanding of information, and of the new technologies which handle it. In fact, the nature of information is very much contested in the contemporary intellectual landscape. As Luciano Floridi writes, 'Information "can be said in many ways," just as being can (Aristotle, *Metaphysics* Γ.2) …' (Floridi 2004: 40). While a detailing of the various theories of and debates about the nature of information lies beyond the scope of this chapter, a brief survey of three distinct approaches to information will suffice to show the implications of this point for Lyotard's aesthetics. These approaches are *reductionist*, *antireductionist*, and *nonreductionist*.[15] Reductionists argue that all forms of information can be reduced to a single concept or theory of information. An example of the reductionist approach is the Unified Theory of Information, the proponents of which insist that all information can be reduced to the mathematical theory of communication (MTC) based on the work of Claude Shannon.

This theory focuses on those aspects of information which can be quantified, and which allow it to be encoded, stored, and transmitted (46). This reductionist approach would appear to be the cause of Lyotard's concern and the proper target of his polemics against information and communication in general.

However, the *antireductionist* and *nonreductionist* approaches to information also have considerable currency in contemporary debates. Antireductionists argue for the radical irreducibility of multiple types of information to any single theory, especially to MTC (Floridi 2004: 41). Nonreductionists take a path between reductionism and antireductionism, seeing information as a distributed network of concepts which are connected, but not reducible to each other or to a single theory (41). I believe it remains an open question whether Lyotard's concern for the possibility of the event in works of art made with new technologies is best served by pursuing nonreductionist or antireductionist strategies.[16] The point I wish to make here is simply that information, and the technologies which concern it, are not necessarily reductive in the way that Lyotard's restricted understanding of information theory led him to believe, insofar as they do not necessarily reduce meaning to what can be communicated according to a single, homogenous form of codification.[17]

This limitation in Lyotard's analysis opens up new possibilities and avenues of exploration for the digital or new media arts. It is Lyotard's own analyses, however, which remain valuable in indicating these new avenues of experimentation. I wish to conclude by briefly indicating two such directions. First, the state of debate regarding the nature of information indicates a role of critical experimentation which might be played by the digital arts. Lyotard himself insisted that the only responsibility the artist has is to the question 'what is art?'[18] This responsibility bears on the particular medium in which the artist works; thus the writer has a responsibility to the question 'what is literature?', the painter to the question 'what is painting?', and so on (Floridi 2004: 41; Lyotard 1982: 67). On this view, then, the digital or new media artist would have a responsibility to the question 'what is art made with new technologies?' Lyotard seeks to distinguish the responsibility of the artist, which is to question art itself and in so doing to produce unexpected aesthetic events, from the demands of culture, which seek a meaning for art in relation to social and political concerns. Nevertheless, I wish to argue, the analysis Lyotard gives of the relations between the postmodern condition, new technologies, and the aesthetic of the sublime suggests a significant avenue of engagement of the new technological arts with the needs of contemporary culture.

As we have seen, the criterion of performativity with which Lyotard is concerned is linked with a 'communicationalist' model of information, one supported by the reductionist approach to information. While models of information are very much in debate, the criterion of performativity itself is arguably prevalent in many areas of contemporary society. Moreover, it would be plausible to suggest that the reductive account of information still operates in conjunction with capitalism to promote this performativity.[19] The new media arts might critically intervene in the logic of performativity, I suggest, helping to undermine this model of information by asking the question 'what is information?' The digital arts, working in sensibility, might critically question the nature of information itself. This is arguably in fact what much new media art already does. Lyotard's aesthetics, then, both provides a philosophical justification for such experimentation in itself, and indicates its vital social significance.

Second, we saw above that a problem that remains for the possibility of sublime feeling in the digital arts is the question of whether *matter* is eliminated through calculation. One way in which experimentation in the digital arts might proceed, asking the question 'what is information?', is to interrogate the nature of matter in the context of information. This is a pertinent question, since much thinking about information construes it as virtual, or conceptual, existing independently of its contingent material supports (see Hayles 1999). As we have seen, moreover, for Lyotard the very possibility of (sublime) aesthetic feeling being aroused by art made with new technologies depends on the possibility that they contain a form of 'matter' which exceeds forms determined by calculation. Lyotard has already sketched out the direction of this development (away from form, towards matter) in the 'traditional' arts such as painting as corresponding to the avant-garde movements of minimalism and abstraction (IN: 141). These artistic movements have developed aesthetic effects which break away from the presentation of recognisable forms. Ways in which the arts can approach abstraction in the digital medium are also being explored. This was demonstrated, for example, by artworks collected in the exhibition *White Noise* at the Australian Centre for the Moving Image in 2005.[20] Works such as Ulf Langheinrich's *Waveform* and *Light* (both 2005) present abstract arrangements of light, sound, and motion with an intensity that produces an effect of sensory overload, inducing an aesthetic experience that defies form. As the title of the exhibition suggests, the matter of information – that element of difference which cannot be pinned down to discrete identities – might be interpreted in one sense as *noise*, data which are not used to transmit a signal encoded as a well-formed meaning, and typically produced in electronic devices by random variations in current or voltage. The matter of information might also be explored through the *material support* or *medium* that carries it.[21]

Lyotard's reflections on the aesthetics of the new technologies are far from conclusive. As we have seen, he offers both problematisations and hesitations regarding art and technology, and the suggestion of positive potentialities. In this chapter I have attempted to draw out these positive potentialities, arguing that art made with new technologies engages an aesthetic of the sublime which is pertinent to the sensibility of the postmodern condition, and moreover that it might act as a site of resistance to performativity by critically questioning the nature of information itself. What is at stake in the question of art and new technologies is the question of whether, and how, such technologies can give rise to events. This is the critical question around which, Lyotard's interventions suggest, an aesthetics of new technologies must revolve.

Notes

1. See 'Answering the Question: What Is Postmodernism?' in PC.
2. See Kluitenberg 2002; Gere 2006. While Gere presents a suitably nuanced reading of Lyotard's engagements with art and technology, he nevertheless states that 'Lyotard did not think art made using new technologies was capable of invoking [...] sublime feeling' (2006: 149). On the contrary, I wish to show that it is precisely technological art's capacity for invoking sublime feeling that Lyotard's thought reveals.
3. Thus, throughout this chapter the term 'new technologies' will refer specifically to these technologies.
4. *The Postmodern Condition* originated as a report on the status of knowledge in the most highly developed societies, commissioned by the president of the Conseil des Universités of the government of Quebec.
5. See Bennington 1988; Readings 1991; Williams 1998.
6. See Lyotard, 'Sublime Aesthetic of the Contract Killer' in A.
7. Organised by Robert Allezaud at the Sorbonne.
8. More precisely, all objective (outward, worldly) presentations must have a *here* and a *now*, but subjective (inward, mental) presentations need only have a *now*, as they do not occupy space, but must still occupy time.
9. In particular, 'Sublime Aesthetic of the Contract Killer' in A and *Peregrinations* (P).
10. This association is also made in 'Something Like: "Communication ... without Communication"', but without the same conclusions being drawn.

11. See Lyotard's discussion of this point in 'After the Sublime, the State of Aesthetics' in IN: 138.
12. This point is developed in Chapter 7.
13. See the discussions of the 'postmodern fable' and the 'Leibnizian hypothesis' in Chapters 1 and 2, respectively.
14. Lyotard in fact explored such possibilities in a concrete fashion through his direction of the exhibition *Les Immatériaux*. See Chapter 7.
15. On these three different approaches I follow Floridi 2004: 40–1. For further information regarding the variety of theories of information now in currency, see this article.
16. Floridi himself, mentioning Lyotard in passing, characterises him along with other French thinkers such as Derrida and Baudrillard as a kind of nonreductionist. See Floridi 2004: 41.
17. For further detail on MTC and Lyotard's critical approach to information theory, see Chapter 2.
18. On this point he follows Thierry de Duve (1996). See Lyotard's reference to de Duve in 'Answering the Question: What Is Postmodernism?' (PC: 75).
19. See the relation of capitalism to the 'monad in expansion' discussed in Chapter 2.
20. Curated by Mike Stubbs, 18 August–23 October 2005.
21. The materiality of the medium of artworks as a site of 'matter' or 'events' is explored by Lyotard in his interpretation of the conceptual art of Joseph Kosuth. See Lyotard, 'Foreword: After the Words' in MTII.

Chapter 6

Immaterial Matter: Yves Klein and the Aesthetics of the Sensible

1. 'And what should one say about Yves Klein's imprints?' (IN: 152).[1] This question is the final sentence of Lyotard's essay 'Conservation and Colour'. The essay breaks off abruptly, and the problem it poses is not one to which Lyotard returns in any detail.[2] What I propose here is to take up the question Lyotard himself does not answer: what *should* one say, not just about Klein's imprints (the Anthropometries and the Cosmogonies) but about all of Klein's works, in the context of Lyotard's aesthetic problematic? My first concern, then, is to sketch a new interpretation of Klein's work on the basis of Lyotard's aesthetic theory. This interpretation will provide an alternative to the common characterisation of Klein as a conceptual artist, as well as lead the reception of his works away from the more religious or mystical aspects of his own self-interpretations. This first concern is a matter of philosophy contributing something to our understanding and appreciation of art.

2. One of Lyotard's persistent concerns in his writings on art and aesthetics was to upset the hierarchical relationship between philosophy and art (and between art criticism and art) frequently imposed, explicitly or implicitly, by aestheticians. For Lyotard, philosophy is not to be thought of as a metadiscourse which is first, foundational, or definitive with respect to other discourses or extra-discursive practises. Philosophical aesthetics does not give art its final meaning in rigorous concepts, beyond the ken of the artist understood as a mere intuitive worker. Rather, the artist, working in the realm of the sensible, poses problems and answers questions with which philosophers and critics are also concerned.[3] Taking my lead from this line of Lyotard's thinking, my second task here is to show how Klein's work

develops and indicates solutions to problems in Lyotard's philosophy. The specific problem I wish to address is one raised by James Williams in his book *Lyotard and the Political* (2000a). Williams is critical of all Lyotard's later work (that is, his writings based around the themes of the sublime and the differend), arguing that it fails from the perspective of the Nietzschean problem of nihilism central to Lyotard's own, earlier, 'libidinal' philosophy. On Williams's reading, in these later works Lyotard appeals to the power of the Kantian aesthetic of the sublime to indicate the limits of Ideas of reason. For Lyotard, such Ideas need to be limited because they attempt to bridge the divide between pure and practical reason, a divide which Lyotard seeks to maintain because of the ethical and political stakes it holds.[4] According to Williams, in pursuing this political task Lyotard's later thought remains bound up with negativity, limitation, and privation, and fails to extend to the life-affirmative creativity advocated by the earlier works as a response to nihilism. Williams suggests that the most promising counter to nihilism in Lyotard's later works is the creative potential suggested by his reflections on matter. Most positively, Williams suggests that

> [t]he limiting function of the feeling of the sublime is balanced by a positive attraction to matter, defined as that which artists and thinkers can exploit in a creative manner in order to testify to the limits of Ideas through the sublime. The politics of Lyotard's later essays would then be about a sensitivity to matter as well as about an ironic undermining of Ideas of reason. The nihilism implied in the latter would be answered by the affirmation of matter ... (Williams 2000a: 132)

Williams concludes, however, that matter itself is conceived by Lyotard primarily in negative terms as the arrest of conceptual thought and the feeling of a privation. My second concern here is to show the way towards circumventing this conclusion and to underscore Williams's positive suggestions concerning Lyotard's later aesthetics by showing how Klein's works act as a clarification and extension of these: Klein *shows* how Lyotard's aesthetics of matter can be directed towards a creative affirmation of life. This second concern is a matter of art contributing something to our understanding and appreciation of philosophy.[5]

3. The relation between art and philosophy I wish to enact here might be expressed by way of an image borrowed from Merleau-Ponty: the chiasm. Two things touch and intertwine, overlap and encroach on

each other, but neither term is dominant.[6] The intertwining of art and philosophy I propose here is mutually productive: Lyotard provides Klein with a philosophically sophisticated situation within the field of contemporary aesthetic theory, while Klein materialises Lyotard's aesthetic philosophy in the realm of the sensible and gives it a thoroughly life-affirmative determination. Together, Lyotard and Klein direct their differing perspectives (philosophy and art) towards the mutual illumination of a common problematic: our understanding of matter and of the sensible in relation to the problem of nihilism. Both lines of approach, I will argue, outline an understanding of matter as paradoxically *im*material, and develop an aesthetics of the sensible, of a sensitivity[7] to this 'immaterial matter' which affirms life.[8]

4. As is well known, and has been discussed in previous chapters, Lyotard argues that the feeling of the sublime provides the key to understanding twentieth-century avant-garde art. For the last century, he believes, the arts have not concerned themselves with the beautiful, but with the sublime.[9] He takes this analysis of the sublime as it pertains to avant-garde art in a number of different directions, taking at different times, it sometimes seems, different sides of the debate that the feeling of the sublime itself engenders. The direction I wish to focus on here is that which explores the *matter* of the work of art. In all aesthetic feeling, judgement must take place without a determinate concept (and thus cannot be a form of knowledge), but with the feeling of the sublime judgement is also deprived of a spontaneous *form* (the imagination cannot present such a form). On this basis, Lyotard explains how sublime avant-garde art challenges the mainstream of art history. He writes that

> [i]t has been a presupposition, or even a prejudice, a ready-made attitude in Western thought at least, for 2000 years, that the process of art is to be understood as the relating of a matter and a form. As the idea of a natural fit between matter and form declines [...] the aim for the arts, especially of painting and music, can only be that of approaching matter. (IN: 138, 139)

Forms, along with concepts, are constitutive of objects: forms allow sensibility to grasp objects, while concepts make them intelligible to the understanding. According to Lyotard's reading, 'form represents the most fundamental case of what for Kant constitutes the property common to every mind: its capacity (power, faculty) to synthesise data, gather up the manifold, the *Mannigfaltigkeit* in general' (IN: 138).

Matter, on the other hand, is that which is '*par excellence* diverse, unstable, and evanescent' (IN: 138). Matter is that which both escapes determination according to calculable parameters (thus escaping the concept) and escapes formation, which Lyotard insists relies on composition according to exact divisions, graded scales, and harmonic temperaments. Sounds and colours, Lyotard writes, can be determined according to the pitch, duration, and frequency of vibrations. They can be given form in compositions which accord value to the note or the colour according to others which surround them in a harmonious fashion. However, Lyotard argues, there are aspects of sonorous and chromatic mater which escape all determination and form. In music, Lyotard emphasises timbre and nuance, those unspecifiable qualities which distinguish a note played on one instrument from the same note played on another. In moving away from the feeling of the beautiful and towards the feeling of the sublime, Lyotard argues, avant-garde art moves away from form and towards matter. In painting, this is a move towards pure colour. The following passage, written in 1870 by Charles Blanc, indicates well the radicality of this artistic and aesthetic move:

> 'The union of design [i.e. form] and colour [i.e. matter] is necessary to beget painting just as is the union of man and woman to beget mankind, but design must maintain its preponderance over colour. Otherwise painting speeds to its ruin: it will fall through colour just as mankind fell through Eve.' (Blanc, quoted in Song 1984: 61–2, quoted in Riley 1995: 6)

5. Yves Klein, I wish to suggest, is the artist of pure chromatic matter *par excellence*. Klein's intentions as a painter of pure colour are clear: he adopted the motto 'For colour, against line and drawing!' and proclaimed his ambition as follows:

> I espoused the cause of pure colour, which had been invaded by guile, occupied and oppressed in cowardly fashion by line and its manifestation: drawing in Art. I aimed to defend and deliver it, and lead it to triumph and final glory. (Klein 1974: 27)

Lyotard quotes Cézanne from one of his letters: 'Form is finished when colour reaches perfection' (IN: 141). This is the state of affairs we find in Klein's works. His earliest experiments and exhibitions show him trying to overcome the problem of form and achieve pure colour. Lyotard explains that colour is synthesised into forms in painting by according colours relative values in comparison with other colours on the same surface. This is the problem of composition, and a problem Klein did not immediately overcome. Klein's first two public exhibitions contained monochrome paintings of different colours;[10] at the second of these, Klein perceived a problem. He writes of this 1956 exhibition:

> At the Galerie Collette Allendy I exhibited some twenty monochrome surfaces, all in different colours: greens, reds, yellows, purples, blues, oranges [...] and so found myself at the start of my career in this style [...] I was trying to show colour, but I realised at the private view that the public were prisoners of a preconceived point of view and that, confronted with all these surfaces of different colours, they responded far more to the inter-relationship of the different propositions, they reconstituted the elements of a decorative polychromy. (Klein 1974: 30)

As Klein's friend and collaborator, the art critic Pierre Restany, notes, this was the time when kitchens were starting to look like Mondrians (Restany 1982: 24), and it was easy for viewers at Collette Allendy's to interpret the different chromatic surfaces as composing a decorative whole. With this, the effect of pure colour Klein was trying to achieve with each individual work was lost in subordination to an unintended, collective formal pattern.

Klein solved this problem with his next exhibition, which marked the advent of his self-proclaimed Blue Period. 'Yves Klein, Monochrome Propositions, Blue Period' at the Galleria Apollinaire, Milan, 1957, consisted of identically proportioned and coloured monochromes. The works were painted in International Klein Blue (IKB), a formula Klein developed with the aid of a chemist, which suspends pure ultramarine pigment in a fixative without the dulling effect that fixatives usually produce.[11] The exclusive focus on one colour allowed viewers to concentrate on the colour itself, overcoming the problem of composition, and hence of form. This movement away from form is accentuated by the fact that Klein's monochromes remain unframed and often have slightly rounded corners, removing sharp edges and allowing colour to spill out into space.

6. By focusing on a single colour, IKB, Klein was able to overcome the mind's tendency to compare colours and thus ascribe a form. In moving beyond form, Klein's blue monochromes allow the viewer to become sensitive to what Lyotard calls matter, the barely perceptible differences in qualities such as nuance and timbre. Klein's monochromes exhibit these material differences in at least two

ways that Lyotard defines as constitutive of matter: in *grain* or *texture*, and in the *variable shadings* of colour itself under different lighting conditions. One of the most notable things about most of Klein's monochromes is that, while often of the same colour and dimensions, their surface texture varies: Klein often applied the paint roughly with sponges or rollers, calling our attention to the concrete materiality of the work, and the subtle material differences between works. Klein creates an almost synaesthetic experience with his monochromes; in viewing them one touches through vision, and feels bodily transported into blue depths. This highlighting of grain or texture is most evident in one of Klein's most original innovations, the 'sponge relief' (Rosenthal 1995: 96), in which Klein attached sponges saturated in IKB directly to the surface of the painting.

Second, as Lyotard tells us, colour is indeterminate because it always looks different under different lighting conditions. Matter is that which *differs* and *defers*, and colour is pure difference without identity because no particular lighting condition can be said to reveal colour in its 'original', 'final', or 'pure' state. As Lyotard tells us, it cannot be demonstrated that a particular way of lighting a painting renders it more beautiful or more 'present' than another (IN: 151). Although International Klein Blue can be made to an exact formula, it appears differently under different lighting conditions, and none can be said to provide it with an absolute identity. This is clearly evident from the different shades of blue that appear in the reproductions of Klein's works, which reflect not only different grades of ink, or chemical variations in photographic processes, but the different lighting conditions under which the photographs of the same works were taken.

7. For both Lyotard and Klein, matter is an *immediate sensory apprehension* which defies concepts and Ideas, and which brings the mind to a shuddering halt. Matter turns the organism away from the conceptual and towards the sensible. Klein explains this immediacy of the sensible in recounting a key moment of insight in his development as a painter: 'A whole phenomenology then appeared, but a phenomenology without ideas, or rather without any of the systems of official conventions. What appeared was distinct from form and became Immediacy. "The mark of the immediate" – that was what I needed' (Klein 1974: 53).

For Lyotard, the aim of painting is to render immediate presence as that which disarms the mind (IN: 151). This immediate presence is the formless, indeterminate, and unconceptualisable 'something' with which one is confronted in the aesthetic feeling of the sublime. Lyotard further explains:

> I use 'matter' to designate this *'that there is,'* this *quod*, because this presence in the absence of the active mind is and is never other than timbre, tone, nuance in one or other of the dispositions of sensibility, in one or other of the *sensoria*, in one or other of the possibilities through which mind is accessible to the material event, can be touched by it: a singular, incomparable quality – unforgettable and immediately forgotten – of the grain of a skin or a piece of wood, the fragrance of an aroma, the savour of a secretion or a piece of flesh, as well as a timbre or a nuance. (IN: 141)

According to Lyotard, sensitivity to matter only becomes possible with the crippling and disaster of conceptual thought.

Klein is frequently characterised as a forerunner of conceptual art; art in which the concept or idea takes precedence over the material instantiation of the work and its sensible qualities. It is perhaps thought that Klein's works have little attraction or make little sense without the ideas he used to justify them, and that these ideas must be the focus of artistic appreciation. If we follow the line of interpretation offered by Lyotard's aesthetic theory, however, Klein appears not at all as a conceptual artist, but as an artist *opposed* to the concept. Klein's works evoke a sensitivity to *matter*, to the aesthetic qualities of the works, which defies conceptual organisation and which can only be effectively felt when the habit of interpreting our sensations via concepts is interrupted.

8. Because matter is indeterminate, unconceptualisable, and formless, Lyotard suggests that it is really, in a sense, *immaterial*. That is, '[i]mmaterial if it is envisaged under the regime of receptivity or intelligence' (IN: 140). This argument is filled out with reference to the 'modern' conception of matter that has been handed down to us from René Descartes, according to which it is understood on the model of the *object*, which stands before and is manipulable by an immaterial subject. In the essay 'Matter and Time' (in IN), Lyotard calls our attention to the obsolescence of the Cartesian notion of matter by comparing it with the image of matter which emerges from more recent developments in physics. Descartes defines matter as extended substance, and distinguishes it from *sensory* qualities, such as weight, hardness, and colour – which he believes are 'mere appearances', and from which the existence of matter is independent. For Descartes, matter is infinitely divisible and contains no smallest

parts (atoms). Moreover – and this point will be pertinent to our consideration of Klein in a moment – for Descartes *matter contains no void* – it is substance through and through. Finally, as Lyotard notes, 'Cartesian matter is a concept – extension – which is perfectly transparent to geometrico-algebraic thought' (IN: 37). That is, it is thoroughly determinable in conceptual terms.[12]

9. Developments in physics since Descartes' time, however, have given us a very different picture of matter. Physicists have discovered atoms, and the fact that atoms are almost entirely empty. Matter, it now appears, is almost entirely void. Around a tiny nucleus of protons and neutrons, electrons orbit, and what we think of as matter in fact consists largely of interactions between electrons. Lyotard quotes the Nobel laureate physicist Jean Perrin: 'all matter is in the end a particular and very condensed form of energy' (IN: 43). Lyotard's suggestion in 'Matter and Time' is that what was once thought of as solid, substantive matter is now coming to be understood in terms of vibrations – a line of thought, we might add, which has been compounded and complexified by the more recent development of string theory, which suggests that particles should be understood as vibrations rather than as points. In the wake of such contemporary developments in physics, Lyotard suggests, the Cartesian dualist picture of the world as divided between matter on the one hand and soul or mind on the other is no longer tenable – instead, we have an 'immaterialist materialism': matter is energy and mind is contained vibration.

10. Klein's meditations on matter also move decisively towards the immaterial in 1958 with the advent of his 'Pneumatic Period'. On 28 April, 3,000 guests attended the Galerie Iris Clert in Paris to view Klein's latest exhibition, only to find an empty room with bare white walls. This famous exhibition, popularly known as 'The Void', in fact had a very precise title: 'The Specialisation of Sensibility in the Prime State of Matter as Stabilised Pictorial Sensibility'. Klein's exhibition was no mere joke or showmanship (although some viewers and critics have been tempted to interpret it this way), but an exhibition of what he conceived to be matter in its prime state. That is, an *im*material state. According to Klein, matter is energy diffused in space, and pictorial, sensible works of art are relative stabilisations of this energy. Monochromes are stabilisations of energy in the colour spectrum. The Void is also a stabilisation of energy to which one might be or become sensitive, but a more refined one – energy is stabilised only by a certain amount of air pressure (hence Klein's naming of his 'Pneumatic Period').

Klein speaks of the Void as the immaterialisation of Blue:

> I had left the visible, physical blue at the door, outside, in the street. The real blue was inside, the blue of the profundity of space, the blue of my kingdom, of our kingdom! [...] the immaterialisation of blue, the coloured space that cannot be seen but which we impregnate ourselves with [...] A space of blue sensibility within the frame of the white walls of the gallery. (Klein 1974: 41)

The relationship between the colour Blue and the Void, in Klein's art and thought, is well expressed in a phrase of Gaston Bachelard's that he was fond of quoting: 'First there is nothing, then there is a deep nothingness, then there is a blue depth' (quoted in Charlet 2000: 88). For Klein, in radical opposition to Descartes, and in closer proximity to contemporary physics, matter is ultimately Void. Moreover, for Klein, the nothingness of the Void should not be understood in a negative sense, but positively, as a pure plenitude, from out of which life and matter appear. While the monochromes call us to matter, to the barely perceptible differences pure colour offers, the Void appeals to an even more refined state of sensibility. As Nicolas Charlet notes, what Klein displays in the Void cannot be seen by the naked eye and 'our perception of it depends on our sensibility' (Charlet 2000: 91). Klein estimated that about 30 per cent of the visitors to Iris Clert's were impregnated by the sensibility of the Void. Considered as matter in its prime state, the nothingness of the Void is that which is ultimately non-objective, formless, beyond conceptual determination, absolute difference and deferral, the finest grain or lightest feather touch to which we might become sensitive.

Further extending his experiment with the immaterial, Klein created and sold Zones of Immaterial Pictorial Sensibility. These 'zones', which had no material manifestation whatsoever, could be transferred from Klein to a buyer by means of a ritual in which a sum of gold was exchanged for a zone, and then the zone of sensibility 'impregnated' the buyer when half the gold was thrown into a body of water and the receipt was burnt. Klein transferred a number of Zones of Immaterial Pictorial Sensibility in this way, often throwing the gold into the Seine.

11. As young men, Klein and his friends Claude Pascal and Armand Fernandez experimented with fasting, and meditated on a rooftop at night, staring at the moon (Stich 1994: 18). Klein read Max Heindel's work on Rosicrucian cosmology (1947) and was a member of the esoteric Christian order the Knights of St Sebastian. He

dreamed of the return to a state of nature in a technical Eden, where machines buried beneath the ground would control the climate of the Earth and nymphs would frolic naked. He made plans and conducted experiments for an 'Architecture of Air' which would realise this dream – privacy and individuality would disappear in a world where walls and roofs would be made of compressed air and fire, and eventually Mankind would be liberated from the earth in levitation and flight.[13]

Much of Klein's yearning for the immaterial thus appears to be bound up with a mystical longing for transcendence from earthly conditions in a spiritual, utopian future. This yearning is expressed by Kandinsky in a way which uncannily seems to speak for Klein: 'The deeper the blue the more powerfully it draws man towards infinity and awakens in him the nostalgia for Purity and for the ultimate suprasensible [realm]' (quoted in Charlet 2000: 85).

In the light of Nietzsche's analysis of nihilism, a powerful influence on Lyotard, these themes appear oppressive and offensive to the very affirmation of life which was so often Klein's goal and motivation. For Nietzsche, the longing for a transcendent realm devalues life in the immanent world of the here-and-now, by setting up an ideal of which the here-and-now falls short.[14] As Kandinsky indicates, this longing for transcendence is often a nostalgic one; it is the feeling that we once existed in a pure state which might be regained. The utopian impulse which Klein exhibits may be seen as the projected regaining of this state of purity in a future world. Having drawn out some resonances between Lyotard's and Klein's reflections on immaterial matter, I now wish to suggest a way in which a Lyotardian reading of Klein's work might act as a corrective to his nostalgic and utopian nihilism.

12. While Lyotard and Klein both develop the paradoxical notion of immaterial matter, the difference in their perspectives is this: Klein emphasises the *immateriality* of mater, while Lyotard emphasises the *materiality* of the immaterial. For Lyotard, the immateriality of matter is nothing other than the fact that matter is anobjective; it is without concept and without form, and thus is not an 'object' (at least insofar as objects are determined in Kant's metaphysics of experience). With this notion of the immaterial, Lyotard gestures towards the nature of sensibility at its limits; immaterial matter is that which we may sense only if we become sensitive enough; sufficiently refined. He underscores the materiality of this idea of sensation at its limits in his following interpretation of Kant's use of the term 'soul' in the *Critique of Judgement*:

> As opposed to forms, and still more figures, colour appears to be withdrawn, at least through its 'effect,' through its potential for affecting feeling, from the circumstances of context, conjecture, and in general, from any plot [...] It is this undoing of the capacity for plot that I should like to call soul. Far from being mystical, it is, rather, material. It gives rise to an aesthetic 'before' forms. An aesthetic of material presence which is imponderable. (IN: 150)

Lyotard, in offering this interpretation of 'immaterial matter', provides the key to situating Klein's works in a thoroughly materialist framework. This situation enables a move in the reception of his work away from those aspects of his own self-interpretation which are seemingly in contradiction with a secular worldview, and thus unpalatable to some, and which also appear philosophically problematic for those who are schooled in the Nietzschean tradition.

13. On the other hand, Klein's optimism, expressed through the direct affective force of his works as well as through his ideas, may work as a corrective to the emphasis on melancholy in the later Lyotard's works. As I mentioned at the outset, James Williams criticises the later Lyotard for focusing on the negativity and privation of the feeling of the sublime in the face of matter: feelings of attraction and repulsion, pleasure and pain cancel each other out, and the interruption of thought leads to a minimal passivity, rather than awakening new creative possibilities. Williams quotes, for example, from Lyotard's essay 'Anima Minima', where the aesthetic experience is portrayed as a kind of paralysis:

> The soul comes into its existence dependent on the sensible, thus violated, humiliated [...] Even while the event brings the soul to life, casts it into the living heart of pain and/or pleasure, no matter how carried away it might be, the soul remains caught between the terror of its impending death and the horror of its servile existence. (PF 243–4, quoted in Williams 2000a: 133)

According to Williams, this construal of the aesthetic experience of matter instils the very nihilism which Lyotard is concerned to subvert.

As Williams indicates, if Lyotard does have a response to nihilism in his later writings, this response centres round the feeling of the sublime and a sensitivity to matter. For Lyotard, nihilism is the devaluation of the sensuous and perceptual, by subsumption to representational structures of thought. In Lyotard's work on immaterial matter, responding to nihilism means underscoring the failure of intelligible representations – 'knowledge', in Kant's terms – implied by the feeling of the sublime. Lyotard's work on Kant thus shows how, in the feeling of the sublime, the sensuous and perceptible are liberated from their subordination to, and devaluation by, the demands of knowledge.

For Kant, knowledge is only possible when a concept may be matched with a sensory form or object, and the constitution of this object depends upon sensations being subject to three syntheses: the synthesis of apprehension in intuition, the synthesis of reproduction in the imagination, and the synthesis of recognition in the concept. The first synthesis is a mere gathering together and apprehension of the manifold of various *sensoria*, of colours, textures, and odours. The second synthesis, that of reproduction in the imagination, imposes on this apprehension an identity through repetition. The imagination reproduces the immediate instant apprehended in the first synthesis. The third synthesis makes knowledge possible by subsuming the formed object under a category of the understanding (causality, purposiveness, reciprocal relationship, etc.). Kant calls these preconceptual syntheses which prepare for knowledge the 'schema'.[15] Lyotard's response to nihilism, in these Kantian terms, is to direct us back to the sensible in its barest apprehension, to the initial syntheses before an object is formed, and, even more radically and potentially problematically, to pure sensation before any synthesis has taken place. Away from the concept, towards the sublime and matter. This direction reconnects us with the *feeling* for life that nihilism devalues, and opens up a more nuanced field of differences, enabling the possibility of richer forms of life.

While Lyotard gives us this formal argument, it is perhaps worthless as a counter to nihilism without the 'evidence' of direct aesthetic feeling – that is, of the capacity of formless matter in works of art to make us feel a heightened sense of vitality. Klein's works, I submit, convey just such an affirmation of life, if one is able to be sensitive to it. Moreover, Klein's notion of the Void as pure plenitude which gives rise to matter and creates forms acts as a corrective to Lyotard's emphasis on privation. If we are able to become sensitive to the smallest differences, which from the perspective of conceptual thought appear to be nothing at all, then in Klein's terms we may be 'impregnated' with sensibility – imbued with a heightened sense of life which drives us to creativity. Despite his own frequent emphasis on privation, Lyotard also indicates the creative potentials of the encounter with immaterial matter in the following passage, where he again takes up the notion of 'soul' in Kant's third *Critique* as the suspension of thought:

It is this suspension that I should like to call soul: when the mind breaks into shards (letting go) under the 'effect' of a colour (but is it an effect?). And then one writes twenty or one hundred pages to pick up the pieces, and one puts together the plot again. (IN: 151)

14. What Lyotard's and Klein's works teach us in their different ways is how to become sensitive to the barely perceptible. What they teach us about sensibility in their insistence on the immateriality of matter is that it is possible to become sensitive to those things we often believe are really 'nothing', because we have forgotten how to feel. As both Lyotard and Klein show, our habit of interpreting the world through conceptual structures is one of the primary means of desensitisation. It is arguably such sensitivity to small differences, however, which gives life its vitality. Lyotard and Klein, if each is allowed to act as a corrective to the other, provide a philosophical aesthetics and an art which help us to shrug off the desensitising effects of our habitual reception of the world through recognisable concepts and objects, and access a level of sensation which heightens the feeling of life. In calling us to an appreciation of the paradoxical notion of immaterial matter, both thus offer a contribution to the resistance to contemporary nihilism.

> Long Live the Immaterial
> And now,
> Thank you for your kind attention.
> > Yves Klein, *The Chelsea Hotel Manifesto*

Notes

1. This chapter is dedicated to Anna Szörényi, who has helped me to appreciate Klein's work in ways both material and immaterial.
2. There are occasional mentions of Klein in Lyotard's aesthetic writings, but never any extended reflections. Notably, documentation for Klein's 'Zones of Immaterial Pictorial Sensibility' was included in *Les Immatériaux*, and it is perhaps also notable that Pierre Restany, a critic who was Klein's most important promoter, wrote a review of the exhibition (Restany 1985).
3. For a good indication of how Lyotard reads artists as contributing to reflection on philosophical problems, see 'The Sublime Aesthetic of the Contract Killer' in A. The philosophical issues at stake here are discussed in Chapter 4.
4. See Chapter 4 for discussion of the reading of Kant underlying Lyotard's later political and ethical thought.

5. As such, the argument of this chapter can be considered as an extension of the argument mounted in Chapter 4, where it was treated in general philosophical terms. This chapter supplements that argument with a particular case example from the arts.

6. See 'The Intertwining – The Chiasm' in Merleau-Ponty 1968.

7. The French term *sensibilité* may be translated as either 'sensibility' or 'sensitivity', terms which have close but differing meanings in English. Klein's frequent use of this term has been translated in both ways. As I am concerned with these terms here, sensibility designates the capacity to receive sensations, while sensitivity indicates a particularly heightened or refined form of this capacity. Rather than consistently render *sensibilité* as either sensibility or sensitivity, I shall alternate between these terms in order to better express the full range of meanings that Lyotard's and Klein's works suggest.

8. While an 'aesthetics of the sensible' may seem like a pleonasm, since 'aesthetic' may be thought to already imply the sensible, in both philosophy and art a separation between them has been introduced (precisely, for example, with the interpretation of Klein as a conceptual artist). The aesthetic of the sensible proposed here thus reaffirms a primacy of sensation in our relation to art.

9. See for example the essay 'The Sublime and the Avant-Garde' in IN. It should however be noted that Lyotard's emphasis on the importance of the sublime in contemporary art is attenuated somewhat in later writings, where he gives greater due to the aesthetic of the beautiful, and to the difficulty of distinguishing between the two aesthetics. See KA.

10. These exhibitions were 'Yves Peintures' (monochromes) at the Club des Solitaires, Paris, October 1955, and 'Yves: Propositions Monochromes', at the Galerie Collette Allendy, Paris, February 1956. Representative works from this period of Klein's career include Monochrome M6 (orange), Monochrome M78 (black), Monochrome M27 (red), and Monochrome M35 (green).

11. In addition to blue pigment, IKB consisted of polymerised vinyl acetate (an industrial transparent binder), alcohol and ethyl acetate (solvents). See Rosenthal 1995: 94.

12. Descartes' views on matter may be found in Part II of his *Principles of Philosophy* ([1644] 1983: 39–77).

13. Klein's utopian dreams are expressed in some of his Anthropometries, such as ANT 96 (*People Begin to Fly*) and ANT 102 (*Architecture of Air*).

14. See for example Nietzsche 1968: §12, 12–14.

15. This brief presentation of Kant follows Lyotard's in *Peregrinations* (P: 32–3). For Kant's own presentation of these ideas, see the 'The Deduction of the Pure Concepts of the Understanding, Section 2: The *a priori* Grounds of the Possibility of Experience' (A edition) (Kant 1929: 129–40).

Chapter 7

Inhuman Arts: From Cubism to New Media

Above all, artists are men who wish to become inhuman. They seek painfully the traces of inhumanity, traces which are never found in nature. These are the real truths, and beyond them, we know no reality.

Guillaume Apollinaire 2012: 11

Contrary to what has been said about them, the avant-garde of the late 19th and early 20th century – Cubism, Futurism, Suprematism, 'De Stijl', etc. – knew that in every great work there exists this relationship with something inhuman in us.

Lyotard 2006

The artwork breaks with convention, with the commonplace, with the flow. It is obtained through a conscious and conscientious labour that relentlessly endeavours to lay bare the ego. Through art the human bends its will to strive toward this inhuman that sometimes forces it wide open.

Lyotard SR: 50

Technical, animal

As outlined in the introduction to this book, Lyotard indicates that there are two meanings to the inhuman: first, the way that the term is used to indicate 'nihilism', the devaluation of our existence by contemporary social, cultural, and technological developments, and second, a meaning of the inhuman which, in one of its most significant forms, issues from the arts, and which indicates a mode of resistance to the first kind of inhuman (IN: 1–7). I am interested here particularly in this second kind of inhuman: in what sense could art be called inhuman? What kinds of arts might be said to be inhuman? And how can such arts act as a response or resistance to the first kind of inhuman, nihilism? The 'inhuman arts' of the title of this chapter should thus be understood in a double sense, and this double sense refers to both 'inhuman' and to 'arts'. First, the inhuman should be understood in both senses of the term Lyotard gave it – as both the dehumanisation effected by our contemporary capitalist and technoscientific system of 'development', and in that sense as a vector of nihilism in its most pejorative sense. On the other hand, it should also be understood as a vector of creativity and of resistance to the first form of the inhuman; the inhuman in the sense in which Apollinaire said that artists seek to become inhuman. Second, 'arts' should be understood in the ambiguous sense of *technē*, as both art and technology (as Heidegger (1977) reminded us in the twentieth century). Keeping these multiple senses in mind, then, this chapter aims to unfold the role of the inhumanising powers of art as a site and mode of resistance to the forces of dehumanisation.

Furthermore, there are two modalities of these inhuman arts evident in Lyotard's work that I wish to explore. His early work on art (around *Discourse, Figure* and *Libidinal Economy*), drawing on Freud and Nietzsche, engaging with Sade, Bataille, and Klossowski, and appealing to libidinal energetics, seems to evoke the animal, the bestial and the 'subhuman' qualities in the human: the unconscious, bodily, physical, affective, irrational remainders of the processes of humanisation and socialisation. To the extent that Freud's revolution may be understood to consist in the undermining of human narcissism by revealing our continuity with the animal kingdom, Lyotard finds a complicity between art as the inscription of the sensible and every other term which has been devalued against the supposed superiority of the intelligible, that is, the *rationality* in the human which had previously been thought to transcend and set us apart from the animal. Art in this sense expresses and inscribes the traces of the inhuman as *the animal* in man. Against reason, the passions: lust, desire, madness, humour, folly. Against a transcendent conception of mind or spirit, the body and materiality. Resistance to nihilism as the assertion of the sensible against the hegemony of the intelligible.

Following a tendency in French philosophy of technology evident at least since Leroi-Gorhan ([1964–5] 1993), Lyotard sees the 'new technologies' of information, communication, and calculation as an *exteriorisation* of mind: following and extending Heidegger, technologies of this kind appear to be the crystallisation of metaphysics, as the rational, subjective determination and control of beings. Hence an association of these technologies with nihilism; with what art ought to *resist*. Yet Lyotard's trajectory of thinking both nihilism and the arts underwent a significant change, and there is an analogous change in these dimensions of his thought attendant to the more well-known (and more obvious) shift between the libidinal philosophy and the philosophy of the differend. As is particularly evident from *The Postmodern Condition* and many of the essays collected in *The Inhuman*, Lyotard's interests turned from the late 1970s and throughout the 1980s to information technologies ('computerisation') and their social and cultural effects. Philosophically, there is a parallel development of interest in the more 'rational' method of the formal analysis of language. And in the domain of the arts, interest in more reasoned, less 'affective' approaches becomes evident at least since the essays on Duchamp he began writing in 1974 (collected in DT).

This interest blossoms in the early 1980s with commentaries which largely analyse artistic effects created through manipulations of formal rules.[1] This development also sees a positive valuation of the arts of mechanical reproduction. Reflecting on Walter Benjamin's famous paper, and his thesis of the decline of experience, Lyotard writes:

> What would he have to say today about the works of music, photography, film, and video, but also painting or dance, theatre, and literature, that explicitly take the useable information unit in the relevant sensorial field as their experimentational material, striving to construct syntaxes as scarcely 'human' as possible!
> I see no decline in this at all ... (MTI: 171)

Lyotard's interest in the confluence of art, rationality, and new technologies reached a remarkable apex in his leading involvement with the exhibition *Les Immatériaux* in 1985. The inhuman character of art appears here in a way diametrically opposed to that in the earlier work: the inhuman is no longer primarily the *animal* remainder in the human, but the *machine*, the exteriorisation of the rational, thinking aspects of the human, divorced from feeling and desire. It is much to Lyotard's credit, and to our great interest, that he was able to recognise that in these *technical* inhuman processes there is as much of interest for the arts as there is in the *animal* inhuman. Yet in Lyotard's last reflections on nihilism and the arts, in the 1990s, he seems to turn once again, back to the 'animal' inhuman, recognising it now – like the technological inhuman – as both source of, and resistance to, nihilism; as both 'good' and 'bad' inhuman. It is these varying modalities of the inhuman arts in Lyotard's work I wish to explore here, in order to uncover a deeper reflection on nihilism and its resistance which persists across a deceptively changing terrain.

Immaterials

Lyotard was the principal director of the exhibition *Les Immatériaux* ('The Immaterials'), held at the Centre Georges Pompidou, 28 March–25 July 1985.

Les Immatériaux is increasingly becoming recognised as a historically significant 'landmark exhibition', not least because it was one of the first major exhibitions of new media arts.[2] It was co-curated with Thierry Chaput and developed under the management of the Centre de Création Industrielle. The exhibition was a major cultural event in France; it took two years of preparation, involved fifty organisers, and was the most expensive exhibition held at the Pompidou Centre to that date. It collected a wide array of 'new materials', including artefacts developed with new technologies, artworks made with such technologies, and the new technologies themselves. It included robots, computers, artificial skin, the world's first showing of a holographic movie, a photocopier, video, film, slides, photographs, a machine that measures the rate of plant growth, a computer that generates poems, and a Japanese sleeping cell, among other things. It put on display the sciences that made new technologies and materials possible: rugosymmetric reproduction, electromicroscopy, spectography, holography, Doppler effects, Fourier series, astrophysics, genetics, and statistics (Rajchman 1991: 105).

These displays were organised according to thirty-one 'zones', some subdivided to give a total of sixty-one 'sites'. Visitors to the exhibition wandered freely between sites, equipped with radio-controlled headphones broadcasting 'commentary' for each zone (often musical passages, or quotations from avant-garde writers and theorists). The exhibition was further organised, in a conceptual fashion, according to a fivefold structure with two levels. First, the exhibition organisers distinguished five terms deriving from the Sanskrit root *mât* (to make by hand, to measure, to build): material, materiel, maternity, matter, matrix. These terms were then related to the 'operational structure' of communication using a model derived from information and communication theory:

- the *material* is the *support* of the message;
- the *materiel* or hardware is what handles the *acquisition*, *transfer* and *collection* of the message;
- *maternity* designates the function of the *sender* of the message;
- the *matter* of the message is its *referent* (what it is about …);
- the *matrix* is the *code* of the message. (Adapted from Lyotard 1985a: 50)[3]

Each of the sites, which explored various aspects of these particular concepts, was given a specific theme that the displays were meant to illustrate or interrogate.

Les Immatériaux involved much supporting material explaining the intentions and themes of the exhibition, including a two-volume catalogue (I1; I2), several books and special journal issues, and various written statements and interviews. Lyotard explains in one interview that what they were trying to evoke was a certain 'postmodern sensibility' concerning the uncertainty and anxiety that the saturation of our world by new technologies evokes (Lyotard 1985b). Such technologies, he contends, evoke uncertainty because they undermine the distinction we have made, at least since Descartes, between subject and object. As such, they question the place of 'Man', as subject in a position of mastery over objects, in the world. Lyotard explains:

> It seems to me that these technologies are interesting, and at the same time troubling, to the extent that they force us to reconsider the position of the human being in relation to the universe, in relationship to himself, in relationship to his traditional purposes, his recognised abilities, his identity. (Lyotard 1985b)

He argues that the relation of the subject to the object, which has been conceived since Descartes as one of domination and control, is subverted by the fact that this attempt to control has been turned back on the subject, constructing the subject as simply another object. This has taken place through the development of neuroscience, as well as the objectification of the functions of the mind (consciousness, the subject) in computer technologies. Lyotard notes:

> The human cortex is 'read' just like an electronic field; through the neurovegative system human affectivity is 'acted' on like a complex chemical organization composed of information transmitted by media and according to diverse codes connected by interfaces where 'translations' take place. (Lyotard 1985a: 49)

By turning the human mind, the supposed seat of subjectivity, into a brain which can be objectively examined, contemporary technoscience undermines the human as essentially subject.[4]

Parahyletisms

Lyotard further contends that the notion of matter or material as object is 'immaterialised' by the new sciences and technologies, which reveal that apparently solid objects are, on a more fundamental level, relations of energy. Moreover, our very relation to objects becomes mediated by technoscience, which represents a reality to us which cannot be perceptually experienced. In a programmatic statement for the exhibition, he explains:

> It is as if a filter has been placed between us and the things, a screen of numbers. [...] A colour, a sound, a substance, a pain, or a star return to us as digits in schemes of utmost precision. With the encoding and decoding-systems we learn that there are realities that are in a new way intangible. The good old matter itself comes to us in the end as something which has been dissolved and reconstructed into complex formulas. Reality consists of elements, organised by structural rules (matrixes) in no longer human measures of space and time. (Lyotard 1985a: 49)

One of the central themes of the exhibition was the way in which matter dissolves not only in quantifiable measurement, but in language and systems of signs in general. The object of perception is 'immaterialised' or 'derealised' through its codification in technologies of information and communication. The intention of the exhibition was to focus awareness on the crisis of perception, of time and space (discussed in Chapters 4 and 5), and to explore this crisis in an artistic, rather than theoretical, manner. It asked, what does 'here' mean, what does 'now' mean? As such, the theme of this exhibition bears directly on the way in which new technologies might open up an aesthetic of the sublime, since such an aesthetic involves a passibility to the lack of the presentation of an object felt when the conditions of space and time are in crisis. The exhibition thus dramatised, *in sensibility*, the same questions dramatised theoretically in many of Lyotard's writings of the period.[5]

Despite this 'immaterialisation' in relation to the modern philosophical conception of mater as object, it is important to emphasise that Lyotard's 'immaterials' are in fact *material*; they are *states of matter*. What he intended with the term 'immaterials' is perhaps better expressed by a term he employs in his later book on Karel Appel: *parahyletisms*, or paradoxes of matter. In this context he introduces the term to indicate the way that matter can affect us, can cause us to feel something, and that this aspect of matter seems irreducible to how matter (as passive substance impressed with form) has typically been understood by the philosophical tradition. He writes that '[i]n the contemporary techno-sciences, we come across what Duchamp, in the manner of Leonardo, had likewise anticipated, namely the parahyletisms, the paradoxes of matter' (KA: 195). In the same place, this paradox of matter is named its *immaterial* quality, which means that matter is 'not presentable in itself' (69). For Lyotard, the experiments artists make with and in matter rely on a paradox, or perhaps a series of paradoxes, regarding how matter is sensed and understood, and aesthetic sensibility requires a 'passibility' to such paradox. In short, this paradox is that something is presented to sensation, but what is presented defies the typical categories through which matter is understood as object: it calls into question time and space, and induces feeling. Yet while the dominant sensations or feelings associated with the reception of parahyletisms may seem 'immaterial', they would not exist without the presentation of some matter, something to be sensed. The immaterials with which Lyotard is concerned, then, must be understood not in the sense of an idealised dematerialisation of the world, as the dreams of techno-spiritualists would have it. Rather, immaterials are states of matter which are paradoxical, which unsettle us in their presentation, drawing attention to the tensions which traverse our understanding and reception of matter, in both concept and sensibility. This includes, then, the new properties conferred on matter by both technoscience and artistic experimentation.

Space–time lost

Insofar as the technosciences are concerned, the immaterials are 'new materials', such as Kevlar and artificial skin, as well as physically instantiated information-processing devices (computers). They are 'immaterial' to the extent that they overturn *a certain conception* of matter – as brute substance, as infinitely divisible and containing no void – which has been philosophically prevalent since Descartes.[6] Moreover, in troubling the direct correspondence of our reason and intuition, they trouble our conception of matter as consisting solely in stable objects presented for our sensibility here and now, in a fixed time and space which corresponds to the body's lived experience. And finally, as we have seen above, the immaterials of technoscience introduce a paradoxical state of matter because of the way they overturn the modern subject–object hierarchy, objectifying the subject by materialising thought, and subjectifying objects by making them capable of calculation and control. Yet the immaterials are material nonetheless, and would be nothing without their material dimension. As always, Lyotard is concerned to draw attention back to the ineradicable remainder of materiality – of sensible presence – which remains, even at the limits of what appears to be a 'dematerialisation'. A first meaning of the inhuman arts, then, is those arts which explore the paradoxes of matter by experimenting with new materials – the arts of the so-called 'new media'.

Yet arts made with new media were not the only ones on display at *Les Immatériaux*. Alongside the latest technologies and arts deploying them were painted canvases, writings of the literary avant-garde, and architectural designs, representative of abstract, minimal, and conceptual artistic modernisms. Artists, writers, and architects collected included Marcel Duchamp, Yves Klein, Giovanni Anselmo, Thierry Kuntzel, Kasimir Malevitch, Samuel Beckett, Antonin Artaud, Marcel Proust, Maurice Blanchot, Henri Michaux, Octavio Paz, Emile Zola, Stéphane Mallarmé, Heinrich von Kleist, Joseph Kosuth, Georges Seurat, Giacomo Balla, Robert and Sonia Delaunay, Larry Bell, Dan Graham, Jorge Luis Borges, Piero Manzoni, Peter Eisenman, François Rabelais, Lewis Carroll, Andy Warhol, Raoul Hausmann, Frank Lloyd Wright, and Jacques Monory, to name some of the more well known.

At least one critic was puzzled by this inclusion of modern art, writing that '[t]he artistically primed viewer [...] could only wonder why so much '60s conceptual art was trotted out, except to illustrate the moribund notion of art's dematerialisation' (Linker 1985: 105).

Yet there was far more to it than this, as the link noted above between technosciences and the arts around the concept of para-hyletisms has already indicated. At one point Lyotard makes this link explicit in the following way: 'The avant-gardes, contemporaries of the crisis of physical and mathematical reason, anticipated the failure of [...] humanism' (MTI: 237). For him, the crisis of time and space opened by the sciences' own discovery of their lack of foundation, and by technological developments alike, had already begun to be explored by the avant-gardes in their experiments with sensibility as such.

This link between the arts and technosciences is developed most extensively in Lyotard's article 'Argumentation and Presentation: The Foundation Crisis', where he writes:

We ought also to analyse in detail how the withdrawal of the presentation of forms opens up the space for artistic inquiry that modern and contemporary art has traversed in every direction through its avant-gardes: abstract, conceptual and minimal art; happenings; installations—all of them investigations of lost space–time and, as such, to be seen as paralleling the crisis of scientific 'rationality'. (Lyotard 2013: 139)

Thus we can see that what was on display at *Les Immatériaux* was the staging of a parallel between questions of materiality and immateriality explored by artists – such as Yves Klein in his 'Zones of Immaterial Pictorial Sensibility', for example – and those same questions as raised by the new materials developed by technoscience. Of relevance here are Lyotard's invocations of some key references to the inhuman in art history and theory, particularly Apollinaire: 'More than anything, artists are men who want to become inhuman'; and Adorno: 'Art remains loyal to humankind uniquely through its inhumanity in regard to it' (quoted in IN: 2). The inhuman in art is the capacity to open ourselves to what exceeds our habitual, 'human' interpretations and perspectives; 'aesthetic facts' about time, space, and matter are analogous to the objective facts science discovers, indifferent to the human and to everyday experience.

Cyborg lament

It is not the cyborg who laments, but the human who laments the coming of the cyborg. The phenomenological body bound in its ambiguous fusion with the flesh of the world who fears the more threatening fusion with silicon and steel. This threat is acutely felt by Paul Virilio, whose thought bears an ambiguous relation to *Les Immatériaux*, one productive to explore. On the one hand, his idea of *overexposure* as an essential characteristic of the contemporary city influenced the conception of the exhibition. On the other hand, his critical stance towards technology, and especially towards contemporary art, stands in stark opposition to Lyotard's own as expressed in the exhibition and elsewhere. This latter opposition in particular helps to illuminate Lyotard's conception of inhuman art, by way of critical contrast.

Virilio was both an inspiration on, and minor participant in, the exhibition itself. In the programmatic statement 'Les Immatériaux' (Lyotard 1985a), and at greater length in the recently published document 'After Six Months of Work …' (Lyotard 2015), Virilio's essay 'The Overexposed City' (Virilio 2002) is discussed in reference to the search for a 'postmodern space–time' which would depart from the modern space–time which has traditionally organised exhibitions. This 'modern' space–time is one in which vision and space are privileged, in which the viewer, as subjective centre, is conceived as an eye, who follows a path through the exhibition, visiting sites conceived of as windows onto the view of what is displayed. The whole structure of the modern exhibition, according to Lyotard, is one which is determined by a didactic intention. The aim being to educate the viewer, the organisation of the exhibition positions the visitor as a protagonist in a *Bildungsroman*, whereby the course through the exhibition constitutes the subject in terms of 'experience' (Lyotard 1985: 53–4, 2015: 45–9).

In contrast to this, Lyotard finds inspiration for an alternative space–time, appropriate to a 'postmodern' exhibition, in Virilio's essay (which, probably not incidentally, cites Lyotard's own theory of the postmodern as the decline of metanarratives – Virilio 2002: 447). For Virilio, the contemporary city is 'overexposed' because it loses the opaque boundaries which used to separate clearly one area from another – for example, the separation of the city itself from the outside of the city, and the opacity of the walls which separate the inside and the outside of buildings. In this way, the postmodern city is divested of spaces of privacy and obscurity. Virilio cites a number of ways in which cities have become overexposed. First, opaque building materials such as wood and brick have increasingly been replaced with the transparency of glass and plastic. Second, with the growth in the populations of cities, the border between the outside and the inside of the city itself has become ambiguous. This has led to the phenomenon of 'conurbation', urban sprawl without a centre, which Lyotard associates with the West Coast of California, 'from San Diego to Santa Barbara' (1985a: 53), for him an important inspiration for postmodern space–time.

Perhaps most interestingly, Virilio links the 'overexposure' of the contemporary city to the televisual screen as a new kind of surface of inscription, one which ceases to separate or divide, but rather provides an *interface* between different spaces. All this means, for Virilio, that space effectively disappears, as distances become virtually crossed, and everywhere becomes reachable in a perpetual present: 'Deprived of objective boundaries, the architectonic element begins to drift and float in an electronic ether, devoid of spatial dimensions, but inscribed in the singular temporality of an instantaneous diffusion' (Virilio 2002: 442).

Lyotard, then, sought to present an 'overexhibition' in the sense that Virilio speaks of the overexposed city (Lyotard 2015: 54), and this can be seen in key aspects of the exhibition design, such as the replacement of walls with semi-transparent 'screens', making the inside and outside of the zones and sites more porous and ambiguous. Virilio's presence was also felt in other, more direct ways in the exhibition. He was quoted on the soundtrack, for Zone 21, and his essay 'L'Immatériel de guerre' (Virilio 1985) was included in one of the publications associated with the exhibition, the book *Modernes et après?*

In Virilio's influence on *Les Immatériaux*, we see that what speaks to Lyotard are the same kinds of concerns regarding the displacement of the body's perceptual relation to space–time with which he was concerned, which I glossed as a 'crisis of perception' in Chapter 4, and a 'crisis of space and time' in Chapter 5. Yet there is a crucial and dramatic difference between Lyotard and Virilio on this issue, which comes to the fore when we consider the latter's polemical diatribes against modern and contemporary art. Virilio's own view of art and technology is at odds with Lyotard's precisely around the notion of the inhuman, where the cyborg may be seen as a figure for the dire threat that Virilio sees technology posing to humanity. Virilio's views on technology and art are exemplified in his highly critical treatment of Stelarc, the Australian body artist whose work experiments with cyborg possibilities, that is, the supplementation and potential replacement of bodily organs with machine technology.[7] For Virilio, a thinker in the phenomenological tradition of Husserl and Merleau-Ponty, the phenomenological body is under threat from technical prostheses and the transformation of perception through new media.

Tortured bodies,

tortured forms

While reflections on art traverse many writings in Virilio's considerable *oeuvre*, perhaps the most illuminating is *Art and Fear* (2003). Here, in asking the question 'what is contemporary art contemporary with?', he answers that it is contemporary with, and symptomatic of, the century of horrors that witnessed the Holocaust. He quotes Jacqueline Lichtenstein's observation that the museum of Auschwitz reminded her of a museum of contemporary art (Virilio 2003: 28), and argues that the violence done to representational form in modern and contemporary art mirrors the violence done to the body's perceptual orientation by contemporary technological media, and – more dramatically – that done to human bodies in war and genocide. He writes:

> Early warning signs of the pitiless nature of MODERN TIMES as portrayed by Charlie Chaplin, the visual arts of that historical period never ceased TORTURING FORMS before making them disappear in abstraction. Similarly others would not cease TORTURING BODIES afterwards to the tune of the screams of the tortured prior to their asphyxiation inside the gas chambers. (Virilio 2003: 87)

For Virilio, the avant-garde experimental movements of the twentieth century, such as abstraction, minimalism, and conceptual art, are 'inhuman art' insofar as they do violence to the human, which he, in traditional humanist fashion, takes to be a natural given and highest in the hierarchy of beings. Virilio then sees no difference between the technoscientific inhuman, which dislocates the organic body's perceptual schema, and the artistic inhuman of the avant-gardes. Moreover, Virilio's critique of the abstractions of modern and contemporary art is motivated by a conviction that art should have a critical vocation in relation to the world in which it is formed, and that such a role can only be played when it presents representations of that world.

The key point of distinction with Lyotard's views – of art in particular, but perhaps ultimately also of technology – revolves around the respective value they place on phenomenological embodiment, as theorised in particular by Merleau-Ponty. While himself a follower of Merleau-Ponty, and continuing to take his lead from the phenomenological philosopher in many respects, Lyotard is critical of aspects of Merleau-Ponty's philosophy from *Discourse, Figure* onwards throughout his writings. Lyotard tends to criticise Merleau-Ponty for attributing the body with too much holistic unity with the world, arguing that the body also experiences dislocations and losses, for example in sleep and orgasm (DF: 131). Moreover, Merleau-Ponty's analysis of the perceptual field relies on the Gestaltist organisation of space in terms of figure and ground, which Lyotard argues is itself the outcome of a secondary rationalisation rather than the most primordial relation between body and world that Merleau-Ponty takes it to be (152–3).

Lyotard then has recourse, in *Discourse, Figure* and later writings, to psychoanalysis to explain the spatiality explored by the avant-gardes, a spatiality in a sense more primordial (because closer to the unconscious, rather than just the 'underside' of consciousness) than that of Merleau-Ponty's 'lived body'. In short, while Virilio sees Merleau-Ponty's phenomenological description of the body as correctly identifying the limits of the human, understood as a natural and primordial given, Lyotard sees both this phenomenological theory and the concept of the human as themselves secondary theoretical constructs. While Virilio sees technology and art as transgressing these natural limits, doing violence to the human, Lyotard sees them as legitimate explorations, since he recognises no such natural given as described by phenomenological humanism. While Lyotard sees the changes wrought by technology as instituting a 'crisis' for perception, he sees the avant-garde arts as effectively confronting this crisis by exploring and elaborating the meaning of this crisis in aesthetic terms. This capacity of the arts to confront nihilism is most directly addressed in Lyotard's last aesthetic reflections – which are also reflections on nihilism – in the works on André Malraux. So let us turn now to these later reflections, where we also see a return to consideration of the 'animal' inhuman.

Nihilism, at the last

> Nihilism is admittedly a pretext for whining: endless discourse about the end of everything – starting with art.
>
> Lyotard SR: 54

A different approach to the problem of nihilism emerges in Lyotard's last works, those written in the 1990s. In several texts he is critical of the approach to the problem taken by the two great voices of this tradition, Nietzsche and Heidegger, and he outlines an alternative canon of thinkers of nihilism. He positions André Malraux as a part of this tradition, and explores his works to find an alternative diagnosis and response to the waning of meaning in the current era. What worries Lyotard about Nietzsche and Heidegger is their apparently nostalgic longing for the return of a lost meaning, a refusal to accept that meaning itself in its 'old' or 'traditional' mode is unrecoverable. And more than anything in their explicit statements, it seems to Lyotard that this nostalgia is inscribed in their *style*:

> Writing in the form of dithyrambs and fragments does not interrupt, rather it reinforces the filiation with Romanticism and Symbolism. Zarathoustra's poetic prose, like the late Heidegger's sibylline writing, is well made for speaking the expected arrival of a 'last god.' (PF: 23)

Here is what Lyotard rejects: the pathos of Zarathustra's struggle to convey his message; his return to the mountain to commune with his animals. Heidegger's retreat to his hut in the Black Forest. Romantic dreams of channelling Being, God, or Nature. Rustic piety.

Instead, Lyotard asserts the irreversible 'conurbanization' of thought, its transmission through information circuits in overexposed, postmodern time–space. These conditions give rise to a new challenge to meaning, a new demand for both thought and style: 'the circumstances are propitious, in the artificial light of the megalopolis, for a laconism without pathos' (PF: 23). Here some names are jotted down to begin a new nihilist canon:

> Wittgenstein, Gertrude Stein, Joyce, or Duchamp seem like better 'philosophical' minds than Nietzsche or Heidegger – by better, I mean more apt to take into consideration the exitless nothingness the West gives birth to in the first quarter of the twentieth century; and by 'philosophical,' I mean, if it is true that philosophizing is an affair of 'style' ... (PF: 23)

In the essay 'The Zone', which I am quoting here, prime place in this canon is given to Max Jacob, who is described as 'one of the most rigorous signs that nihilism [...] has made in literature' (PF: 22).

Jacob is taken up again in Lyotard's works on Malraux, of which the little book *Soundproof Room: Malraux's Anti-Aesthetics* is of particular interest. This book effectively constitutes a last reflection on nihilism in Lyotard's oeuvre: a reconsideration of what constitutes it, what resists it, and the role of art in this resistance.[8] It is a very beautifully written but gnomic text. Interestingly, a clearer version of much of the argument presented in it can be found in an earlier paper, 'Being Done with Narrative by Cubism and André Malraux' (Lyotard 1996). The working-over of much of this text, which effected a loss in conceptual clarity but a gain in writerly finesse, suggests the seriousness with which Lyotard took the above comments concerning the importance of style for philosophy. Yet the style of *Soundproof Room* is far from a 'laconism without pathos'; nihilism is here again reworked from a different angle, that of bodily abjection, and with it, the identification of a style at the limits of writing which would witness it. With the stinking decomposition of the body of the dead God, 'nihilism ceases to be a sceptical or disabused turn of mind to become the experience of a soul and a body exposed obstinately to abjection' (SR: 10). Writers who have explored nihilism from the depths of abjection and at the limits of writing include Céline, Bataille, Artaud, and Camus. Lyotard states that his intention is to append Malraux's oeuvre to this group (SR: 10). Yet the work begins with the issue of the construction of meaning in modernity through the temporal modes of narrative and historicity.

Larval existence,

abject repetition

> [O]nly the inhuman – and not the superhuman – can carry out the murder of God because it seeks its nourishment on the putrefaction of his cadaver.
>
> Lyotard SM: 213

Lyotard presents God as the narrator, 'the Voice'. The Voice leaps into time. The narrator inserts himself into the story being narrated, exposing himself to the dangers of contingency, but lending vitality to the historical drama. What is at stake is what happens *in* the world, in the unfolding of the historical narrative, oriented towards a future, but significant *here and now*. The Voice promises a solution to the suffering of experience at the end of time, a salvation, a satisfying denouement to the tale we tell through living our lives. The modern decision is that God (the narrator) is *in* history, not outside it. It is essentially Christian: the Voice in time is God incarnated in the flesh. But it takes secular form in the Enlightenment metanarratives.

Nihilism tells of the silencing of this Voice, its quieting to the point where we can no longer hear it. For whatever reason (and every diagnostician of nihilism has their own story to tell), the Voice has lost its power, leaving us alone, vulnerable, abject. All that unfolds now in history is a meaningless, redundant repetition; cycles of birth and death, of civilisations as well as of microbes and larvae, stars and molluscs. Through Malraux and the theme of abjection Lyotard sees a modification of Nietzsche's thought of the eternal return as 'the heaviest burden', the crystallising and catalytic thought of nihilism which would force us to succumb or drive us to overcome. He writes: '[T]he worst is this: that in the ostensibly mute swamp where everything gets engulfed, larvae stagnate by the billions, fomenting renewal. Plants, animals, humans, and cultures: everything will begin again' (SR: 12). The world without meaning appears here not as death, but precisely the contrary, the continual renewal of 'mere life'. Maggots infesting the dead God's corpse, existence reduced to the blind reflexes and instincts of larvae, a never-ending repetition of abject, meaningless, living matter. An imagining of immanent existence in time without purpose, meaning, or goal which is more (or less) than a rational judgement, but which provokes a *physical disgust*. Nihilism as horror at existence registered in the flesh. A meaningless vitalist materialism.

Lyotard summarises the significance, in his reading, of what he discovers with Malraux for the nihilist problematic as follows:

> Malraux is more than a nihilist. Not only is God dead, but so is Man, like a figure of the voice incarnated in history. But what they leave after them is not a void; it's a vitality swarming with larvae, spiders, octopi, and soft crabs; a nightmare in which the cycle of putrefaction and regeneration endlessly repeats itself. Without end and without purpose. The stars in the sky form a spider's web, indifferent and threatening; and 'more interior in one-self than the self,' man does not discover the voice of God, as Augustine thought, but horrifying beasts vegetating in the bottoms of pits. The nihilism here is not philosophical; it's the body that experiences it like a filthy Repetition. (Lyotard 1996: 87)

Lyotard traces Malraux's response to this abject nihilism along at least two significant lines. The first deals with questions of subjectivity, while the second – which is the line I am concerned to follow here – delineates an inhuman art.[9] This is approached by way of Malraux's interest in the cubist poets.

Jewel

> [T]he prose poem is a jewel.
>
> Max Jacob 1981: 129

Malraux felt an early attraction to the masters of cubist poetry: Apollinaire, Jacob, Reverdy, Cendrars. The principles of cubist poetics were outlined by Max Jacob in his preface to *The Dice Cup*. While Jacob applies these principles specifically to the prose poem, for the reading of Malraux's anti-aesthetics that Lyotard develops they may be generalised to outline a theory applicable to any kind of artwork. These principles may be summarised as follows:

- The artwork is a dicethrow (a result of blind chance).
- The artwork means nothing.
- The artwork is a singular, unexpected arrangement of its constituent elements (words in literature; shapes and colours in painting).
- The artwork doesn't represent anything (no reference, history, event, or perceptual reality that might have come before it).
- The artwork doesn't express the subjectivity of the artist.
- The artwork has no symbolism.
- The artwork is a 'fact' [*fait*]: it is composed of materials 'unset from contexts and usages and grouped into a little dense and hard mass like a "jewel" '.
- The artwork develops from the will to *exteriorize* oneself.

(Paraphrased from Lyotard 1996: 83 and SR: 46–8)

In addition to this list, Jacob accentuates two key features of cubist art: it is worked by *style* (such that it gives the sensation of being self-enclosed), and it is *situated* (it gives a 'shock' from a margin that surrounds it).

First, style in this sense is the *elimination of the man*, that is, the removal of the artist him- or herself as much as possible from the work. In Jacob's words, '[s]tyle is here considered the setting of materials into a work and the composition of the ensemble, not the language of the writer' (Jacob 1981: 128). Cubist art is openly opposed to surrealism, the difference being that it is not intended as a release or expression of unconscious forces. The cubist artwork is conceived as an 'objective fact', separated from the subjectivity of its author. As such, it is not the product of a self, but of the 'I without Self', a modality of existence below conscious intention. Processes of chance play a role in the composition of the work, but these are not conceived as allowing the entry of unconscious forces into the creative process, as is the case for the surrealists, but as an ascesis of the subjectivity of the artist as such. Hence, art is understood to be 'inhuman', in Apollinaire's sense.

Second, the 'situation' of the work. Lyotard explains this idea as follows:

> The situation of the work is what removes it from the avid reader's impatience to appropriate it for himself: it puts in his way a 'spiritual margin,' and this delay, necessary for artistic emotion, does not in any way arise from an aesthetic of surprise (or from shock, in the Baudelairian sense), nor from a seductive maneuver. It results from the autonomy, let us not say the transcendence, of the prose poem in relation to all motivation. Let us say: to its autography. (Lyotard 1996: 84)

Thus, while style removes the subjective identity of the artist from the work he or she creates, situation 'brackets', or puts out of play (to phrase it phenomenologically), the network of meanings and significances which traverse the world of human culture. It is these cultural meanings which allow us to 'identify' the meaning of artworks by embedding them in a framework of historical and cultural relevance, as is typically done by art historians and art critics, but as the average viewer or reader is also inclined to do in interpreting the work. The 'situated' work is thus subtracted as much as possible from the human world and its significances, and surrounded by a 'spiritual margin' which is the marker of this separation. This meditation on cubism allows Lyotard an entry point into Malraux's anti-aesthetics, which he then elaborates as a countermovement to the nihilism with which Malraux was also preoccupied.

Raptor swoops

Soundproof Room, the title of the English translation of Lyotard's book *Chambre sourde*, is potentially misleading (or at least relatively uninformative). The title should rather be approached in the following way. The French *Chambre sourde* may be contrasted with Roland Barthes's *La Chambre claire*, translated as *Camera Lucida* (1993), which Lyotard references and calls 'a silly little book whose singular intensity leaves us transfixed' (SR: 102). The 'chambre claire' is a primitive camera, which allows the entry of a controlled amount of light in order to produce a clear image, often taken as a realistic representation of reality. Lyotard's 'chambre sourde' is best thought of not as a room – an anechoic chamber – but in contrast with the primitive camera, as a 'little case' (104) which does not allow any sound to penetrate, which isolates silence and makes it resonate: 'Style excavates the audible at its limit and fashions a singular little case in which the vibrations that the eardrum refuses just might be harnessed' (104).

The chambre sourde is an allegory for an artwork in the form of a little, soundproof box. Any artwork, since 'sound' is treated synaesthetically in this text for any and all sensation: '[p]ainting is not for seeing; it demands this listening: the eye listens to something beyond the harmonious music of the visible' (SR: 100). The book's subtitle (L'Antiesthétique de Malraux) situates the approach to aesthetics which Lyotard finds in Malraux as consistent with the aesthetics he pursues under different rubrics elsewhere, the aesthetics of the 'presence' of something insensible, or at least unsensed, in the midst of sensation. As already indicated, here this unsensed is pursued by using sound as a synecdoche for all sensation; it is the inaudible in the audible. It is announced through the theme of stridency, sound so violently loud that it cannot be properly heard: '[h]igh frequency, mighty amplitude, its vibration swoops down on the eardrum like a raptor, shaking it furiously. A front of sound so offensive that the frail membrane fails to enter into resonance with it' (76). Silent or strident, it makes no difference: the senses are deprived of their 'ordinary' data and cannot process it as 'everyday experience'.

Lyotard calls the artwork a 'fact',[10] following Reverdy's idea of a 'poetic fact' and Braque's of a 'pictorial fact'. It is self-enclosed, situated, surrounded by a spiritual margin – like a soundproof box. This 'fact' continues the emphasis in Lyotard's philosophy of art on the *singularity* of the work; it extends the opposition to structuralism which conceives meaning as a network of deferral beyond the work itself. The fact extracts the work from this network; it 'frames' it by isolating it from the world, from meaning and sense. Lyotard explains:

> The 'poetic fact' is not a human, social, psychical, or historical fact; it is not natural and it is not supernatural. It has the violence of an event: the pure occurrence of a group of words, previous to its capture in explanatory or interpretive discourses; the simple enigma that *there are* words. (Lyotard 1996: 84)

Here then, in the development of the cubist aesthetics which Lyotard calls Malraux's anti-aesthetics, we see another sense in which art may be considered inhuman: the artwork conceived as fact or event is inhuman insofar as it subtracts itself from the world of the human and its interests (or 'intrigues', as Lyotard calls this network of significances in *What to Paint?*).

Vacuum

According to Malraux's anti-aesthetics the artwork is constituted as a 'hole' in perceptual space–time and discursive reason. As this naked fact, as that which merely exists, yet insists, it is that which resists. Lyotard outlines how this inhuman notion of art constitutes a response to nihilism, as Malraux understands the problem:

> more than ever, within this vacuum of meaning, literature and the arts practice their arrangement of materials into works, confident as they are that works still stupefy, have always stupefied, by putting forward no secret in the investigation and no objection against it. Because it is made for questioning, form (or whatever stands in for it) harbors and suggests the *beyond* of answers – silence, being zero. Thus the artwork is *here*: fact invulnerable to redundancy, the tiresome repetition of motifs. (SR: 54)

The significance of 'the fact' in relation to nihilism is then this: it isolates something from the meaningless, abject repetition of existence, and makes it 'significant' without recourse to narrative and 'meaning'. Thus, it responds to nihilism on its own terms. The same strategy as the sublime, but in a different register. Instead of responding to nihilism by using the technical device of narrative to carve out a 'meaning' for a 'human being' (Man as the protagonist of history), inhuman art isolates materials from the cacophony of narratives, *subtracting* them from meaning.

If meaning is given by Voice (God, the narrator), inhuman art isolates the inaudible, using an alternative technical device: the 'soundproof chamber'. In this chamber, the inaudible insists. It is a 'fact' because it is like an event, it rips materials from the world in which their meaning is inscribed, allows them to resonate in such a way that something entirely new and unexpected is created (it ensnares our attention, stupefies us, gives rise to aesthetic feeling without meaning and even without sensible reception according to established codes); this 'something' causes ripples in the fabric of being, which resonate with other 'facts'. But the 'inhuman artwork' itself is complicitous with nihilism, sutured to nothingness:

> Aphonic, perhaps, or diaphonic, a *beyond* touches these throats for an instant but only inasmuch as they have been masked, inasmuch as

> a mold molded over nothingness opens the soundproof room of their
> concavity lying in wait for that which is almost unheard. The outer
> appearance, the artwork's facies, seems to doom it to simulation, dis-
> simulation, lying. But its empty inside allows the mask to pick up the
> truth – nothingness – in the form of strident apparitions. (SR: 104)

Thus the fact responds to nihilism from a place as immanent to nihilism itself as does the aesthetic of the sublime (see Chapter 4) insofar
as it does not mean anything, and is as foreign to narrative meaning
as the very nihilism which announces the end of meaning. God is
dead, the human is dead, yet aesthetic 'facts' continue to accumulate
which testify that there is something more than the abject repetition
of biological life and death. A fact for which we have artists to thank.

Protean memory,

stellar crucible

This theme of the fact or event bears directly on the issue of historicity.
We set out on the path of nihilism by considering modernity and its
deconstructions: in Lyotard's thesis of the end of metanarratives and
the attendant decline of history understood as a narrative meaningful
in human terms, and in his later reconstruction of Malraux's nihilism
as the silencing of the Voice of God, and then of Man as his successor,
in the historical narrative. Lyotard notes that Malraux formulates an
early response to nihilism in his 1927 work 'D'une jeunesse europée-
nne' (SM: 77). The problem of nihilism as it is expressed here is the
meaninglessness that is revealed through recognition of the repetition
of life, akin to the abject repetition discussed earlier, but here the same
drama is played out primarily in terms of human history: cultures
are born and die like living beings (the thesis of Spengler's *Decline of
the West* ([1918] 1932)), and the meanings and values which orient
those cultures and give human beings a purpose within them also die
as their horizons collapse. Yet artworks, understood in the inhuman
sense outlined above, resist this cycle of the births and deaths of horizons of cultural meaning insofar as they already subtract themselves
as much as possible from such horizons.

While we must not forget that Lyotard is commenting on Malraux, it is clear that he countersigns the latter's aesthetic response to
nihilism when he writes:

> [art]works, at least, do not perish along with the cultures from which
> they appear to emanate; and, because the modern West has rendered

itself incapable of any beliefs or any symbolics, because it ignores man's purpose, it can accept all forms attempted and can imagine still others. (SM: 77)

Thus, if there is some advantage to the nihilism in which our contemporary Western (and perhaps now becoming global) culture has fallen, it is at least this: that artworks are liberated from their cultural and historical contexts, their fixed symbolisms and meanings, and we have been rendered open to multiple varieties of aesthetic experience and artistic experimentation. Thus, in the contemporary world,

> [t]he nihilist disaster turns back into privilege: the first civilization that cannot name its ending can marvel at the bust of an Egyptian scribe, a Dogon mask, or a Malevitch in the same way. All are indeed marvels sprung from oblivion thanks to the 'style' and the 'situation' demanded by Max Jacob. (Lyotard 1996: 88)[11]

We can find here a return to the place from which we began in our exploration of inhuman art, 1985 and *Les Immatériaux*. We have already noted that some were puzzled by the juxtaposition of the latest technoscience and earlier twentieth-century avant-garde works, and have shown that this was well motivated insofar as, to Lyotard's mind, art from cubism to new media can bear the character of the inhuman. But there was even older and more foreign art on display at that exhibition. Lyotard later reflected:

> By what I hear, people wonder how we, in Europe, can be sensitive to the bas-relief of Nectanebo II, now 2,500 years old, that adorned the entrance of *Les Immatériaux*. The question betrays the lowliness of the thinking of art when it is submitted to historicism, that is, precisely, to the hegemony of narrative closure and absentness. (WP: 121; translation modified)

According to Lyotard and Malraux, the modern human has a memory like Proteus, able to assume multiplicitous forms, to appreciate arts from multiple cultures and histories. But only to the extent that it gives up its own cultural horizons and constitution as a 'self', that it 'bends its will to strive toward this inhuman that sometimes forces it wide open' (SR: 50).

In what, exactly, does 'meaning, value, or significance' consist, in inhuman art? Or in other words, what exactly is it that resists nihilism? We must say that it is a non-narrative, even non-discursive kind of meaning. Lyotard's late works on Malraux are thus a final expression of the intuition already motivating *Discourse, Figure*, the notion that there is an aesthetic form of meaning or significance not reducible to discourse. Given this resistance, its meaning is difficult to narrate, or to capture in discourse. Instead, it is something that must be *felt*. Lyotard's argument that art has a power of resistance to nihilism must thus be understood in its most general terms in contrast to Virilio, and others who insist that art can only have relevance by weaving narratives from the stuff of the world to which it is contemporary: the artwork does not resist nihilism by constructing a narrative meaning, by instituting an identity for 'the human', or the communal experience of a culture, but through direct aesthetic experience itself, however minimal, however tenuous. It is such an *aesthetic*, rather than narrative, response to meaninglessness that Lyotard consistently proposes, in the technoscientific experiments of *Les Immatériaux* as in the anti-aesthetics of Malraux. As Max Jacob wrote, '[a] work of art receives validity from itself and not from any possible comparison with reality' (Jacob 1981: 130). To summarise briefly: inhuman art is the construction of a 'soundproof chamber', a device (*dispositif*) opposed to the narrative device, which functions to allow the persistence and resistance of art in the face of nihilism and the end of modernity. Inhuman art is able to explore permutations of the sensible, of time–space–matter, which are as meaningless to human concerns as the births and deaths of stars in distant galaxies.[12]

Notes

1. See for example the essays 'A Game of Painting', 'On the Constitution of Time through Colour in the Recent Works of Albert Ayme', and 'Beyond Pathos' in MTII.
2. After several decades of little interest, several recent commemorative events, projects and publications are giving renewed attention to this exhibition. These include two events at the Pompidou Centre in 2005 to commemorate its twentieth anniversary: '*Les Immatériaux* Vingt Ans Après', 20 June 2004 and 'Retour sur *Les Immatériaux*', 30 March 2005; and several symposia to commemorate its thirtieth: '30 Years After *Les Immatériaux*: Art, Science & Theory' at the Centre for Digital Cultures in Lüneburg, 21–22 May 2014; '*Les Immatériaux*: Towards the Virtual with Jean-François Lyotard' at the Courtauld Institute of Art, London, 27–28 March 2015; and '*Les Immatériaux* trente ans après' at the Centre Georges Pompidou, 27 November 2015. A volume of essays based on the Lüneburg symposium, *30 Years After Les Immatériaux*, edited by Yuk Hui and Andreas Broeckmann, was

published by Meson Press in 2015. A retrospective exhibition, '"*Les Immatériaux*" for Instance' was held at the Kunstverein, Düsseldorf, 5 April–10 August 2014. The growing recognition of the significance of *Les Immatériaux* is further indicated by the fact that several papers were dedicated to it in the 'Landmark Exhibitions' special issue of *Tate Papers* (12, Autumn 2009): http://www.tate.org.uk/research/publications/tate-papers/issue-12 Artist and scholar of the new media arts, Randal Packer, cites *Les Immatériaux* as one of the first exhibitions to explore the intersection of information technology, art, industry and culture. Packer, who visited the exhibition, says that it was responsible for fuelling his interest in new media. Packer is cited in Spingarn-Koff (2001).

3. Lyotard names Harold Lasswell and Norbert Wiener, as well as Roman Jacobson, as sources for the model of communication theory he employs (Lyotard 1985a: 49).

4. The rhetoric of 'mastery' which *Les Immatériaux* sought to question is still very much alive in popular narratives of technoscientific advancement. See for example Michio Kaku's BBC documentary 'The Intelligence Revolution' in the *Visions of the Future* series.

5. Curiously, Lyotard does not discuss the aesthetic of the sublime in his writings and interviews concerning *Les Immatériaux*, despite its importance in his aesthetic theory of the same period and the clear connections which may be made between the two. Paul Crowther (1992) has correctly identified this connection.

6. See the discussion of this in the preceding chapter.

7. See for example the chapter 'From Superman to Hyperactive Man' in Virilio 1995.

8. This reading of the work, insofar as it centralises the problem of nihilism, follows Williams 2000b and Crome 2013.

9. The dimension of subjectivity in Lyotard's encounter with nihilism through Malraux has been treated by Williams 2000b and Crome 2013. Williams sees Lyotard as grappling with the problems of the subject after its postmodern deconstruction, and the personal struggles of a self facing the prospect of death, identifying an 'I without Self' in Lyotard's Malraux as a 'refuge from nihilism'. Taking a more historical perspective, Crome argues that Lyotard's confrontation with nihilism here consists in throwing the modern subject into crisis by confronting it with the bodily affectivity of the voice, which it is unable to hear as itself, and as such is irreducible to the self-transparent ideal of modern subjectivity and reason. While operating in somewhat different registers, both highlight subjectivity pushed to an extreme limit in confrontation with nihilism.

10. *Fait* – which can be rendered as either 'fact' or 'event', and has been rendered as event in some published translations of Lyotard's writings. (See for example 'The Pictorial Event Today' in MTI.) I choose 'fact' here in order to distinguish from the other French term for

event, *événement*, which Lyotard also frequently uses. However, the clear resonances in meaning between the terms fact and event (*fait* and *événement*) in the context of Lyotard's aesthetic discussions should nevertheless be kept in mind.

11. Interestingly, we can find here something of an implicit reply to the questions Ray Brassier makes Lyotard ask (see Chapter 1): what, if anything, of 'the human', or of 'thought', can persist without a horizon? For Lyotard, it is the work of art which persists, but only if it is understood in its 'inhuman' dimensions.

12. 'Stellar Crucibles' [*Creusets stellaires*] was one of the Zones (number 17) in *Les Immatériaux*. It presented stars as laboratories where elements are transformed into other elements. The brief catalogue describes it as follows: 'On a big circular screen close to the floor, projection of an audiovisual of astrophysics. On a vertical semi-circular screen alongside the first, presentation in caption of the corresponding formulas and commentaries' (Lyotard and Chaput 1985: 8).

The Judgement of the Inhuman

With the megalopolis, what the West realises and diffuses is its nihilism. It is called development. The question it asks of the philosopher is: what remains that is worthwhile when the presentation of every object is stamped with the unreality of its passage?

Lyotard PF: 22

The best possible time to contest for what the posthuman means is now, before the trains of thought it embodies have been laid down so firmly that it would take dynamite to change them.

N. Katherine Hayles 1999: 291

The preceding chapters have presented perspectives on how we might think the inhuman condition with Lyotard through the entwined themes of nihilism, information, and art. Lyotard's responses to nihilism are searching, minimal, elusive. For him, we still live in the horizon of decline, and our defences must take the form of resistances. Lyotard avoids all attempts to overcome nihilism in terms of a 'unity' which would mend the breach of the divide – however it is construed – between life and what gives it value. It is this move, on my reading, which constitutes Lyotard's significant difference to other (currently more fashionable) philosophies which seek to heal the wound of existence. I share with Lyotard the suspicion that such moves are both implausible and dangerous, and think the path that he takes is more fruitful for exploration – a path that seeks to think the abyss in its abyssal state, to try to find 'meaning' *in* the meaninglessness of the contemporary situation.

What is vital, novel, and important about Lyotard's stance on nihilism, then, is his refusal of salvation, his refusal of any nostalgia for unity, whether it be the unity of a leading meaning of being which would restore our being-at-home-in-the-world (Heidegger), the earth (Husserl), a univocity of Being in the principle of difference itself (Deleuze), an immanent auto-affection of non-objectified Life (Henry), any infinite thought of totalising speculative reason, any pure immanence, or any return to a consoling religion, including that religion which takes a political form. Instead, Lyotard opts for an interesting gambit: to accept, and even to accentuate, the abyss, the non-self-co-incidence of life and thought, of being and meaning. To attempt to think – and to live – them as incommensurable. The philosophical reflections which result from such a path do not constitute a unified and systematic philosophy, but consist of a series of heterogenous, micrological reflections. Lyotard never took himself to have had the last word on nihilism, and we should never take him at his word. Yet Lyotard's interventions are apposite, and if *thought* is one of the things nihilism threatens, Lyotard's texts perform this very resistance and perpetuate it by inflaming our own thinking.

The contemporary nihilism that Lyotard seeks to think is marked by technoscience, which enacts a further blow to human narcissism (after the first three that Freud enumerated – those of Copernicus, Darwin, and Freud himself (SE XVII: 135–44)):

> Through contemporary techno-science, s/he learns that s/he does not have the monopoly of mind, that is of complexification, but that complexification is not inscribed as a destiny in matter, but as possible, and that it takes place, at random, but intelligibly, well before him/herself. (IN: 45)

Various contemporary theories attempt to think this displacement and its consequences under names such as the transhuman, the posthuman, the inhuman, the metahuman, the nonhuman – and so on. Arguably, the dominant trend in contemporary continental philosophy is to reassess more positively the role of technoscience and the relation of the arts and humanities towards it; to reverse the overly reactionary resistances characteristic of phenomenology, existentialism, hermeneutics, and critical theory. Brian Massumi names this as a move from *constructivism* – which focuses on the creative forces of culture – to *inventivism*, which also takes into account extra-cultural, natural processes (Massumi 2012: 21–2).[1] This move is essential: philosophy has always needed to think in relation to science and current culture, and to be willing to let go of its long-held prejudices when the times demand it. And it is high time continental philosophy – in its anglophone form at least – took science seriously. Yet (and this is also an arguable point) this currently seems to be taking the form of a widely prevalent move in the direction of a problematic kind of naturalism and scientism. This is certainly not a new reductionist positivism, but consists rather in collapsing Hume's famous gap between the *ought* and the *is*. There is, it seems to me, a growing assumption that ethical and political values are either directly inscribed in, or can be summarily derived from, naturalistic processes identified by science and a science-inspired metaphysics.[2]

It is here that Lyotard's work presents a heterodox perspective which I see as decisive for current debates around the trans/post/in/human. Crucially, for Lyotard, thinking the inhuman maintains a critical distance from science: it acknowledges and attempts to think the displacements of the human that science effects, but resists any collapse into a scientism or naturalism which sees no difference between 'natural' processes and political, ethical, or vitalist principles; between metaphysics and ethics, between the 'ought' and the 'is'. Lyotard's work then offers us a powerful, more critical, more prudent (but no less inventive) manner of thinking the posthuman than many of those currently in vogue. Here is where the imperative force of his legacy lies, and why he must be (re)read and (re-)engaged in the contemporary scene.

Lyotard's approach to nihilism, at least from the 1980s, *eschews all anthropologism* in attempting to think alternatives and resistances. The unity of the human is fractured in the plurality of language games, or of faculties (akin to Deleuze's fracturing of the 'I' in the transcendent use of the faculties, but without regrounding the whole in the unity of difference, which would supposedly save us from nihilism). This is the originality and value of the 'purely formal' attempts to think the event through the heterogeneity of language games, paradox, and paralogy. This formalism strips the critique of nihilism of anthropomorphic prejudices and confronts technoscientific rationality on its own terms. The appeal of the formal for Lyotard is that it allows the location of its limits at aporetic points: an awareness of these limits then transports thought beyond what can be achieved through the application of rules, to the alternative modes of thought and feeling he elaborates, such as *judgement, anamnesis,* and *passibility*. Unlike rule-governed thinking, these modes of thinking and feeling cultivate an openness to the *event*.

In her conclusion to *How We Became Posthuman*, N. Katherine Hayles speculates that the notion of distributed cognition allows us to imagine that in our posthuman future numerous sophisticated judgements might be made by intelligent machines (Hayles 1999: 287). While by 'judgements' she perhaps means 'decisions' in a broad and general sense, this claim allows us to draw attention to what Lyotard believes remains a limit for technological, computational processes: precisely judgement, as he understands it. While many processes previously believed to belong exclusively to thought have been successfully externalised, materialised, and automated in computational processes, judgement – understood as thought that proceeds without criteria, guided by feeling, on a case-by-case basis – is what remains intractable to such automation, precisely because it cannot be formalised. While the 'distributed cognition' Hayles discusses – which conceives of systems composed of both human and technological elements (such that the system itself might be considered posthuman) – is certainly conceivable, Lyotard reminds us that what allows judgements in such systems must be other than rule-governed computation, even where sophisticated calculating devices are used to provide information regarding what is to be judged. Such judgement is the only kind of thought which can adequately approach questions of value and meaning, of ethics, politics, and aesthetics. The inhuman condition in which we find ourselves today calls for precisely such judgement, without which we are delivered over mercilessly to the 'monstrous' inhuman of the autonomous global system, governed by nothing other than the logic of capital and technoscience, the rule of performativity.

Following Lyotard, we can see that we need to assess the complexities of the inhuman condition not simply with appeals to science or to speculative metaphysical systems which purport to ground valuations in naturalistic phenomena, but in terms of *judgements* of values. A judgement is precisely that which proceeds without appeal to rules such as those which, in varying ways, metaphysical structures or algorithms provide. Yet a suspicion immediately arises here: *what* does the judging? Following the 'canonical' reading of Kant, following Heidegger's critique of values (that value thinking is necessarily subjectivising[3]), it may seem that the only possible answer could be 'the subject'. Or – following Foucault's analysis – the 'empirico-transcendental doublet' which the category 'the human' indexes in the current era (Foucault 1970). However, Lyotard very clearly resists this, and develops – through a close and detailed, if consciously heterodox, reading of Kant – a model of judgement which is a combination of thinking and feeling precisely *not* grounded in a subject. Commenting on 'aesthetic reflection', the form of judgement analysed in the first part of the *Critique of Judgement*, Lyotard writes:

> It is striking that little mention is made of a subject in the great majority of Kant's texts that touch on reflection. [...] the notion of a 'subject' in its substantive form does not seem necessary to the understanding of what reflection is. The notion of actual thought [...] is sufficient. (LAS: 14)

This stands in contrast to Kant's analysis of knowledge in the first *Critique*, in which a 'transcendental subject of apperception' is posited as necessary in order to unify the field of experience in which objects are known. According to Lyotard's interpretation, judgement as aesthetic reflection is 'tautegorical'; it is a thought accompanied by a feeling (a sensation of pleasure or pain) which is 'of' nothing but itself: it signals itself, and judges itself in the feeling it has of itself (LAS: 13). Aesthetic reflection is thus self-sufficient, not needing a subject as a principle of grounding and unification.[4] Significantly, Lyotard's heterodox reading of Kant argues that this understanding of judgement as aesthetic reflection, as thought guided by feeling, is the model of all critical thought and philosophy as such.

Similarly, 'the human' cannot be taken as a *fixed* notion of what judges, or underlies judgement, as a stable point of value – as we have seen, for Lyotard the human is itself a construction, displaced by the technosciences. *What judges are inhuman thoughts and feelings*, inhuman in the sense of what Lyotard calls childhood, infancy, or *infantia* (that which, in the human, is other to both the human, and the 'bad' inhuman of development). The thoughts and feelings involved in judgement are 'prior' or 'deeper' than the complex construction of the human; they are what is systematically trained, organised, and repressed in order to produce the human, thereby remaining 'proper' to it (IN: 2). The 'judgement' of the inhuman in the title of this conclusion, then, should be read in the double sense of the genitive: it is the inhuman nature of our contemporary condition which needs to be judged, but what does the judging is itself inhuman.

The inhuman nature of thoughts and feelings has long been in evidence in the field of the arts. As we have seen in the preceding chapters, Lyotard has approached this inhuman as a passibility to sensation at the level where sensory data impact sensitive receptors prior to the unity of a subject, prior to the unity of the faculties which constitutes 'the human' transcendentally, and prior to the cultural intrigues which constitute a normalised structure of experience and a concept of the human. This is the region of the sensory event. While it can never be grasped immediately, it can be identified through the evidence of the remainders in experience, the body, culture, and language which mark its impossible presence. Art testifies to this inhuman, and functions as a countermovement to nihilism by resisting the demand to give up everything to that which can be calculated, a functional demand made everywhere today in the interests of performativity and in the name of development.

If Lyotard does not see the inhuman condition as entirely nihilistic and negative, it is because in some respects it releases these inhuman powers of creativity and judgement which are only confined and repressed by the old humanisms. The avant-gardes had already approached this inhuman throughout the twentieth century. Lyotard sees it in the experiments with colour and line, form and volume, which divest us of the familiarity of the everyday and plunge us into an experience of the visual or the sonorous where, as though we have just been born, we again have to struggle to see and to hear. Yet it is the new media arts which confront most directly the specificity of the nihilism of the contemporary age. The concept of 'information' is of central important to Lyotard's concerns, because it gives us a theory, based in a technology, of *meaning independent of support (the sensible object, here and now)*.[5] The informational turn thus indexes the 'crisis of perception' or the 'foundation crisis' insofar as it negates the value of the sensible given by reducing it to an exchangeable support for 'cognitive' (semantic) content. As I have tried to show here, this is precisely why the aesthetic of the sublime comes to the fore in Lyotard's reflections on art in the 1980s onwards: it highlights the insistence of the sensible event in an informational era in which 'the presentation of every object is stamped with the unreality of its passage' (PF: 22).

It is to be hoped that part of Lyotard's legacy would be to wrest the problem of 'nihilism' – regardless of whatever one wishes to call it – from the legacy of romanticism, nostalgia, fusional community, closed cultural horizons, determinate ideas of the human and what is good for it, and so on. Without necessarily believing that he has 'the answers' (a danger which in any case he rails against), Lyotard helps us to think the contemporary situation of our 'nihilism', the informational inflation which encompasses us, eclipses the human, and continues to leave us wondering 'how to live, and why' (PF: vii). Such questions are a persistent existential demand, but they also admit of a specific form appropriate to our times. In this sense, as I hope to have shown here, Lyotard continues to be a philosopher for ours.

Notes

1. Massumi explains that with constructivism, '[w] hat is constructed are fundamentally perspectives or paradigms, and the corresponding subject positions. Within the 1990s constructivist model these were understood in terms of signifying structures or coding, typically applying models derived from linguistics and rhetoric. This telescoped becoming onto the human plane [...] Constructivism does not have

the resources even to articulate effectively the issue of the non-human necessarily raised by ontogenesis, let alone begin to resolve it. All the less so in that the figure of the non-human is ultimately that of matter, and the question of matter that of nature – which is radically bracketed by constructivism for fear of falling into a "naïve realism"' (2012: 21). For Massumi, following Simondon, it is precisely a theory of information, in conjunction with a thinking of matter, which allows a move away from constructivism's restriction to cultural significations and a thinking of the non-human through 'inventivism' (22).

2. Regardless of whether or not this is ultimately an adequate characterisation of his thought, Gilles Deleuze's influence here appears to be paramount. As Paul Patton notes, for example, there is a 'structure of evaluation built into the conceptual figures developed in *Mille Plateaux* that gives the text its ethical character' ([1986] 2001: 1156). These conceptual figures are at the same time metaphysical, and many draw significantly on scientific discourse.

3. See for example Heidegger 1977: 141–2.

4. More technically, Lyotard argues that if it is believed that sensation needs a substrate to 'bear' it, then for the Kant of the third *Critique* such a substrate is not a subject, but only the regulative Idea of a supersensible substrate, about which we can have no knowledge (LAS: 13).

5. The π Research Network write that 'the profound importance of the language of information is that it has altered the way we think forever. The key to this alteration is in the abstraction away from the peculiarities of a particular unique physical object in front of you' (2013: 14).

Bibliography

Adams, Frederick R. (2003), 'The Informational Turn in Philosophy', *Minds and Machines*, 13.4: 471–501.

Adriaans, Pieter (2012), 'Information', *The Stanford Encyclopedia of Philosophy* <http://plato.stanford.edu/entries/information/#Rel> (last accessed 20 July 2015).

Ansell Pearson, Keith (1994), *An Introduction to Nietzsche as Political Thinker: The Perfect Nihilist*, Cambridge: Cambridge University Press.

Ansell Pearson, Keith (1997), *Viroid Life: Perspectives on Nietzsche and the Transhuman Condition*, London: Routledge.

Apollinaire, Guillaume (2012), 'Aesthetic Meditations on Painting: The Cubist Painters', in Guillaume Apollinaire, Dorothea Eimert, and Anatoli Podoksik, *Cubism*, New York: Parkstone International.

Badmington, Neil (2000), *Posthumanism*, New York: St. Martin's Press.

Bamford, Kiff (2012), *Lyotard and the 'figural' in Performance, Art, and Writing*, London and New York: Continuum.

Bar-Hillel, Yehoshua and Rudolph Carnap [1953] (1964), 'An Outline of a Theory of Semantic Information', in Yehoshua Bar-Hillel, *Language and Information: Selected Essays on Their Theory and Application*, Reading, MA and London: Addison-Wesley.

Barthes, Roland (1993), *Camera Lucida: Reflections on Photography*, trans. Richard Howard, New York: Vintage.

Bataille, Georges (2014), *Inner Experience*, trans. Stuart Kendall, New York: SUNY.

Bateson, Gregory (2000), *Steps to an Ecology of Mind: Collected Essays in Anthropology, Psychiatry, Evolution, and Epistemology*, Chicago: University of Chicago Press.

Beavers, Anthony F. (2012), 'A Brief Introduction to the Philosophy of Information' <https://www.academia.edu/1230161/A_Brief_Introduction_to_the_Philosophy_of_Information> (last accessed 20 July 2015).

Bennington, Geoffrey (1988), *Lyotard: Writing the Event*, Manchester: Manchester University Press.

Bergson, Henri (1911), *Matter and Memory*, trans. Nancy Margaret Paul and W. Scott Palmer, London: George Allen & Unwin; New York: Macmillan.

Bergson, Henri (1946), *The Creative Mind*, trans. M. L. Andison, New York: Philosophical Library.

Bernstein, Richard J. (2002), *Radical Evil: A Philosophical Interrogation*, Cambridge: Polity.

Bickis, Heidi and Rob Shields (eds) (2013), *Rereading Jean-François Lyotard: Essays on His Late Work*, Farnham: Ashgate.

Boeve, Lieven (2015), *Lyotard and Theology*, London and New York: Bloomsbury.

Bousso, Raphael, Ben Freivogel, Stefan Leichenauer, and Vladimir Rosenhaus (2011), 'Eternal Inflation Predicts that Time Will End', *Physical Review D*, 83.2.

Brassier, Ray (2003), 'Solar Catastrophe: Lyotard, Freud, and the Death Drive', *Philosophy Today*, 47: 421–30.

Brassier, Ray (2007), *Nihil Unbound: Enlightenment and Extinction*, Houndmills: Palgrave Macmillan.

Bryant, Levi, Nick Srnicek, and Graham Harman (eds) (2011), *The Speculative Turn: Continental Materialism and Realism*, Melbourne: RePress.

Caygill, Howard (1995), *A Kant Dictionary*, Malden: Blackwell.

Chaitin, G. J. (2004), 'Leibniz, Information, Math and Physics', *Wissen und Glauben/Knowledge and Belief. Akten des 26. Internationalen Wittgenstein-Symposiums 2003*. Herausgegeben von Löffler, Winfried/ Weingartner, Paul. ÖBV & HPT, Wien: 277–86 <http://www.cs.auckland. ac.nz/~chaitin/kirchberg.html> (last accessed 20 July 2015).

Chaitin, G. J. (2007), 'The Halting Probability Ω: Irreducible Complexity in Pure Mathematics', *Milan Journal of Mathematics*, 75: 291–304.

Charlet, Nicolas (2000), *Yves Klein*, Paris: Vilo/Adam Biro.

Coole, Diana and Samantha Frost (eds) (2010), *New Materialisms: Ontology, Agency, and Politics*, Durham, NC: Duke University Press.

Cordeschi, Roberto (2004), 'Cybernetics', in Luciano Floridi (ed.), *The Blackwell Guide to the Philosophy of Computing and Information*, Malden: Blackwell.

Crome, Keith (2004), *Lyotard and Greek Thought: Sophistry*, Houndmills: Palgrave Macmillan.

Crome, Keith (2013), 'Voicing Nihilism: Lyotard on Malraux', in Heidi Bickis and Rob Shields (eds), *Rereading Jean-François Lyotard*, Farnham: Ashgate.

Crowther, Paul (1992), '*Les Immatériaux* and the Postmodern Sublime', in Andrew Benjamin (ed.), *Judging Lyotard*, London: Routledge.

Crowther, Paul (1999), *The Kantian Sublime: From Morality to Art*, Oxford: Clarendon Press.

Davis, Todd F. and Kenneth Womack (eds) (2001), *Mapping the Ethical Turn: A Reader in Ethics, Culture, and Literary Theory*, Charlottesville: University of Virginia Press.

De Duve, Thierry (1996), *Kant After Duchamp*, Cambridge, MA: MIT Press.

De Garis, Hugo (2005), *The Artilect War: Cosmists vs. Terrans: A Bitter Controversy Concerning Whether Humanity Should Build Godlike Massively Intelligent Machines*, Palm Springs, CA: ETC Publications.

Deleuze, Gilles (1983), *Nietzsche and Philosophy*, trans. Hugh Tomlinson, New York: Columbia University Press.

Deleuze, Gilles and Félix Guattari (1983), *Anti-Oedipus*, trans. Robert Hurley, Mark Seem, and Helen R. Lane, Minneapolis: University of Minnesota Press.

Deleuze, Gilles and Claire Parnet (2006), *Dialogues II*, 2nd edn, London: Bloomsbury.

Derrida, Jacques (1973), *Speech and Phenomena, and Other Essays on Husserl's Theory of Signs*, trans. David B. Allison, Evanston: Northwestern University Press.

Descartes, René [1644] (1983), *Principles of Philosophy*, trans. Valentine Rodger Miller and Reese P. Miller, Dordrecht: D. Reidel.

Dummett, Michael (1993), *Origins of Analytical Philosophy*, London: Duckworth.

Fischer, Joschka (ed.) (1989), *Ökologie im Endspiel*, Munich: Fink Verlag.

Floridi, Luciano (2002), 'What Is the Philosophy of Information?', *Metaphilosophy*, 33.1/2: 123–45.

Floridi, Luciano (2003), 'Two Approaches to the Philosophy of Information', *Minds and Machines*, 13.4: 459–69.

Floridi, Luciano (2004), 'Information', in Luciano Floridi (ed.), *The Blackwell Guide to the Philosophy of Computing and Information*, Oxford: Blackwell.

Floridi, Luciano (2005), 'Is Information Meaningful Data?', *Philosophy and Phenomenological Research*, 70.2: 351–70.

Floridi, Luciano (2008), 'Data', in William A. Darity (ed.), *The International Encyclopedia of the Social Sciences*, 2nd edn, Detroit: Macmillan.

Floridi, Luciano (2011), *The Philosophy of Information*, Oxford and New York: Oxford University Press.

Floridi, Luciano (2013), 'Semantic Conceptions of Information', *The Stanford Encyclopedia of Philosophy* <http://plato.stanford.edu/entries/information-semantic/> (last accessed 20 July 2015).

Floridi, Luciano (2014), *The Fourth Revolution: How the Infosphere Is Reshaping Human Reality*, Oxford: Oxford University Press.

Floridi, Luciano (2015), 'An Interview with Luciano Floridi on the Philosophy of Information', *Five Books* <http://fivebooks.com/interviews/luciano-floridi-on-philosophy-information> (last accessed 20 July 2015).

Foucault, Michel (1970), *The Order of Things: An Archaeology of the Human Sciences*, New York: Vintage.

Garber, Daniel (1998), 'Leibniz, Gottfried Wilhelm (1646–1716)', in Paul Edwards (ed.), *The Routledge Encyclopedia of Philosophy*, vol. 5, London and New York: Routledge.

Gasché, Rodolphe (2001), 'The Sublime, Ontologically Speaking', *Yale French Studies*, 99: 117–28.

Gere, Charlie (2006), *Art, Time and Technology*, Oxford and New York: Berg.

Germain, Gil (2009), *Spirits in the Material World: The Challenge of Technology*, New York: Lexington Books.

Golan, Amos (2002), 'Information and Entropy Econometrics – Editor's View', *Journal of Econometrics*, 107.1–2: 1–15.

Gould, Stephen J. (1990), *Wonderful Life: The Burgess Shale and the Nature of History*, New York: W. W. Norton and Co.

Grusin, Richard (ed.) (2015), *The Nonhuman Turn*, Minneapolis: University of Minnesota Press.

Habermas, Jürgen (1971), 'Theorie der Gesellschaft oder Sozialtechnologie? Eine Auseinandersetzung mit Niklas Luhmann', in Jürgen Habermas and Niklas Luhmann, *Theorie der Gesellschaft oder Sozialtechnologie. Was leistet die Systemforschung?*, Frankfurt a.M.: Suhrkamp.

Hadot, Pierre (1995), *Philosophy as a Way of Life: Spiritual Exercises from Socrates to Foucault*, ed. Arnold I. Davidson, trans. Michael Chase, Oxford and Cambridge, MA: Blackwell.

Harris, Paul (2001), 'Thinking @ the Speed of Time: Globalization and Its Dis-contents or, Can Lyotard's Thought Go on Without a Body?', *Yale French Studies*, 99: 129–48.

Hassan, Ihab (1977), 'Prometheus as Performer: Towards a Posthumanist Culture?', in Michael Benamou and Charles Caramella (eds), *Performance in Postmodern Culture*, Madison: Coda Press.

Hayles, N. Katherine (1999), *How We Became Posthuman: Virtual Bodies in Cybernetics, Literature, and Informatics*, Chicago and London: University of Chicago Press.

Heidegger, Martin (1962), *Being and Time*, trans. John Macquarrie and Edward Robinson, Oxford and Cambridge: Blackwell.

Heidegger, Martin (1977), *The Question Concerning Technology and Other Essays*, trans. William Lovitt, New York: Harper & Row.

Heidegger, Martin (1981), *Nietzsche, Vol. 1: The Will to Power as Art*, trans. David Farrell Krell, London and Henley: Routledge & Kegan Paul.

Heidegger, Martin (1987), *Nietzsche, Vol. IV: Nihilism*, trans. David Farrell Krell, San Francisco: Harper & Row.

Heidegger, Martin (1993), 'The Way to Language', trans. David Farrell Krell, in David Farrell Krell (ed.), *Martin Heidegger: Basic Writings*, San Francisco: HarperCollins.

Heidegger, Martin (1998), 'Traditional Language and Technological Language', trans. Wanda Torres Gregory, *Journal of Philosophical Research*, XXIII: 129–45.

Heindel, Max (1947), *Cosmogonie des Rose-Croix*, Paris: Leymarie.

Herbrechter, Stefan (2013), *Posthumanism: A Critical Analysis*, London: Bloomsbury.

Horton-Parker, Skip (2007), 'Tracking the Theological "Turn": The Pneumatological Imagination and the Renewal of Metaphysics and Theology in the 21st Century', *PentecoStudies*, 6.1: 47–77.

Hudek, Antony (2009), 'From Over- to Sub-Exposure: The Anamnesis of *Les Immatériaux*', *Tate Papers*, 12 <http://www.tate.org.uk/research/publications/tate-papers/over-sub-exposure-anamnesis-les-immateriaux> (last accessed 20 July 2015).

Hui, Yuk (2015), 'Anamnesis and Re-Orientation: A Discourse on Matter and Time', in Yuk Hui and Andreas Broeckmann (eds), *30 Years After Les Immatériaux*, Meson Press.

Hui, Yuk and Andreas Broeckmann (eds) (2015), *30 Years After Les Immatériaux*, Meson Press.

Husserl, Edmund (1981), 'Foundational Investigations of the Phenomenological Origin of the Spatiality of Nature', trans. Frederick Kersten, in Peter McCormick and Frederick A. Elliston (eds), *Husserl: Shorter Works*, Notre Dame: University of Notre Dame Press.

Husserl, Edmund (1991), *On the Phenomenology of the Consciousness of Internal Time*, ed. and trans. J. B. Brough, Dordrecht: Kluwer.

Jacob, Max (1981), '1916 Preface', trans. Judith Morganroth Schneider, in Sydney Lévy, *The Play of the Text: Max Jacob's* Le Cornet à dés, Madison: University of Wisconsin Press.

James, Ian (2012), *The New French Philosophy*, Cambridge: Polity.

Jencks, Charles (1996), *What Is Post-Modernism?*, 4th edn, London: Academy Editions.

Jones, Graham (2013), *Lyotard Reframed*, London and New York: I. B. Tauris.

Kant, Immanuel (1914), *Critique of Judgement*, trans. J. H. Bernard, London: Macmillan.

Kant, Immanuel (1929), *Immanuel Kant's Critique of Pure Reason*, trans. Norman Kemp Smith, Houndmills and London: Macmillan.

Kellner, Douglas (1999), 'Questions from "Cadernos de Filosofia Contemporanea"', *Illuminations: The Critical Theory Project* <http://pages.gseis.ucla.edu/faculty/kellner/Illumina%20Folder/kell33.htm> (last accessed 12 February 2012).

Klein, Yves (1974), *Yves Klein, 1928–1962: Selected Writings*, ed. Jacques Caumont and Jennifer Gough-Cooper, trans. Barbara Wright, London: Tate Gallery Publications.

Klein, Yves (2007), 'The Chelsea Hotel Manifesto', in *Overcoming the Problematics of Art: The Writings of Yves Klein*, trans. Klaus Ottmann, Washington, DC: Spring Publications.

Klossowski, Pierre (2005), *Nietzsche and the Vicious Circle*, trans. Daniel W. Smith, London and New York: Continuum.

Kluitenberg, Eric (2002), 'Transfiguration of the Avant-Garde: The Negative Dialectics of the Net', *Noema* <http://noemalab.eu/ideas/essay/transfiguration-of-the-avant-garde/> (last accessed 20 July 2015).

Knopf, A., C. Schuchert, A. F. Kovarik, A. Holmes and E. W. Brown (1931), *Physics of the Earth IV: The Age of the Earth*, National Research Council, Report of the National Academy of Sciences.

Korycansky, D. G., G. Laughlin and F. C. Adams (2001), 'Astronomical Engineering: A Strategy for Modifying Planetary Orbits', *Astrophysics and Space Science*, 275: 349–66.

Krauss, L. and G. Starkman (2000), 'Life, the Universe, and Nothing: Life and Death in an Ever-expanding Universe', *The Astrophysical Journal*, 531.1: 22–30.

Lacey, A. R. (1989), *Bergson*, London and New York: Routledge.

Laruelle, François (2013a), *Philosophy and Non-Philosophy*, trans. Taylor Adkins, Minneapolis: Univocal.

Laruelle, François (2013b), *Principles of Non-Philosophy*, trans. Nicola Rubczak and Anthony Paul Smith, London and New York: Bloomsbury.

Lasswell, Harold (1948), 'The Structure and Function of Communication in Society', in L. D. Bryson (ed.), *The Communication of Ideas*, New York: Harper.

Leibniz, Gottfried Wilhelm (1956), *Philosophical Papers and Letters*, ed. and trans. Leroy E. Loemker, Chicago: University of Chicago Press.

Leroi-Gourhan, André [1964–5] (1993), *Gesture and Speech*, trans. Anna Bostock Berger, Cambridge, MA: MIT Press.

Linker, Kate (1985), 'A Reflection on Post-Modernism', *Artforum*, 24.1: 104–5.

Littlefield, Melissa M. and Janell M. Johnson (eds) (2012), *The Neuroscientific Turn: Transdisciplinarity in the Age of the Brain*, Ann Arbor: University of Michigan Press.

Longinus (1985), *On the Sublime*, trans. James A. Arieti and John M. Crossett, New York: E. Mellen Press.

Luhmann, Niklas (1989a), *Ecological Communication*, trans. John Bednarz, Chicago: University of Chicago Press.

Luhmann, Niklas (1989b), 'Ökologische Kommunikation – Ein Theorie-Entscheidungsspiel', in Joschka Fischer (ed.), *Ökologie im Endspiel*, Munich: Fink Verlag.

Lyotard, Jean-François (1977), 'The Unconscious as Mise-en-scène', in Michael Benamou and Charles Caramella (eds), *Performance in Postmodern Culture*, Madison: Coda Press.

Lyotard, Jean-François (1978), 'Notes on the Return and Kapital', *Semiotext(e)*, 3.1: 44–53.

Lyotard, Jean-François (1980), 'Deux métamorphoses du séduisant au cinéma', in Maurice Olender and Jacques Sojcher (eds), *La Séduction*, Paris: Aubier Montaigne.

Lyotard, Jean-François (1981a), 'The Works and Writings of Daniel Buren: An Introduction to the Philosophy of Contemporary Art', trans. Lisa Liebmann, *Artforum*, 19.6: 56–64.

Lyotard, Jean-François (1981b), 'Theory as Art: A Pragmatic Point of View', in Wendy Steiner (ed.), *Image and Code*, Ann Arbor: Rackham School of Graduate Studies, University of Michigan Press.

Lyotard, Jean-François (1982), 'Presenting the Unpresentable: The Sublime', trans. Lisa Liebmann, Artforum, 20.8: 64–9.

Lyotard, Jean-François (1983), 'Presentations', trans. Kathleen McLaughlin, in Alan Montefiore (ed.), *Philosophy in France Today*, Cambridge: Cambridge University Press.

Lyotard, Jean-François (1985a), 'Les Immatériaux', *Art & Text*, 17: 47–57.

Lyotard, Jean-François (1985b), 'Les Immatériaux: A Conversation with Jean-François Lyotard', interview with Bernard Blistène, Flash Art, 121: 32–9. Reproduced at <http://www.art-agenda.com/reviews/les-immate-riaux-a-conversation-with-jean-francois-lyotard-and-bernard-blistene/> (last accessed 20 July 2015).

Lyotard, Jean-François (1986), 'Complexity and the Sublime', in *Postmodernism: ICA Documents 4 and 5*, ed. Lisa Appignanesi, London: Institute of Contemporary Arts Publications.

Lyotard, Jean-François (1986–7), 'Rules and Paradoxes and Svelte Appendix', *Cultural Critique*, 5: 209–19.

Lyotard, Jean-François (1988), 'An Interview with Jean-François Lyotard', with Dick Veerman and Willem van Reijen, *Theory, Culture, and Society*, 5: 300–1.

Lyotard, Jean-François (1989), 'Judiciousness in Dispute, or Kant after Marx', in Andrew Benjamin (ed.), *The Lyotard Reader*, Oxford and Cambridge: Wiley-Blackwell.

Lyotard, Jean-François (1990), 'L'Inarticulé, ou le différend même', in Michel Meyer and Alain Lempereur (eds), *Figures et conflits rhétoriques*, Bruxelles: Université de Bruxelles.

Lyotard, Jean-François (1994a), 'Nietzsche and the Inhuman', interview with Richard Beardsworth, *Journal of Nietzsche Studies*, 7: 67–130.

Lyotard, Jean-François (1994b), 'A Postmodern Fable on Postmodernity, or: In the Megalopolis', in W. J. Lillyman, M. F. Moriarty, and D. J. Neuman (eds), *Critical Architecture and Contemporary Culture*, New York and Oxford: Oxford University Press.

Lyotard, Jean-François (1996), 'Being Done with Narrative by Cubism and André Malraux', trans. Leonard Hinds, in Robert Newman (ed.), *Centuries' Ends, Narrative Means*, Stanford: Stanford University Press.

Lyotard, Jean-François (1999), 'Freud, Energy, and Chance: A Conversation with Lyotard, Jean-François', interview with Richard Beardsworth, *Tekhnema*, 5 <http://tekhnema.free.fr/5Beardsworth.html> (last accessed 20 July 2015).

Lyotard, Jean-François (2002), 'Emma: Between Philosophy and Psychoanalysis', trans. Michael Sanders (with Richard Brons and Norah Martin), in

Hugh J. Silverman (ed.), *Lyotard: Philosophy, Politics, and the Sublime*, New York: Routledge.

Lyotard, Jean-François (2006), 'Resisting a Discourse of Mastery: A Conversation with Jean-François Lyotard', interview with Gary A. Olson, *JAC*, 15.3.

Lyotard, Jean-François (2013), 'Argumentation and Presentation: The Foundation Crisis', trans. Chris Turner, in Peter W. Milne, Rob Shields, Heidi Bickis, and Kent Still (eds), *Rewriting Lyotard: Figuration, Presentation, Resistance*, special issue of *Cultural Politics*, 9.2: 117–43.

Lyotard, Jean-François (2015), 'After Six Months of Work ...', in Yuk Hui and Andreas Broeckmann (eds), *30 Years After Les Immatériaux*, Meson Press.

Lyotard, Jean-François and Thierry Chaput (1985), *Les Immatériaux* (petit journal), Paris: Centre Pompidou.

Lyotard, Jean-François and Élie Théofilakis (1985), 'Les Petits récits de chrysalide: entretien', in Élie Théofilakis (ed.), *Modernes et Après: Les Immatériaux*, Paris: Éditions Autrement.

Marcuse, Herbert (1962), *Eros and Civilization: A Philosophical Inquiry into Freud*, New York: Vintage.

Martin, William (2009), 'Re-programming Lyotard: From the Postmodern to the Posthuman Condition', *Parrhesia*, 8: 60–75.

Massumi, Brian (2012), ' "Technical Mentality" Revisited', in Arne De Boever, Alex Murray, Jon Roffe and Ashley Woodward (eds), *Gilbert Simondon: Being and Technology*, Edinburgh: Edinburgh University Press.

Maturana, Humberto and Francisco Varela (1980), *Autopoiesis and Cognition: The Realization of the Living*, Dordrecht: D. Reidel.

Meillassoux, Quentin (2009), *After Finitude: An Essay on the Necessity of Contingency*, trans. Ray Brassier, London and New York: Continuum.

Merleau-Ponty, Maurice (1968), *The Visible and the Invisible*, ed. Claude Lefort, trans. Alphonso Lingis, Evanston: Northwestern University Press.

Merleau-Ponty, Maurice (2012), *Phenomenology of Perception*, trans. Donald A. Landes, New York: Routledge.

Miccoli, Anthony (2010), *Posthuman Suffering and the Technological Embrace*, Plymouth: Lexington.

Milne, Peter W., Rob Shields, Heidi Bickis, and Kent Still (eds) (2013), *Rewriting Lyotard: Figuration, Presentation, Resistance*, special issue of *Cultural Politics*, 9.2.

More, Max (2003), 'Principles of Extropy: An Evolving Framework of Values and Standards for Continuously Improving the Human Condition', Version 3.11. *Extropy Institute*, archived at <https://web.archive.org/web/20131015142449/http://extropy.org/principles.htm> (last accessed 20 July 2015).

More, Max and Natasha Vita-More (2013), *The Transhumanist Reader*, Oxford: Wiley-Blackwell.

Mullarkey, John and Anthony Paul Smith (eds) (2012), *Laruelle and Non-Philosophy*, Edinburgh: Edinburgh University Press.

Nietzsche, Friedrich (1968), *The Will To Power*, ed. Walter Kaufmann, trans. W. Kaufman and R. J. Hollingdale, New York: Vintage.

Nietzsche, Friedrich (1993), *The Birth of Tragedy*, ed. Michael Tanner, trans. Shaun Whiteside, London: Penguin.

Nietzsche, Friedrich (2001), *The Gay Science*, ed. Bernard Williams, trans. Josefine Nauckhoff and Adrian Del Caro, Cambridge: Cambridge University Press.

Nietzsche, Friedrich (2006a), *On the Genealogy of Morality and Other Writings*, ed. Keith Ansell Pearson, trans. Carol Diethe, revised 2nd student edn, Cambridge: Cambridge University Press.

Nietzsche, Friedrich (2006b), *The Nietzsche Reader*, ed. Keith Ansell Pearson and Duncan Large, Oxford: Blackwell.

Odenwald, Sten F. (2002), *Patterns in the Void: Why Nothing Is Important*, Boulder: Westview Press.

Patton, Paul [1986] (2001), 'Deleuze and Guattari: Ethics and Postmodernity', in Gary Genosko (ed.), *Deleuze and Guattari: Critical Assessments of Leading Philosophers*, London and New York: Routledge.

Plato (1977), *Plato's Phaedo*, trans. G. M. A. Grube, Indianapolis: Hackett.

Prigogine, Ilya and Isabelle Stengers (1985), *Order Out of Chaos: Man's New Dialogue with Nature*, London: Flamingo.

Quine, W. V. O. (1970), *Philosophy of Logic*, Englewood Cliffs, NJ: Prentice Hall.

Rajchman, John (1991), 'The Postmodern Museum', in *Philosophical Events: Essays of the '80s*, New York: Columbia University Press.

Readings, Bill (1991), *Introducing Lyotard: Art and Politics*, London: Routledge.

Regis, Ed (1990), *Great Mambo Chicken and the Transhuman Condition*, New York: Perseus.

Restany, Pierre (1982), *Yves Klein*, trans. John Shepley, New York: Harry N. Abrams.

Restany, Pierre (1985), 'Immateriaux', *Domus*, 662: 60–1.

Ridley, Aaron (2007), *Routledge Philosophy Guidebook to Nietzsche on Art*, London and New York: Routledge.

Riley, Charles A. (1995), *Color Codes: Modern Theories of Color in Philosophy, Painting and Architecture, Literature, Music, and Psychology*, Hanover: University Press of New England.

Rosenthal, Nan (1995), 'Out of the Blue: Comic Relief', *Artforum*, 33.10: 92–7.

Saul, L. J. (1958), 'Freud's Death Instinct and the Second Law of Thermodynamics', *International Journal of Psychoanalysis*, 39.5: 323–5.

Sawyer, Dylan (2014), *Lyotard, Literature and the Trauma of the Differend*, London: Palgrave Macmillan.

Simondon, Gilbert (1989), *L'Individuation psychique et collective*, Paris: Aubier.

Schmidhuber, Jürgen (1997), 'A Computer Scientist's View of Life, the Universe, and Everything', in C. Freksa, M. Jantzen, and R. Valk (eds), *Foundations of Computer Science: Potential – Theory – Cognition*, Lecture Notes in Computer Science, Springer: 201–8.

Schrift, Alan D. (1990), *Nietzsche and the Question of Interpretation: Between Hermeneutics and Deconstruction*, New York: Routledge.

Sellars, Wilfrid (1963), 'Philosophy and the Scientific Image of Man', in Wilfrid Sellars, *Science, Perception and Reality*, London: Routledge and Kegan Paul.

Shannon, Claude E. (1993), *Collected Papers*, ed. A. D. Wyner and Neil J. A. Sloane, Hoboken, NJ: Wiley-IEEE Press.

Shannon, Claude E. and Warren Weaver [1949] (1963), *The Mathematical Theory of Communication*, Urbana: University of Illinois Press.

Shröder K.-P. and Robert Cannon Smith (2008), 'Distant Future of the Sun and Earth Revisited', *Monthly Notices of the Royal Astronomical Society*, 386.1 (May): 155–63.

Sim, Stuart (1997), *Lyotard and the Inhuman*, London: Icon.

Sim, Stuart (ed.) (2011), *The Lyotard Dictionary*, Edinburgh: Edinburgh University Press.

Slocombe, Wil (2006), *Nihilism and the Sublime Postmodern: The (Hi)Story of a Difficult Relationship*, London and New York: Routledge.

Song, Misook (1984), *Art Theories of Charles Blanc*, Ann Arbor: University of Michigan Press.

Spengler, Oswald [1918] (1932), *The Decline of the West*, trans. C. F. Atkinson, London: Allen & Unwin.

Spingarn-Koff, Jason (2001), 'Art and Tech, Together Again', *Wired News*, archived at <http://archive.wired.com/culture/lifestyle/news/2001/02/42037> (last accessed 20 July 2015).

Stich, Sidra (1994), *Yves Klein*, Ostfildern: Cantz; New York: Distributed Art Publisher.

Stiegler, Bernard (1986), 'Technologies de la mémoire et de l'imagination', *Réseaux*, 4.16: 63–87.

Stiegler, Bernard (1998), *Technics and Time 1: The Fault of Epimetheus*, trans. George Collins and Richard Beardsworth, Stanford: Stanford University Press.

Stiegler, Bernard (2009a), *Technics and Time 2: Disorientation*, trans. Stephen Barker, Stanford: Stanford University Press.

Stiegler, Bernard (2009b), *Acting Out*, trans. David Barison, Daniel Ross, and Patrick Crogan, Stanford: Stanford University Press.

Stiegler, Bernard (2010), *Taking Care of Youth and the Generations*, trans. Stephen Barker, Stanford: Stanford University Press.

Stiegler, Bernard (2011), *The Decadence of Industrial Democracies: Disbelief and Discredit 1*, trans. Daniel Ross, Cambridge: Polity.

Stiegler, Bernard (2012), *Uncontrollable Societies of Disaffected Individuals: Disbelief and Discredit 2*, trans. Daniel Ross, Cambridge: Polity.

Stiegler, Bernard (2013), *What Makes Life Worth Living: On Pharmacology*, trans. Daniel Ross, Cambridge: Polity.

Stiegler, Bernard (2014a), *The Lost Spirit of Capitalism: Disbelief and Discredit 3*, trans. Daniel Ross, Cambridge: Polity.

Stiegler, Bernard (2014b), *States of Shock: Stupidity and Knowledge in the Twenty-First Century*, trans. Daniel Ross, Cambridge: Polity.

Stiegler, Bernard (2014c), *The Re-Enchantment of the World: The Value of Spirit against Industrial Populism*, trans. Trevor Arthur, London: Bloomsbury.

Stiegler, Bernard (2014d), *Symbolic Misery Volume 1: The Hyperindustrial Epoch*, Cambridge: Polity.

Stiegler, Bernard (2015a), 'Automatic Society 1: The Future of Work – Introduction', trans. Daniel Ross, *La Deleuzeana*, 1: 121–40.

Stiegler, Bernard (2015b), 'In the Shadow of the Sublime: On *Les Immatériaux*', in Yuk Hui and Andreas Broeckmann (eds), *30 Years After Les Immatériaux*, Meson Press.

Stiegler, Bernard (2015c), *Symbolic Misery Volume 2: The Catastrophe of the Sensible*, Cambridge: Polity.

Stiegler, Bernard with Frédéric Neyrat (2012), 'Interview: From Libidinal Economy to the Ecology of the Spirit', trans. Arne De Boever, *Parrhesia*, 14: 9–15.

Swimme, Brian and Thomas Berry (1992), *The Universe Story, From the Primordial Flaring Forth to the Ecozoic Era*, San Francisco: Harper.

Tarkovsky, Andrei (1989), *Sculpting in Time*, Austin: University of Texas Press.

Taylor, Stuart Ross (1992), *Solar System Evolution: A New Perspective*, Cambridge: Cambridge University Press.

The π Research Network (2013), *The Philosophy of Information: A Simple Introduction* <http://www.socphilinfo.org/teaching/book-pi-intro> (last accessed 20 July 2015).

Théofilakis, Élie (ed.) (1985), *Modernes et après?: Les Immatériaux*, Paris: Éditions Autrement.

Tipler, Frank J. (1994), *The Physics of Immortality: Modern Cosmology, God, and the Resurrection of the Dead*, New York: Doubleday.

Vandenabeele, Bart (2007), 'Kant and Lyotard on Sublime Togetherness', in Barbara Bolt, Felicity Colman, Graham Jones, and Ashley Woodward (eds), *Sensorium: Aesthetics, Art, Life*, Newcastle: Cambridge Scholars Publishing.

Virilio, Paul (1985), 'L'Immatériel de guerre', in Élie Théofilakis (ed.), *Modernes et après?: Les Immatériaux*, Paris: Éditions Autrement.

Virilio, Paul (1995), *The Art of the Motor*, trans. Julie Rose, Minnesota: University of Minneapolis Press.

Virilio, Paul (2002), 'The Overexposed City', in G. Bridge and S. Watson (eds), *The Blackwell City Reader*, Chichester: Wiley-Blackwell.

Virilio, Paul (2003), *Art and Fear*, trans. Julie Rose, London and New York: Continuum.

Welsch, Wolfgang (2007), 'The Human – Over and Over Again', trans. Jim Scott, in Santiago Zabala (ed.), *Weakening Philosophy: Essays in Honour of Gianni Vattimo*, Montreal and Kingston: McGill-Queen's University Press.

Westphal, Kenneth R. (1998), 'Kant on the Sublime', in Michael Kelly (ed.), *Encyclopedia of Aesthetics*, vol. 3, New York: Oxford University Press.

Wheeler, John A. (1990), 'Information, Physics, Quantum: The Search for Links', in W. Zurek (ed.), *Complexity, Entropy, and the Physics of Information*, Redwood City, CA: Addison-Wesley.

White, Alan (1987), 'Nietzschean Nihilism: A Typology', *International Studies in Philosophy*, 14.2: 29–44.

White, Richard (2006), 'Lyotard and Posthuman Possibilities', *Philosophy Today*, 50.2: 183–9.

Wiener, Norbert (1949), *The Human Use of Human Beings*: Cybernetics and Society, Boston: Houghton Mifflin.

Wiener, Norbert (1964), *I Am a Mathematician: The Later Life of a Prodigy*, Cambridge, MA: MIT Press.

Wiener, Norbert [1948] (1968), *Cybernetics, or Control and Communication in the Animal and the Machine*, Cambridge, MA: MIT Press.

Williams, James (1998), *Lyotard: Towards a Postmodern Philosophy*, Cambridge: Polity Press.

Williams, James (2000a), *Lyotard and the Political*, London: Routledge.

Williams, James (2000b), 'The Last Refuge from Nihilism', *International Journal of Philosophical Studies*, 8.1: 115–24.

Wittgenstein, Ludwig (1967), *Zettel*, ed. G. E. M. Anscombe and Georg Henrik von Wright, Oakland: University of California Press.

Woodward, Ashley (2006), 'Answering the Question, "What is an Event?"', *antiTHESIS*, 16: 12–25.

Woodward, Ashley (2009), *Nihilism in Postmodernity: Lyotard, Baudrillard, Vattimo*, Aurora, CO: The Davies Group.

Woodward, Ashley (2013), 'Testimony and the Affect-phrase', in Heidi Bickis and Rob Shields (eds), *Rereading Jean-François Lyotard: Essays on His Later Works*, Farnham: Ashgate.

Woodward, Ashley (forthcoming), 'Circuits of Desire: Lyotard and Stiegler', in *Philosophy After Nature*, ed. Rosi Braidotti and Rick Dolphijn.

Young, Julian (1992), *Nietzsche's Philosophy of Art*, Cambridge: Cambridge University Press.

Zuse, Konrad [1970] (2012), 'Calculating Space', in *A Computable Universe: Understanding & Exploring Nature as Computation*, Singapore: World Scientific.

Index

Adorno, Theodor W., 7, 35,
    89, 173
aesthetics, 8, 71, 99, 115,
    119–20, 121, 134–49,
    151–63, 182, 191
affect, 6, 76, 80, 100, 161, 166,
    167, 169, 189
anamnesis, 95–9, 101, 191
animal, 5, 48, 76, 78, 91, 165–7,
    176, 179
Ansell-Pearson, Keith, 12, 21–7,
    34–5, 107, 121
Apollinaire, Guillaume, 155,
    165–6, 173, 180–1
Aristotle, 36, 45, 67, 146
art
    conceptual, 151, 157, 172,
        175
    inhuman, 165–86
    new media, 8, 135, 147–8,
        168, 194

Bar-Hillel Carnap paradox, 67–8
Bateson, Gregory, 65
Benjamin, Walter, 167
Bennington, Geoffrey, 2, 44, 123
Bergson, Henri, 45, 47–50, 53–4
Brassier, Ray, 12, 26–36

capital, 5, 17, 23, 25, 45,
    52–5, 82, 87, 90–2, 97,
    108, 124, 134, 136–7,
    148, 166, 192
code, 55–6, 59–60, 62–3, 65–6,
    168–9, 183
complexity, 12–14, 16, 18,
    20–1, 24–6, 42, 48, 53–4,
    75, 83–4
correlationism, 27–31, 34
crisis of perception/foundations/
    time and space, 102, 113–20,
    135, 137–8, 142, 146, 170,
    172, 175, 194
Crome, Keith, 7, 64, 128
cubism, 18, 165, 180–1, 185
cybernetics, 5, 7, 56, 61, 74,
    82–3, 85–6, 136
cyberphilosophy, 43–4

data, 43, 50, 52, 54, 56–64,
    66, 99, 114–20, 127,
    136, 139, 148, 153,
    182, 193
Deleuze, Gilles, 44, 76, 81, 189,
    191, 195
Derrida, Jacques, 2, 3, 20, 44,
    87–8, 90, 99

Descartes, René, 1, 47, 157–9,
169, 171
desire, 27, 74, 75–82, 87,
90–3, 100–2, 111–13,
118, 123, 167
differend, 57, 75, 95, 99–101,
113, 121, 123–4, 152, 167
distributed cognition, 191–2
Duchamp, Marcel, 167, 170,
172, 177

ecology, 82–6, 93
energy, 13–20, 31–2, 76–80,
83, 86, 91–3, 100,
158, 170
entropy and negentropy, 12–13,
16, 18, 22, 24–6, 60, 65, 75,
82, 85–6, 94, 101
eternal return, 76, 80–1, 179
event, 9, 41, 44, 46–7, 51–8,
60, 64–9, 71, 76, 85–6,
96, 99–101, 113, 118,
128, 137–8, 140–2,
146–9, 157, 161, 182–4,
191–4
evolution, 5, 14, 20, 24–6, 88
experimentation, 102, 126–8,
135, 146–8, 167, 171,
185
extinction, 30–3

fact (*fait*), 180–4
Floridi, Luciano, 41–3, 55,
59–60, 62–3, 69–70,
146–7
Foucault, Michel, 3, 192

Freud, Sigmund, 18, 26, 31–3,
70, 75–82, 85–6, 90,
92, 94–6, 98, 100,
105, 109–13, 118–19,
166, 190

Habermas, Jürgen, 85
Hadot, Pierre, 11–12, 36
Hayles, Katherine N., 74, 82,
148, 189, 191–2
Heidegger, Martin, 7–9, 19–20,
35, 61–2, 64, 67, 80, 82, 86,
89, 93, 96, 98–9, 116–17,
144, 166, 177, 189, 192
historicity, 15–16, 19, 26, 35–7,
178, 184
human, 4–36, 45, 49, 51, 53–4,
64, 69–71, 74–9, 85, 88, 89,
91, 93–4, 102, 106, 107,
125, 127, 166–76, 179,
181–6, 190–4
Husserl, Edmund, 7, 11–12,
19, 36, 88–9, 98, 143,
175, 189

Immatériaux, Les, 8, 65–6, 70,
97–8, 167, 168–75, 185–6
information
general definition of, 63
philosophy of (PI), 7, 41–4, 55,
58, 69, 70–1
theory, 2, 7–8, 12, 42–4,
58–60, 64–5, 68, 86, 135,
147; *see also* mathematical
theory of communication,
the (MTC)

informational turn, 2, 41–2, 58,
    62, 66, 69, 70–1, 194
inhuman, 4–9, 16–20, 23–7, 68,
    75, 87, 102, 134, 146,
    165–86, 189–94

Jacob, Max, 177–8, 180,
    185–6
Jencks, Charles, 18–21, 35–6
judgement, 3, 36–7, 67, 86,
    99–100, 106, 113–14, 117,
    122, 138–41, 144, 153,
    179, 191–4

Kant, Immanuel, 3, 8, 27–8,
    34–7, 42, 86, 98–100, 105,
    109, 113–18, 120–6, 128,
    134, 138–44, 152–3,
    160–2, 192–3
Klein, Yves, 151–63
Klossowski, Pierre, 81, 166

language, 14, 16, 28, 34, 42–4,
    53–8, 60–8, 81, 94–8,
    123, 128, 134–7, 167,
    170, 191, 193
Laruelle, François, 32–4
Leibniz, Gottfried Wilhelm,
    45–8, 50, 52–5, 57, 68,
    82–3, 87, 102
Leroi-Gourhan, André, 50, 88
libidinal economy, 75–82, 85–7,
    90–3
Luhmann, Niklas, 82–5, 100

Malraux, André, 176–86

Marcuse, Herbert, 81, 90–1
Massumi, Brian, 190
mathematical theory of
    communication, the (MTC),
    58–67, 146–7; see also
    information: theory
matter, 13, 16, 20, 30, 39,
    47–50, 53, 83, 102, 114,
    120, 138, 140, 145,
    148–9, 151–63, 168–73,
    179, 186, 190
meaning, 4, 8, 9, 11, 15, 19,
    24, 26, 27–8, 30, 34–6,
    43, 51, 56–66, 69–71,
    78, 87, 89–90, 93–102,
    106–12, 116–17, 119,
    121, 127–9, 136–7, 141,
    146–7, 149, 151, 177–86,
    189–90, 192, 194
Meillassoux, Quentin, 27–31
memory, 14, 42, 46–51, 53,
    57, 64, 85, 87–8, 94–101,
    184–6
Merleau-Ponty, Maurice, 11–12,
    36, 152, 175–6
metaphysics, 1, 15, 17, 28–9,
    35, 41, 47, 53, 55, 80,
    82–3, 86–8, 98, 100–1,
    107, 115, 119–20, 124,
    139, 160, 166, 191
Monory, Jacques, 117, 172

Nietzsche, Friedrich, 2–3, 7–9, 12,
    17, 22–7, 34, 70–1, 75–81,
    94, 100, 105–17, 120–9, 152,
    160–1, 166, 177, 179

nihilism, 2, 5–9, 12, 19, 27–8, 34, 36, 71, 77–9, 87, 89, 90, 92–5, 101–2, 105–29, 152–3, 160–7, 176–9, 181, 183–6

object, 14, 28–32, 46–7, 51, 67, 76, 88, 90–2, 95, 97, 99, 111–12, 114, 116–20, 122, 125, 138–45, 153, 157, 159–63, 169, 170, 171, 173, 193–4
organology (general), 89–90, 93

paradox, 57, 67–9, 102, 120, 128, 170–1, 191; *see also* Bar-Hillel Carnap paradox
parahyletisms, 102, 169–73
paralogy, 57, 67, 191
passibility, 126, 138, 141–3, 145, 170–1, 191, 193
performativity, 5, 18, 45, 68, 135–7, 146, 148–9, 192–3
phenomenology, 18, 27–8, 34, 156, 190
Plato and Platonism, 1, 21, 24, 80, 87, 98, 106, 109–11
posthuman, 4–7, 26, 68, 70, 74–5, 82, 102, 189–92
postinformation, 55, 57–8, 68

postmodern, 1–4, 8, 12, 17, 19, 23, 57, 115, 128, 134–6, 138, 142–3, 145, 146–7, 149, 169, 173–4, 177
presence, 87, 101, 117, 119–20, 156–7, 161, 172, 182, 193

schemata, 97–9, 162
science, 4–5, 11–12, 17, 22–6, 29, 34–6, 42, 50, 56, 63, 74, 80, 106, 118, 135–7, 145, 168–9, 172–3, 190–1
Shannon, Claude, 58–60, 62, 65–6, 146
Simondon, Gilbert, 89
Sophists, 3, 67–8
speculative realism, 28, 32
Stelarc, 175
Stiegler, Bernard, 1, 45, 50–3, 64, 75–6, 87–102
subject, 1, 15–18, 26, 41, 47, 70, 81, 83, 99, 125, 127, 142, 144, 157, 169, 171, 173–4, 179–81, 192–3
sublime, 8–9, 102, 105–29, 134–5, 142–9, 152–4, 157, 161–2, 170, 183–4, 194
systems theory, 12, 74, 82–4, 89, 100

technology, 9, 12, 22, 45, 51–6, 61, 64, 70, 74, 85, 118, 135–6, 142, 145, 149, 166, 173, 175–6, 194 technoscience, 5, 8–9, 50, 54, 82, 99, 101, 136, 169–73, 185, 190, 192–3

time, 11–37, 44–55, 64, 87–9, 95, 102, 116–17, 126–7, 134–9, 142–6, 170–9, 183, 186

transhuman, 5, 6, 12, 21–6, 35–6, 190

unpresentable, 118, 120, 124, 134

Valéry, Paul, 93

Virilio, Paul, 173–6, 186

Weaver, Warren, 58–61

Wiener, Norbert, 13, 61, 65–6

will to power, 24, 79, 80, 112, 128

Williams, James, 105, 152, 161

Wittgenstein, Ludwig, 20, 36, 58, 113, 177

EU Authorised Representative:

Easy Access System Europe Mustamäe tee 50, 10621 Tallinn, Estonia

gpsr.requests@easproject.com

Printed and bound by CPI Group (UK) Ltd, Croydon, CR0 4YY

10/03/2026

02068810-0001